THROUGH THE REMEMBERED GATE

THROUGH THE REMEMBERED GATE

Stephen Chalke

FAIRFIELD BOOKS

This book is dedicated to all those who have helped Fairfield Books,
especially those who have taken no public credit:
Ron Deaton and David Smith, for their wise advice,
Bob Mitchell, for his invaluable support in selling the books,
Rob Taylor, for his design work and always excellent guidance,
Martha Lewis, for not letting me take myself too seriously,
and Susanna Kendall.

Fairfield Books
17 George's Road, Bath BA1 6EY
Tel 01225-335813

Text © Stephen Chalke

Jacket image © Susanna Kendall

Most of the photographs in the book were taken by Susanna Kendall.
The following appear by kind permission of their copyright holders:
Huddersfield landscape – Ken Taylor
Bomber Wells at Cheltenham College – Christopher Bentall
Mark Wagh in the pavilion – Sam Bowles
Helen Castor and Stephen Chalke – Dave Allen

First published 2019

ISBN: 978 1 9996558 9 1

Printed and bound in Great Britain by
CPI Antony Rowe, Bumpers Way, Chippenham SN14 6LH

Contents

We shall not cease from exploration
And the end of all our exploring
Will be to arrive where we started
And know the place for the first time.
Through the unknown, remembered gate
When the last of earth left to discover
Is that which was the beginning ...

TS Eliot, Little Gidding

Introduction

The idea for this book came from a talk I gave to an MCC Library Supper in the summer of 2018 in the Writing Room at Lord's. With examples from my work I reflected on the challenges of being an oral historian, focusing in particular on the problems of memory, the significance of language and the crucial importance of trust. Teasing out of someone their life story, then giving it shape in written form, requires sensitivity, and it carries with it responsibility. When it works well, it can be a richly therapeutic experience for the subject.

My journey into this work was an accidental one, the story of which I tell here. To give readers an inkling of who I am and how I came to this work, I have also given glimpses of my own back pages. In my writing I have always tried to capture the testimony of my subjects without distortion, but inevitably, in shaping that testimony, my perspective and my values have been present.

I have worked with some fascinating men, men whose life stories would otherwise have gone unrecorded, and I have learned so much. As one who is captivated by social history and inclined to philosophical musings, I have found myself asking questions, and from time to time in this book I have explored these questions. I am not one who wants to turn back the clock, I am deeply suspicious of politicians who invoke past glories to drum up popular support, but I do believe that, in our modern throwaway culture, we are often too dismissive of experience.

This journey of mine has led me to become not only an oral historian of cricket but a publisher of my own and others' works. I tell that story as well, with all its ups and downs. Hidden in my account there may be a few dos and don'ts for others wanting to go down this road.

In writing and shaping the material of this book, I have perhaps done to myself what I have done to others, creating an ordered whole out of the myriad experiences of my life. There is always a degree of contrivance in that task, not least in the way one focuses on those experiences that are instructive or entertaining to recount.

These last 23 years of writing and publishing have had their share of drudgery and angst but, all in all, as I hope you will realise from reading this memoir, they have been great fun and most fulfilling.

1

Never too old to learn

If I had hit the ball properly, none of this would have happened.

If I had come off with a sparkling 20 not out, seen us home in a thrilling run chase in our last game of the season, if I had been surrounded by joyous team-mates clapping me on the back, the hero of the hour, I would have gone home happy. I would have spent the winter months reliving the glory, looking forward to another summer of cricket. I would never have become a cricket writer.

But it did not happen like that.

*

It was late September 1993. I was 45 years old, working in adult education in Bristol. With Sue and our daughter Martha, I had just moved to Bath, and I was playing my cricket for a wandering club, The Journeymen, whose fixture list of 29 matches ruled my summer. A group of friends, we travelled all over the country: a Whitsun tour of Norfolk, a long weekend in Derbyshire, three days at Cambridge University's Fenner's ground, a week in the West Country and this last weekend in Essex, finishing on the Sunday at Great and Little Warley, a picturesque if rather decaying ground on the outskirts of Brentwood.

The old wooden pavilion with its verandah had seen better days, the field – on a shelf above the M25 – was plagued by rabbits, and the club was starting to suffer from its refusal to play in the local league. They were clinging to a dying form of the game, a 1990s version of country-house cricket, and they did not quite have the pizzazz to do it.

In Warley's innings of 151 I had bowled seven wicketless overs of gentle away swing and, down to bat at number eight, with the score on 103 for two, I was not expecting to play any further part in the match. Then, within a few minutes, it was 113 for six and I was walking across the soft outfield grass, telling myself to have a look at the bowling ... get used to the pitch ... play myself in. There was plenty of time.

The departing batsman, a newcomer, was clearly not familiar with our strict club rule: 'There will be no questioning of umpiring decisions.' On being given out stumped, he stood for an age, looking at his feet, then glaring at the umpire. Eventually he began his huffy departure, by which time I had reached the edge of the square.

Was my concentration broken by the profuse apologies I had to offer to the fielders? Or was I distracted by the low sun that twinkled through the chestnut trees, with their half-bare branches, behind the bowler's arm?

I fully intended to play the first ball with a straight bat. But it was such a bad ball, thrown up high and dropping well short of a length, and at the last minute I changed my mind. I went to pull it over short mid-wicket's head, it came off the pitch more slowly than I expected, and the ball lobbed in a gentle arc into the fielder's hands. It looked, and felt, utterly pathetic.

'Davis's stay at the crease after his dismissal,' our match report recorded, 'lasted longer than Chalke's one-ball innings.'

Nobody said a word when I got back to the pavilion. Not a 'Bad luck', nothing. They were all looking the other way.

*

On the long journey home the melancholy set in.

Early in the summer in Derbyshire I had hit 84 not out, my highest ever score, and I had driven home full of hope that this was to be the year when everything would click into place for me. During the course of that innings I weathered a fearful over from a fast bowler, full of short-pitched deliveries that were accompanied by much swearing and gesticulation. At the end of it the bowler ran off the field, grabbed his bag from the pavilion and drove out of the ground at high speed. Had my resolute batting really upset him that much? "It's nothing personal," the wicket-keeper explained. "He's gone to conduct choral evensong."

After that my season went rapidly downhill. For the first time I was struggling with back problems, paying regular visits to a chiropractor. Perhaps it was time to call it a day. "Don't go on and on like Dad did," a voice started telling me. "Don't make a fool of yourself. Retire now before it gets worse."

Over the following weeks another voice started to answer back. "Don't be silly. Dad was 62. You're only 45. You're not ready to walk away from it all, the friendships, the fun."

At my college we ran a set of courses for mature students, to raise them to the standard necessary to go to university. We had some heart-warming successes, with milkmen, roofers and typists turning themselves into computer programmers, physiotherapists and housing officers. At the start of each course I would give a talk, telling them not to feel self-conscious about being students; the modern world of work required lifelong re-skilling. "You're never too old to learn," I said.

So, as I reflected on my summer's cricket, I thought, "Why don't I work on my game, get some coaching?"

*

I rang 3-D Sports, a mail-order company in Cheltenham, and they gave me the telephone number of a coach called Ken Biddulph who had played for Somerset for some years. The name hardly rang a bell, but I looked him up in *Wisden* and there he was: *Biddulph, K.D. (Som.) b May 29, 1932.* I rang his number and explained who I was.

"What did you have in mind?" he asked.

"Well, I could get off early on Friday afternoons. Perhaps I could come up for half an hour each week and work on my bowling."

"Half an hour?" he repeated. "You can't do anything in half an hour."

"Well, an hour perhaps."

He rang back later in the week. "Stephen, I've booked the Stratford Park Leisure Centre in Stroud for Friday afternoon, 4 to 5.30."

There was no mention of money, and I started to become anxious. I worked two evenings a week and was usually tired by Friday lunch-time. I would have to drive home from Bristol, change and get up to Stroud where I would be on my own in a net, bowling for an hour and a half. Did he understand what an ordinary cricketer I was?

Our first session was scheduled for the fifth of November. With it due to end at 5.30, I promised to be home by seven so that we could go as a family to the fireworks display at Bath University.

*

Just before four o'clock I made my way, cricket bag in hand, to the main entrance of the leisure centre where I was greeted by a tall, slim, erect man. He had a good head of wavy, silver-grey hair and wore a Somerset blazer over some old-fashioned cricket whites.

"Stephen? Nice to meet you. I've got some good news. There's nobody in after us till six o'clock."

He asked me to show him my bowling action. "It's very good," he said. Then he proceeded to make some alterations. He got me picking my knees up higher. He made some footmarks with chalk on the floor and asked me to land in them. He made me more side-on, with a greater swivel of the hips and my front arm reaching higher. In no time I was so disorientated by the changes that the ball started to fly all over the place: into the side of the net, even onto its roof.

"That's much more like it, Stephen. Now we're getting somewhere."

I had my doubts, but I soon realised that he knew what he was doing. And I loved his enthusiasm. It did not matter to him that I had only limited ability.

"I understand what you want," he told me. "If I can get you a few more runs, a few more wickets, keep you enjoying the game for a few more years, you'll be happy, won't you?"

By six o'clock I was exhausted. The staff at the centre pushed back the net, and the room was turned over to five-a-side football. Ken collected up his paraphernalia, and I followed him up to the balcony where, with my shirt dripping wet on my back, we half-watched the footballers while I listened to Ken talking about his days as a county cricketer.

For him, I suspect, this was the high point of the session.

*

As a boy I had watched Hampshire, where my first hero was the bespectacled Roy Marshall, a white West Indian who thought nothing of hitting the first ball of the match for four. He would cut in-swingers to the third-man boundary or drive the ball imperiously through the covers. It all seemed so easy, and there was never much running between the wickets, just a blaze of boundaries. What a groan went round the ground when he was out!

"Roy was a great bat, very entertaining," Ken said. "He used to enjoy my bowling; he hit me all over the place. I got him out at Bournemouth. For 212. Second new ball. What a wonderful player. I used to lie awake the night before the Hampshire match, dreading having to bowl at him."

Suddenly he had transported me across the boundary.

"I got him out for nought once," he went on. "In the first over. I had him caught at short leg." When I got home, I looked for it in the old *Wisdens* I had kept from my childhood.

Taunton. 22 July 1959
R.E. Marshall c Lomax b Biddulph 0

"I'm like a cat with ten tails; I've got Roy out first over for nothing. At the end of the over I go down to field at fine leg, my usual place, for Bill Alley to come up and bowl. And there was an entrance down at that side, and the old turnstile was clicking. People coming in. There was a group came in, and one of them turned and looked up at the scoreboard. 'I say,' he says, 'Marshall's out. I've come all the way from Southampton to see Marshall bat, and some silly bugger's got him out.'"

Talk of Hampshire led him on to their Old Etonian captain, Colin Ingleby-Mackenzie, how the Hampshire twelfth man was forever running messages to the local bookmaker and coming onto the outfield with the latest race results. Early one summer, Ken told me, Ingleby-Mackenzie hit a very quick hundred. In those days there was a prize of £100 for the fastest century of the summer, and he managed to get a bookmaker to give him odds of 4/1 that his own effort would be beaten before the summer was out. He placed a bet of £25, ensuring that one way or another he would finish up with £100. Later in the summer, against Somerset inevitably, he beat it himself, so he finished up with two cheques for £100.

Bournemouth. 18 June 1958
A.C.D. Ingleby-Mackenzie not out 113 in 61 minutes
Biddulph 2 wickets for 82 runs

"In the evening we were eating in the hotel," Ken said. "The Hampshire team were on the next table, and the waiter came over. 'Excuse me, gentlemen,' he said. 'Everything is on Mr Ingleby-Mackenzie.'"

The stories continued to flow. Fred Trueman, Colin Cowdrey, Frank Tyson, the cricketers of my childhood were coming alive, one after another. Not just the cricketers, either, but their whole way of life.

"We had one year when we went everywhere by train. Can you imagine going by train from Taunton? We spent about 400 hours at Bristol Temple Meads, waiting for connections. You'd finish a game at 4.30 or 5 on the final day, then you had to go to Bristol before you could get anywhere. By the time you got to the hotel, you wouldn't get a hot meal; you'd be lucky if you got a sandwich. I remember arriving at Old Trafford after three in the morning."

My damp shirt dried out, and I hardly noticed that my back was stiffening up. The five-a-side football ended, and the badminton nets came out. When I finally looked at my watch, it was nearly half past seven. I found a phone box and rang home. "I don't think I'm going to make it for the fireworks. You'll have to go on without me."

I paid Ken £20. By the time he had settled up for the net, and adding in our session on the balcony, I think he must have earned about £1.50 an hour. But that was Ken for you.

"See you next Friday, Stephen."

2

Finding a specialism

"Well, you can cut out all those opening paragraphs. That's how they teach you to write in universities. By the time you get to the guts of the article, you'll have no readers left."

Three years on from my first net with Ken Biddulph, I had embarked on another attempt at self-improvement: a University of Bath extra-mural evening class, 'An Introduction to Feature Writing'.

Hazel the tutor, a middle-aged Jewish lady who had stumbled into journalism by accident, fizzed with a slightly mad energy. She had no organised plan for developing our skills over the eight sessions, as became clear in the second week when one of the class arrived with the transcript of an interview he had conducted with his next-door neighbour, a newly elected city councillor who was dying from breast cancer. Hazel, on the spur of the moment, had the pages photocopied and told us that our homework for the week was to create a 700-word article out of the transcript. It was a ferociously difficult task, at a point at which we had barely started the course. The following week, to make matters worse, we had to read aloud our efforts.

The subject of the interview had spoken extensively about her funeral, how she wanted her ashes to be scattered in the Rift Valley in Kenya, 'the cradle of mankind'. This theme was taken up by one of the first readers in our class, a well-spoken elderly woman whose opening paragraphs consisted of a lengthy anthropological overview of funeral rites around the world.

This provoked Hazel's withering putdown about 'how they teach you to write in universities', as a result of which we all grew more nervous in our seats. The majority of the class were women, and mostly their pieces focused on the breast cancer, often with the underlying theme that only women could understand what the dying woman was going through. Each time Hazel listened carefully; each time she offered points for improvement. Occasionally she ventured a minor compliment, softening the criticism, but there was no flannel, no concern to protect our feelings.

Three or four of the group, including the elderly woman with the discourse on funeral rites, never came again. But I already knew that it was what I needed. On and off for years I had been working on a set of autobiographical short stories; my writing was crying out to be shaken out of its introspective preciousness.

She called me last of all, after a succession of dark and depressing pieces, all of which left me feeling that my unread offering was that of 'a typical man': shallow and insufficiently empathetic. I dreaded the feedback as I reached my final joky paragraph:

> Brave and outspoken even in death, she has been working on her own funeral arrangements. "Typical of you," one of her friends joked. "Bossy to the last. Making sure you get things done the way you want them." But Sue's reply is quick and to the point: "It's my funeral, and I'm going to be the star of the show."

There was a long silence in the room, a silence that filled me with terror. Then Hazel delivered her verdict.

"How wonderful. You see what he's done, don't you? He's the only one of you who has done it. He's caught her strength, her sense of being alive."

*

The Friday afternoons with Ken became an unmoveable part of my week. Initially it was just the two of us, including a session in which Ken brought in a video camera and filmed my bowling. At six o'clock we went in search of a television screen on which to view the film, finishing up in the upstairs gym where various runners and cyclists, pounding away to a video of 'Boom Shake The Room', suddenly found themselves staring at repeated sequences of me running in to bowl.

"You're looking a bit like Derek Shackleton," Ken said, summoning up another of my childhood Hampshire heroes. Thereafter, much to my delight, he would occasionally refer to me as 'Shack': "Come on now, Shack, get those arms up high."

Ken began to introduce other cricketers till there were six of us, including one winter my younger brother Andrew, who was in Bristol that year and who had always been a better cricketer than me. We could all bat and bowl, with a variety of left and right-handers, pace, swing and spin. Ken got us to warm up carefully, and he ensured that, when we went in to bat, we played ourselves in; when we bowled, we analysed each batsman and talked about how we were going to get him out. Such was the magic he weaved that, if he ever missed a week, we all turned up and did everything just as thoroughly.

Always there would follow an hour or more on the balcony. The others would stay for a while, listening to Ken, but never as long as I did. I could never get enough of his stories.

In 1948, as a 16-year-old growing up in Chingford in Essex, he had been sponsored by the *Evening News* to attend Saturday afternoon sessions with Alf Gover, the great Surrey and England fast bowler who ran a pioneering coaching school in Wandsworth, South London.

"Once we'd had our lesson, we'd hang around in the hope that we could bowl at somebody else. There were four nets: with four batsmen and four coaches. We'd bowl at anybody and everybody. I remember once, when I was 17 or 18, I was bowling at this chap and he didn't look very good. There was a club cricketer in the next net, and I said to Alf, 'Excuse me, Mr Gover, do you think I could go and bowl at that feller next door?' 'All right, old boy.' Everybody was 'old boy' to Alfred. 'But what's the matter with this one?' 'Well, he isn't very good.' Isn't very good. Afterwards, he said to me, 'That's Peter May.'"

In time Ken was offered a contract by Somerset, where he started just as the great Harold Gimblett, the highly-strung opening batsman, was calling it a day. Gimblett's last appearance for the county was in early May 1954, when in mental turmoil he walked away in mid-match. The game started on a Wednesday morning during Ken's first week on the staff.

"They were playing Yorkshire, I remember. I went down to the ground nice and early to bowl in the nets. Half past nine, maybe. And walking through the main gates in St James Street, I bumped into Harold Gimblett. All these small boys came running up for his autograph. So he was signing away, and I was standing to one side, waiting. Then they turned to me. 'Can we have yours?' 'Oh no,' I said, 'you don't want mine.' And I started to walk through the gates. It was the first time anybody had asked for my autograph."

The young boys in the Stratford Park Leisure Centre ran past him now without a second look.

"Gimblett didn't half give me a bollocking. 'You sign. You sign those autographs. Don't you ever refuse a boy an autograph.' 'But they don't even know who I am. They've never seen me play.' 'Yes, and when they have seen you play, they probably won't want your autograph.'"

That was Ken all over. None of his stories ended in personal triumph, and I loved that. I also loved the light he was shining on that long-lost world of an England still rebuilding after the ravages of war.

"I remember at Somerset, going along to the office to get a ball at the beginning of my time there, and I had to sign for it. And it wasn't a new ball, either. That was my ball; I was responsible for it. I'd take it home and polish it up every evening. By the middle of July it had been hit in the river a few times, and it was getting a bit tatty. So I went to see if there was any chance of another ball. 'Another?' he said. 'What have you been doing to it? You've only had that this summer.'"

With Ken's coaching, my cricket improved in leaps and bounds. At the back of each year's diary I recorded my performances, and my tally of wickets rose from 23 in 1993 to 39 the next year, then to 50. In 1996, at the age of 48, I had my best-ever season, taking 82 wickets and averaging over 30 with the bat. I was not playing at a high level but, as Ken had said at the start, "If I can get you a few more runs, a few more wickets, keep you enjoying the game for a few more years, you'll be happy, won't you?" And I was. Very happy.

*

I was less happy at work. As a result of government reform, the college was no longer under supervision from the local authority. It was now a free-standing institution, required to balance its books, and the new principal, brought in to supervise this changeover, belonged to that school of management that meets every challenge with a structural reorganisation.

At first I benefited from this, winning promotions in two shake-ups, but the college became a confused and unhappy place, and I finished up with an almost impossibly heavy workload, caught between an out-of-touch senior management, with no day-to-day responsibilities, and a demoralised workforce turning increasingly to trade union militancy. A government inspection came to the conclusion that the college had had too many reorganisations and needed a period of calm. It was a verdict that was reported with some embarrassment at the start of a meeting called to outline the next full-scale reorganisation.

We were given a choice: to apply for a post in the new structure or to take a generous redundancy package. The principal pleaded with me to stay, but the personnel department said that there was to be no discrimination in who was and was not offered the package. So, with no job to move on to, with a mortgage and a family, I took my life in my hands and left. I had no idea what the future held, but I was emotionally drained and the redundancy money was enough for me to take a short break. I bought a new computer and taught myself how to use it, I got back to half-marathon running and lost a stone in weight, and I decided to have another shot at some writing. And so it happened that I was sitting in Hazel's evening class.

"You need to specialise," she said one week when the course was nearing its end. "Find a subject where you can develop some expertise."

In one of the many strange twists of Hazel's life, while working on a river boat teaching art to disturbed children, she had talked her way onto *Newsnight* as an expert on the safety of the London Underground. On another occasion she had persuaded *The Times* to send her to Paris, this time as somebody

17

qualified to report on an international pharmaceutical conference. With a delightfully infectious spirit she made anything sound possible for an aspiring feature writer, but deep down I knew I did not have her bravado.

My mind drifted away for a while, and I found myself thinking about Ken and his wonderful stories. Perhaps I could interview him for an article.

But Ken Biddulph? He played 91 games for Somerset between 1955 and 1961, never got close to playing for England. I could not imagine the sports editors sitting up with excitement at such a piece. Then I thought, "I could ask him to tell me about the best game of cricket he ever played. I could write it as a short story."

So it was that, on Thursday 21 November 1996, I sat with Ken at a rickety wooden table in The Old Fleece Inn, just south of Stroud.

"I'm going to choose Yorkshire at Bath in '59, towards the end of the season," he said when we settled with our pints of beer. "The reason I pick that one is that in those days it was a great achievement to beat Yorkshire. It's the only occasion I was on the winning side against them."

Little did I know it, as the tape in my pocket cassette recorder started revolving, but in that moment a new life, a life that would last for more than twenty years, was beginning.

3

They could not be beaten

"Funny man, Closey. He could be both a brilliant genius and thick at the same time."

I had watched Brian Close as a cricketer, but beyond that I had little insight into him as a man. I read the occasional cricket book, I subscribed to the magazine *The Cricketer*, and sometimes I attended the meetings of the Gloucestershire Cricket Lovers in Bristol. But Ken was taking me somewhere different, bringing alive the players of my youth in a way that was new to me. Over the years since then, I have listened to so many stories about Brian Close – he remains the greatest character of post-war English cricket – but I am not sure I have heard a better one-line summation of him, 'a brilliant genius and thick at the same time', than Ken offered across the table of The Old Fleece.

Ken told me about a time when he was running a pub in the north-east. He and Close had developed a friendship, leading on one occasion to the Yorkshireman asking Ken to accompany him to court where he faced a driving charge. All the way there Close cursed the pettiness of the summons. He had been doing "about 80 miles an hour" on the motorway, that was all. Only when the evidence was presented in the court room did Ken discover that Close had been in the fast lane, driving at nearly 90 with an out-of-control caravan in tow.

"The thing about Closey is that, if you listened to him, he was never wrong. You tended to get into the habit of believing everything he said was right."

In Ken's chosen match, at Bath in August 1959, Yorkshire were top of the championship table, up against one of the minnows of the circuit, a county that had not beaten them in their last 66 encounters, not since 1903. It was a David and Goliath story, and on the last afternoon Goliath was in control. Chasing 255 for victory, Yorkshire were 133 for two.

Then the balance of the game started to shift. Brian Langford, Somerset's young off-spinner, was turning the ball on the responsive surface. "A superb bowler," Ken said, "but he was a little excitable. He wasn't a great thinker of the game. He needed the experience of our captain." Wickets fell, and Somerset, unfancied Somerset, triumphed by 16 runs. Then, to round off a glorious three days, Ken was awarded his county cap.

"I had to buy a couple of bottles of champagne to go round the dressing room. Invite the visiting team in for a quick glass of bubbly. And I remember I couldn't afford it. I had to get it on credit from Bill Moor the caterer. I think it took me about a month to pay for it."

With a match next day in Bristol, some of the Yorkshire team stayed in Bath for drinks. "Closey was one of them. We sat listening to him for half an hour. How it would have been different if Fred Trueman hadn't been away at the Test match. How they should have lapped Brian Langford. How the game was there for the taking. We'd beaten Yorkshire for the first time for 56 years, I'd been awarded my county cap but, after half an hour of listening to Closey, we thought we were the ones who'd lost. They could not be beaten."

I took my tape recorder home and copied out what Ken had said. His memories of the game itself, 38 years on, were patchy so there was a challenge for me in writing it up as a story. I decided to visit the Central Library in Bath, where they stored back copies of *The Times* on microfilm, and to my joy I found detailed reports of the three days.

> Bath has a ground of natural beauty, and here it was that the destiny of Yorkshire cricket was to be shaped in an environment so essentially different from the chimneys of Bradford or Sheffield ... When Close arrived, his approach, his immense skill, which was evident from the beginning, and some Somerset bowling far short of the standard required, enabled Yorkshire to prosper ... Yorkshire had got their teeth into Somerset and were not letting go ... Then Langford began spinning to his heart's content.

The game ran through my veins: the twists and turns of a great contest, the players that Ken had brought alive, the moments of personal drama. And I could not help looking at the stories on the other pages of the paper: the plan to extend the new M1 from Rugby to Doncaster, the battle between Debenham's and the House of Fraser for control of Harrod's, the advertisement for Phosdrin, an organo-phosphorus insecticide with 'dramatic killing power'.

How was I going to write it up? "You've got to hear a voice reading it," Hazel had told us. "You've got to catch a rhythm." I worked for hours to weave together the various strands: the *Times* reports, the titbits of contemporary life and, above all, Ken's voice. "You've got to go on and on editing it until it sounds right."

On quiet days I had been going back to my set of short stories, trying to revive a sad fantasy that, if I could only get them right, the collection would be as good as James Joyce's *Dubliners*. I even had fifteen of them, the same as

Joyce. That autumn I had recast them all in the present tense, and I liked the immediacy that created. So I tried the same with Ken's game.

> The sun shines on the Bath Recreation Ground. A week earlier, there have been floods in the West Country, but summer has re-asserted itself. It is August 1959. Yorkshire have just gone top in the championship table. It is their chance to end Surrey's seven-year reign, and they have not lost to Somerset since 1903, not since the days of Lord Hawke and Lionel Palairet.
>
> "Yorkshire were a hard team to play," Ken remembers. "The atmosphere was always a bit different. They had this self-belief. When you went in to bat, they used to look at you as if to say, 'How dare you come out here!' They could not be beaten."
>
> It is August 1959. Harold Macmillan is preparing for his 'Never had it so good' election, the Queen is expecting her third child and Cliff Richard is top of the hit parade with 'Living Doll'.

When I read my first draft to Sue and Martha, I could hear the rhythm of it, the way the elements bounced off each other, the humour in Ken's voice, the gathering tension of the match.

Sue's heart sank each time I returned to my short stories, she knew nothing would ever come of them, but that evening her enthusiasm seemed genuine. She said, "I think you might be onto something with that."

I called it 'They Could Not Be Beaten' and sent it to Ken. "You *have* been working hard," he said at our next net. "You know more about the game than I do." And he was away again, about what Tony Lock and Alec Bedser said to him the next day and the time he met Harold Macmillan at a charity match at Haywards Heath. "I sat next to him at tea. I was dying to know what it was like to be a prime minister. He didn't want to know, though. All he wanted to do was to talk cricket. He wanted to know what it was like being a professional cricketer."

I found a scorecard of a 1955 charity match, in which Macmillan had played. He was hit wicket bowled Hearne, 2. The Hearne in question was Richard, television's Mister Pastry. I added that to the piece.

But what on earth was I to do with it? Who would publish 2,500 words about a county match in 1959? I sent it to a friend, Rich, and he liked it. "It's like I'm watching the match as I read it," he said. "Only the match is forty years ago, and the person chatting away next to me is playing in it." Still somewhat in the dark about what I was doing, that was a formulation that I found helpful. An exceptionally bright bloke, Rich contributed articles on the history of South African cricket to an obscure, subscription-only magazine called *Cricket Lore*, and he suggested that I should try to get my piece published in that. "The editor is always on the lookout for new contributors."

Meanwhile I continued to research the game at Bath. I found a passage in Brian Close's autobiography, recalling the last afternoon, how he told Ronnie Burnet, a 40-year-old chemical engineer who had never played first-class cricket before taking on the Yorkshire captaincy, to counter Langford's off-spin by sweeping him:

> I said, 'For God's sake get your left foot down the pitch and hit Langford anywhere between mid-on and fine leg. He's hardly likely to get you lbw and you can pull him anywhere in that arc with reasonable safety.' Well, Ronnie got his leg down the pitch all right but somewhere outside the line of the leg stump! The whole lot went over – and he blamed me. 'You told me to do that,' he complained.

Then I discovered a book of Yorkshire reminiscences, which included Burnet's own version of this:

> As a 'business stroke' the sweep was virtually unknown, unlike today. Closey gave us all a demonstration, there and then in the dressing room, on how to execute it ... the art of sweeping, and three of us were out playing the shot. I am convinced to this day that, if we had batted in an orthodox manner, we would have won.

I was writing a gentle piece about a good game of cricket, recreating a long-lost world. Little did I realise how seriously people in Yorkshire took such matters.

*

Pleased with my effort and with Ken's response to it, I hatched the idea that I could interview other cricketers and write up their most memorable matches. Perhaps I could cover all 17 counties and put them together as a book, a portrait of county cricket in days gone by. It would not be on a par with Joyce's *Dubliners*, but it might be easier to sell to a publisher.

The editor of *Cricket Lore* accepted my piece for his next issue so I reckoned that, even if I did not make a go of the book, I had an outlet for my efforts. Apart from Rich, nobody seemed to have heard of the magazine, but I was going to be in print. It felt like a step forward.

I asked Ken if he could recommend anybody for me to interview: people like him with a good memory, a telling turn of phrase and a sense of humour. Without a second thought he suggested Worcestershire's Martin Horton. "I think he'd be your sort of person." He gave me Martin's address, and I wrote to him, enclosing a copy of my write-up of Ken's game.

The telephone rang the next morning. "I'd love to help you," Martin said. "Would it be a problem if I also chose a match when we beat Yorkshire?"

Not long afterwards I was sitting with Gloucestershire's Arthur Milton in his front room in Bristol. "There was a game at Cheltenham when we beat Yorkshire," he started, and I found myself thinking, "Shall I call the book *The Day We Beat Yorkshire*?" It seemed to be every old cricketer's favourite memory. But I decided against that. "Let's pick another match," I said. "I've done Yorkshire twice already."

*

I still turned up every Friday afternoon for Ken's net sessions, but they did not fit into the rhythm of my self-employed lifestyle as easily and, in any case, our little group had broken up. My brother was no longer in Bristol, the two talented sixth-formers were now in full-time employment, and a relentlessly accurate left-arm bowler, an intense character who was forever complaining about the bad umpiring he had suffered the previous summer, took it badly when Ken demonstrated how he was taking a half-step to leg as a fast bowler ran in. "I'm not having that, he's humiliated me in front of the youngsters," he told me, and we never saw him again.

Early in the summer, making a mess of a catch, I sustained a hairline fracture of my left thumb. Three days later, ignoring the pain, I played again, and I dropped another catch. This one left my thumb, in the surgeon's words, 'smashed to smithereens'. It was rebuilt under general anaesthetic, and I walked around for weeks with a great staple-like contraption sticking through it. At the end of the summer I had taken just 14 wickets.

All my cricketing energy was going into my book, which was published with the title *Runs in the Memory* in October 1997.

*

Three months later the Yorkshire cricketers gathered at the funeral of David Bairstow, their popular wicket-keeper who had committed suicide.

Don Wilson, Yorkshire's slow left-armer, had played in the 1959 match. "Have you seen this book *Runs in the Memory*?" he asked Brian Close during the wake. "It's got about that game at Bath where you had us all playing the sweep shot and we lost." In the midst of this most mournful of occasions Close responded by launching into a loud justification of his strategy, complete with foot movements and a waving of an imaginary bat, demonstrating how none of them had played the shot properly. "What I said was to get your foot across like this," he insisted, lunging his leg forward as the room around him fell silent. "Not down the line like this."

He could not be beaten.

4

The unheard voices

It was an extraordinary four months. From January to April I was driving about England and Wales, talking to county cricketers of the 1950s. I read all the books I could find, I discovered the British Newspaper Library in North London, and I sat at my computer, just as Hazel had told me to do, editing and re-editing the chapters till they sounded right.

"Have you found a job yet?" my neighbour Adrian asked one day.

"I've got a job," I replied defiantly. "I'm writing a book."

"That's not a job. That's only a hobby."

I was determined to prove him wrong. I had stumbled on a good idea, I had enough of my redundancy money left, and I was going to make a success of it.

I decided that all the games in the book would take place in the 1950s, though my choice of decade stemmed from nothing more than the accident of knowing Ken Biddulph. It certainly was not a decade whose values and way of life chimed especially with the mood of the times. We were in the dying days of John Major's government, when Tony Blair was telling us that things could only get better, and the prime minister was regularly mocked for his nostalgia for the 1950s: for his images of warm beer, old maids bicycling to holy communion, long shadows on cricket grounds.

Yet that had been the decade in which I had spent my childhood up to the age of eleven, years when I had hardly understood the adult world about me. There was a fascination for me in returning to it.

I do remember the Suez crisis; during it a master at my prep school explained to us about the atom bomb, and I could not get to sleep that night. I remember a scientist at the local Porton Down Research Establishment dying of the bubonic plague; his wife was a cook at our school, but nobody seemed to worry. And I remember the 1959 General Election. A group of boys descended on me, one pulling my tie tight and pushing me up against some coat pegs: "Conservative or Labour?" they demanded menacingly. I had little idea what it all meant, though I suspect that I knew what I was supposed to say. Loyally I stuck to the party line of my father. "Liberal," I choked out. They conferred for a while, then let me go. "Liberal, he's not worth bothering with."

One day in the summer of 1955, when I was still in the pre-prep school, our teacher Mrs Dowson drew a pattern of straight lines on the blackboard. She handed out sheets of paper and told us to copy the lines carefully. Then she explained how it was a grid for scoring a cricket match, demonstrating how it had to be filled in. After lunch we trooped across in a crocodile to the prep school, where we sat on a bank and under her supervision scored the beginning of a match.

It had a mystery about it, a sense of ritual and magic. And soon I came to realise how it mattered so much to everybody, the playing well and being a good sport. In my childish imagination, becoming a cricketer had something to do with growing up and becoming a man.

Our father was in his sixties – we were the children of his second marriage – and I never saw him play. But all his life he was in love with the game, and he encouraged my interest. Peter, my older brother, was not sporting at all; he was happier making a wooden fort in the carpentry shed or building a tree house, but soon enough I taught my younger brother Andrew the basics, and by the time he was old enough we were playing cricket all the time in the garden. One summer we staged a full five-match Test series, England versus Australia, when we had to bowl fast or slow depending whether we were Trueman or Laker and, for the lower-order batsmen, we had to turn round and bat left-handed.

In the summer of 1956 I collected the set of 35 cards that appeared in Barratt's sweet cigarette packets: 'Test Cricketers by EW Swanton'. There were the 17 touring Australians and 18 assorted Englishmen: a puppy-faced Colin Cowdrey, a smiling Brian Statham, a determined Bob Appleyard.

We went to watch the Australians at the end of that summer. We were on holiday in Eastbourne, and Dad took us to the Hastings Festival. My memory is of a sunny day, but *Wisden* says 'a biting wind blew across the ground' and 'rain spoiled the match'. Dickie Dodds and Arthur Milton opened the innings for an England XI; I would meet both of them on my travels in 1997.

The following year, 1957, I developed a grumbling appendix. In bed I listened to the first day of the First Test on the radio, in what I have since worked out was the inaugural broadcast of *Test Match Special*. Sonny Ramadhin, West Indies' magical spinner, bowled England out for 186, and I recorded every ball in my *Compactum* scorebook. Then in the operating theatre, as the surgeon hovered above me with his anaesthetic needle, he asked, "Do you like cricket?" It seemed that the game was everywhere. "I'll bowl you an over," he said and he imitated John Arlott. "Miller comes in to bowl the first ball. It's full on the off stump, and Chalke comes forward. He plays it carefully into the covers." By the fourth ball I was far away.

I started playing organised matches at school. We had nets at the end of the day, and there was a team to be selected for Saturday afternoon. I can still remember my shock and excitement when the master announced that I would be opening the bowling.

Dad introduced a system of payments: threepence if we scored 10 and a penny for each run thereafter, and threepence for each wicket or catch. Peter rarely troubled Dad's pockets. I did rather better: 14 runs here, two wickets there. Then Andrew made a fortune: "I got 47 today, Dad ... I took nine wickets." Dad's business might have been losing money, but he always paid out with a smile.

Here I was, in the early months of 1997, returning to that long-lost, barely understood world through the memories of the cricketers whose scores I had read each day in the *News Chronicle*. There was Harold Rhodes in Derby, Don Shepherd on the Gower peninsula, Ken Taylor in Norfolk, Jim Parks in Hove. I taped the conversations, 55 hours spread across 17 counties.

"Why don't you interview some more famous names?" a friend asked. "Nobody is going to buy the book otherwise."

I made my decision at a meeting of the Gloucestershire Cricket Lovers in Bristol. Trevor Bailey was the speaker, and I took along a letter I had prepared for him, outlining my project and asking for an interview. But, as I listened to him, I realised that I had heard most of it before, in print and on the radio, and I left the letter in my pocket. "No," I thought. "I should be looking for the unheard voices, people like Ken Biddulph."

Martin Horton fitted the bill perfectly. He was a good county cricketer who had played just two Tests for England. He scored 2,468 runs in 1959, and twice he did the double of 1,000 runs and 100 wickets in a season.

I was nervous as I drove up the M5. I was not sure that my project was going to work and, though I had swotted up on the Worcestershire players, I was afraid I was going to get them all mixed up and make a fool of myself.

I need not have worried. Martin, a shortish man, almost bald, with a round, cheerful face, settled into his armchair and talked without inhibition, with a Worcester accent that had a warm burr in the vowels and a wry, observant chuckle. I arrived at eleven o'clock, expecting at most a couple of hours of his time, and found his wife Margaret preparing a two-course lunch, complete with a bottle of wine. It was nearly four o'clock when I left.

"It didn't feel like an interview," he told me some years later. "It was just a very enjoyable conversation." I soon realised that that was the best way: keep it relaxed, make the minimum of fuss about the tape recorder.

England had recently completed a tour of Zimbabwe which had been something of a disaster on and off the field, and we started by talking about that. Martin had just retired as the cricket professional at the Royal Grammar School, Worcester, whose team he had taken some years earlier to Zimbabwe, and he could not understand the way the England team had shut themselves away inside their hotel. "Whenever I took a tour, I always told the boys, 'Make sure you enjoy yourselves; you may never come here again.' You can't go wrong in Zimbabwe. Everything is so free-and-easy out there. You can go to functions in shorts and sandals."

In his party had been Dean Headley, who by the time of our conversation was getting close to the England team. As the only non-white in the school side and the grandson of the great George Headley, the 'black Bradman', he attracted much attention. "The first match was at a club just outside Harare. Afterwards we were all in this little bar, with its thatched roof, and there was one of the locals serving the drinks. Somebody said, 'What sort of player is Dean Headley? Do you think he'll do any good?' Dean was very thin; he bowled quick, but he needed building up. So I said, 'Yes, I think he's going to be a really good bowler. But he needs plenty of beef, plenty of beer and a good woman.' And the bloke behind the bar, he wasn't even part of the conversation. 'My Christ,' he said. 'You're the manager for me.'"

We were already laughing, and we had not started. It was a good sign.

"So you've chosen this match against Yorkshire in 1956?"

"That's right. At Kidderminster. You've got the book there, haven't you? So just fire away."

It was my first interview with a stranger.

"Well," I said hesitantly. "What do you want me to ask you?"

I sometimes think those first interviews, when I knew nothing, were the best I did. I made no assumptions; I got them to talk through everything.

I was already fascinated by the relentlessness of their summer-long county round: two three-day games every week, often with long journeys between them. At Worcestershire, Martin said, they travelled in a team coach, long after the players at other counties were using their own cars. They lobbied for a change, and in 1957 the committee, still haunted by the death of a player in a car crash in 1939, reluctantly agreed to an end-of-season experiment. On their way up to London, a four-hour journey with a bottleneck in High Wycombe, one of them stopped for a few drinks too many and finished up demolishing several bollards in Oxford Street. When the rest of the team arrived at Lord's the next morning, they were greeted by a newspaper placard: 'County Cricketer Spends Night in Jail'.

Martin chuckled. "It was back to the coach for a few more years after that."

I got him to tell me about all the Worcestershire players, as cricketers and as men, and he soon got on to Roly Jenkins, the highly-strung leg-spinner who chattered away incessantly. "He was a real worrier about everything. He used to phone Jim Laker up at The Oval. 'I've lost it, Jim. I can't bowl well.' And Jim would say, 'What the hell do you expect me to do, Roly? I can't see you bowling. I don't know what you're doing wrong from 100 miles away.' ... I could go on for an hour, just telling stories about Roly."

"Go on then," I said.

He told of a three-day match in Scotland when Roly bowled with no luck to the Reverend Jimmy Aitchison. "They say you're a vicar?" he said at the end of one over. "Well, with your bloody luck, you'll finish up as Archbishop of Canterbury." Soon afterwards, when his finger became sore, he turned to the umpire and said, "I'll borrow the one you're not using."

"He broke down in the end. He sat down in the middle of the pitch with tears streaming down his face. 'I can't bowl anymore.' He had to come back with the twelfth man on the train. He didn't play again for a month."

I found the game, at Glasgow in 1955, and it all fitted. Aitchison hit 81, and Roly was missing from the team for a full month afterwards.

The stories flowed, and the best ones were where Roly's quick tongue punctured the absurdities of the English class system, as when he wrote an article on spin bowling for an MCC book for young cricketers and was congratulated by RWV 'Cock' Robins, a pillar of the Lord's establishment or, as Martin put it, 'a snob'.

"That was a very good article, Jenkins. Who wrote it for you?"

"I wrote it myself, sir. Who read it for you?"

I was still laughing to myself as I wrote it all up:

> One innings he is run out by RES Wyatt, another influential figure in the game. "Say something," Roly says with exasperation, "even if it's only goodbye." "I'll see you at lunch, Jenkins," comes the stern reply.

My friend Chris of the Journeymen was not impressed. "They're just stories," he said. "He'd never have said a thing like that. Not at that time."

Who knows? We can only reach the past through memories, and they may be faulty; they may have been embroidered down the years. But when Martin told me the stories, I believed the essence of them. I still do.

There was a warm glow in everything Martin said. He was indeed 'my sort of person', as Ken had suggested. He did not sentimentalise the past or say it was better than the present. He recognised the improvements in the game and, for all the tut-tutting and head-shaking of his fellow committeemen at Worcester, he knew the modern generation were no worse behaved than his had been.

He had the happiest of memories of his years of playing cricket – "I'd have played for nothing if I could have afforded to" – but he could also convey the claustrophobia of spending every day with the same team-mates.

"Roly had so many of these little sayings. I remember one of the ones he used to come out with: 'We're given memories so that we can have roses in December.' ... Of course they do wear on you when you get the same ones all the time, week after week."

Roses in December. There was the title of my chapter.

*

I found Arthur Milton's number in the Bristol telephone directory. He had always fascinated me as a character since I had read an article about him by Frank Keating. He was the last man to have played both cricket and football for England, and in later life he had become a postman.

Arthur seemed happy for me to come round. And yes, Thursday suited him fine. "What time would you like to come?"

"Well, I'll come early if you like. Say, nine o'clock."

"Oh no, don't come that early. I've got three paper rounds to get done."

Three paper rounds! Arthur had been a good-looking and intelligent sportsman who today would have had an agent negotiating a fortune for him: to appear in advertisements, to take part in television chat shows, to give talks at corporate dinners. Yet here he was, getting up every morning at half past six, riding his bicycle over Durdham Down, delivering newspapers, mostly to the elderly with whom he would often stop and talk.

"It keeps me fit, gets me out of bed," he told me in his lovely Bristol drawl. "And it's magical on the Downs. There's always early moisture on the grass and, when the sun comes up over the horizon, it draws it up and forms this low mist that runs all across the Downs. I love it. I shall do it as long as I can."

I sat on the sofa in his front room. After I had deflected him from another victory over Yorkshire, he opted for a match at Leyton in 1959 when Sam Cook, Gloucestershire's last man, a plumber from Tetbury, was on strike in the last over with one run to win. "Cooky wasn't the worst with the bat," Arthur said. "He made a hundred when he was in the 'raff', at a place called Bulawayo. He always used to talk about his hundred at Bulawayo."

These matches, I was starting to realise, were short stories, and what more could you want from a short story than a thrilling climax? When I wrote up the chapter, interweaving several newspaper reports, I had some fun.

'Cooky', he scored a hundred at Bulawayo and he has just one run to score now. He almost squeezes the next ball through the three short legs, but 'Williams, with the spectators shrieking in excitement, scrambled along the ground to cut it off.'

Three balls left. Knight bowls a perfect in-swinger, it lifts a little and catches the glove. It flies low to Joe Milner's left in the leg trap.

"If I remember right," Arthur says, "he was quite an athletic sort of lad." He flings out his left arm as he dives across the turf and, with every breath in the Ilford ground stopping for a second, the ball lodges in his outstretched palm. It is all over. A tie. The first one in county cricket since 1955. There will not be another for eight years.

It is 'the catch of the season' in the *Daily Mirror*. 'As Milner sprung up off the turf,' the *Walthamstow Guardian* describes, 'he did a passable imitation of a South African war dance.' "I don't think it was quite as good a catch as that," Arthur recalls, "but it makes a good story, doesn't it?"

"Wonderful days in the sun," Arthur said with a contented sigh. "The days were never long enough." When he decided that he had talked enough about himself and his cricket, he took to interviewing me. Where had I been working? And how soon would I be getting back to a proper job?

That was what I liked most about Arthur. Not the fact that he was a double international. Nor that he talked so engagingly about the sport he had played. No, it was the way he had lived another life after it, and that life had made him look very differently at his time as a sportsman.

"It was a bad period for me when I finished. I hadn't got myself trained for anything. I had nothing to go to, and I didn't have much money. I'd played sport because I loved it; I felt it was born in me to do. And you never think you're going to get old, do you? But then the Post Office came along, and that turned me right around, did me the world of good, because I had to serve somebody else. In my lifetime as a player, although I was interested in other people, I'd had to perform, to think about myself to stay in the game."

*

Martin and Arthur had a special status in my life as a writer. They were my first two interviews with strangers, and I felt a bond with them.

I met Arthur a few times over the following years, and he often reflected on the choice he had made in becoming a sportsman. Part of him wished he had gone up to Oxford to study maths instead of signing for the Arsenal. And, fondly though he spoke of his years in the sun, he regretted that they had taken him away from his three boys when they were growing up.

"I don't really believe in professionalism in sport. I'd have liked to have worked *and* played. I think that's what sport is for. Recreation and exercise. Away from what we do most of the week."

I had one session when he told me about his footballing days. He said how his best spell was when he was on the right wing for Arsenal and the Scottish international Jimmy Logie was inside him. Then in November 1954 they played an evening friendly against Spartak Moscow at Highbury, several years before British clubs played in European competitions.

"It was very sad. The Russian referee refused us a penalty when we were 2-1 down. After the match Jimmy refused to shake his hand, and he never played for Arsenal again. He ended up selling papers on Piccadilly."

I found myself thinking, "What would happen if they ran football clubs like that today?" They would have nobody to pick from.

I also kept in touch with Martin, who took me one afternoon to see Olive Jenkins, Roly's widow.

I had been given a tape of Roly talking on BBC Radio Hereford and Worcester, in which he had started with the story of his birth, how he was one of ten children: "When they went to bed together, my mum and dad, my dad used to say, 'Shall we go to sleep or what?' And she said, 'What?', and that's why I'm here."

Olive recalled that in June 1949 Roly had been given a week off to get married, though he only missed games against Cambridge University and the Royal Navy, and he sent the team a postcard from their honeymoon in Llandudno. On it he wrote the words, 'They say it's sunny outside.' When he returned to the cricket, he was in the brightest of moods: "I never realised," he told them, "that you could have so much fun without laughing."

In preparation for that afternoon with Olive, I had looked up Roly in *Wisden*. During the previous winter, 1948/49, he had been the star of the MCC tour of South Africa, taking more than 100 wickets in all matches and topping the averages both in the Tests and for the whole tour. Then in 1949 he took an astonishing 183 wickets, scored 1,183 runs and held 27 catches. Yet in the Test series that summer England picked six different slow bowlers, three of them leg-spinners, and Roly did not play once. It seemed incomprehensible.

Olive produced an envelope marked 'Unpublished Article', and in it were eight pages of typed script. Somebody had once started writing up Roly's life story, and the unfinished result had lain buried deep in a drawer.

> There are those who assert that he was omitted because of a frivolous (and harmless) remark made while batting for MCC in a friendly match. He was certainly carpeted at Lord's for his levity and, it seems, lost his Test place because of it.

"What on earth did he say?"

"Ah well, I don't suppose it matters to repeat it now. He was batting on the last morning, and he said to this fancy cap, 'I'm going to play as an amateur today. I want to catch the early train back to Worcester.'"

We sat for a moment in silence. Roses in December, certainly, but also the stab from the thorn. Was it really only fifty years earlier that England had been like that?

5

From the Gower to North Norfolk

Like the county cricketers of the 1950s I was driving back and forth all over England and Wales. One day I would be on the Gower peninsula, drinking soup with Glamorgan's Don Shepherd, looking out across the magnificent Three Cliffs Bay. Another day I would be driving up and down a remote lane in North Norfolk, trying to find the house where Yorkshire's Ken Taylor lived. I ate home-made cake in front of a log fire in the Cotswolds with Hampshire's Malcolm Heath and lunch in a noisy pub near Sandown Park racecourse with Surrey's Bernie Constable. Warwickshire's Tom Cartwright talked to me during a break in a coaching day at a sports hall in South Wales, and Dennis Brookes welcomed me into his house six doors down from the gates of Northampton's County Ground, a house that felt like a time warp of the 1950s; his wife served tea from a trolley just like the one my mother had.

When I rang to explain what I wanted, I was apologetic, imagining that they had many such requests and that they might be irritated by me pushing into their lives. "I'll only need an hour or two," I would say in reassurance. It took me a while to realise that, for many of them, their years in the public eye were long gone. They enjoyed my interest.

After my first three pieces – with Ken, Martin and Arthur – I had a strong sense of what I was trying to achieve. These were short stories, each centred on a single game, and my task was to tease out memories of the game itself, of the key players and of their way of life. Inevitably, forty years on, much had been forgotten, but I devised ways to fill in the gaps, sometimes finding a second voice to add an extra flavour.

One match, a tragi-comic encounter at the Ind Coope ground at Burton-on-Trent, was chosen both by Derbyshire's Harold Rhodes and Hampshire's Malcolm Heath. On a damp pitch made treacherous by a hot sun burning down on it, a record 39 wickets fell in one day, a disaster for Jack Green, the groundsman, in his one big match of the season. When I discovered that Jack Green's son David was playing in the match, home from university, I drove to Marlborough and interviewed him as well.

Still recovering from the war, with rationing not ending till 1954, Britain in those years lacked the wherewithal to prevent such calamities, yet, as Malcolm said, "It was a tremendous game of cricket. It's stood in people's memories."

Harold and Malcolm were both bowlers, of course, unlike Tom Cartwright who chose a match at The Oval when, as a fresh-faced 17-year-old opening batsman, he scored 0 and 9 in an innings defeat that was all over inside a day. "I think I learnt more in my time at the wicket in that game," he said, "than I learnt in any period of any other game."

Tom was not alone in believing that the skills required to play in the 1950s were greater than those in the 1990s, by which time the covering of pitches during rain breaks, the improvements in drainage and ground equipment and the abandonment of so many idiosyncratic out-grounds had produced a standardisation that, for the generation I was interviewing, had removed so much of the unpredictable charm of the game.

"You came in on the first day," Malcolm Heath said. "You took your tie off, and you stuck it on the peg. And there was this glorious uncertainty of not knowing what was going to happen."

Much has improved since those years and, as a consequence, we have come to expect everything to work, everything to be just as it should be.

*

In the end I needed 12 matches to span the 17 counties, and eight of those chosen twelve took place at out-grounds: Bath, Blackheath, Brentwood and Burton; Huddersfield, Kidderminster, Leyton and Stroud. Now only Kidderminster is used by the first-class game, and only in an emergency when the Worcester ground is flooded.

With fewer cars on the road and people more settled in their lives, with television in its infancy, county cricket went out in search of its audience. As John Arlott, from Basingstoke, wrote of the game at Stroud, 'The folk there speak of "the cricket" as we did when I was a boy and the cricket sometimes came to us, seeming – like the circus elephants when they paraded through the main street – a very large matter indeed in our small country town.' As one who grew up in a village outside Salisbury, I can relate to that.

The process of finding people to interview was a haphazard one. I asked Martin Horton to recommend a Derbyshire player, and he put me onto Harold Rhodes. Then I asked Harold for a Yorkshire name, and he suggested Ken Taylor. "I think he's teaching somewhere in Norfolk," he said, and I tracked him down through the phone books in Bath's Central Library.

Ken would become a major figure in my life in the years that followed, a good friend, but my interview with him that day was not my best. He made me very welcome, cooking me lunch and showing me his art work, but his memories of the game at Hove, when Yorkshire clinched their first title for ten years, were not great. To compound my difficulty, he kept wandering across the room, standing in front of the fireplace, out of range of my cassette recorder. When I rang up his great friend Bryan Stott the next week, I wished I had started with him.

Bryan was running his family plumbing business in Leeds, and my phone call interrupted his morning's work. Yet he was soon in full flow with his memories of the Hove match and of the aftermath when, as newly crowned champions, they drove up to Scarborough. The demands of his business were clearly not going to disturb that flow.

"The one thing that still gets to my heart and soul, Stephen, was the reception back in Yorkshire. We got to Scarborough about 2 or 2.30 in the morning ... I'm tied up at the moment, just put it down there, will you? ... We were all in different cars so we arrived in penny numbers. But everybody was waiting up for us. All along the streets and outside the hotel. It will stay with me for ever ... Just down there, please ..."

The following morning they were asked to field first, and the Yorkshire team walked to the middle through a long tunnel of cheering supporters.

"I'm almost in tears now thinking about it, Stephen ... Just a minute, will you, I'm on the phone ... I remember thinking to myself, 'My gosh, this is something I'm never going to forget.'"

I scribbled down his words as best I could. Almost forty years had passed, but the emotions of that morning were as intense as ever.

*

The day before my meeting with Ken Taylor, I visited Dickie Dodds in St Neot's. I had spoken on the phone to his Essex captain Doug Insole about Arthur Milton's Leyton game, and I asked him to recommend an Essex player. "Preferably somebody with a good sense of humour."

"Well, if you like your humour bucolic," he replied, "you could try Tonker Taylor. Or if you'd prefer it religious, there's Dickie Dodds."

'Religious' caught my imagination, it sounded different, so Dickie Dodds it was.

"I've written out some notes on the players and the game," he said when I arrived at his door. "It will save us both a lot of time."

My heart sank. I wanted his natural voice to flow out of conversation, and as politely as I could I insisted on starting from scratch.

Dickie was an active proponent of Moral Rearmament, believing strongly that all progress stems from the individual human spirit, not from political movements, and that people are at their best when they let the Holy Spirit flow freely through them. For him, this interview was an opportunity for him to promote his beliefs.

"The highest form of prayer I knew was to play beautiful shots for a creator who loved beautiful things. My job was to give recreation to those who came to watch. Re-creation. Lift their spirits. I believe that we can all find re-creation when we glimpse creativity. But if what we see is materialism, it will be dull."

He had stayed on the periphery of cricket in later life, seeking out people who might respond to his message. One was the Middlesex batsman Wilf Slack, whose career he transformed. Another in whom he saw potential for conversion was Ian Botham, whose words after one of his great innings had been given to Dickie by a friend, a priest: "You've got to enjoy it, let it go, let it speak for itself, let it take you over. You've got to set it free and not get in its way."

"That," the priest said, "is a perfect expression of the Holy Spirit."

Compton, Sobers, Lara all played the game as he believed it should be played, but not Ken Barrington – "I wouldn't have crossed the road to see him bat" – and not his Essex team-mate Trevor Bailey: "Bailey to me was an enigma. Whatever it was that drove him, I never found it. I still don't know. Nobody knew where he came from. He was a complete mystery."

The denouement of his chosen game, at Brentwood in 1952, was centred on Bailey. On strike with nine wickets down, and three runs needed off four balls, he attempted to hit a straight six. The catch was dropped in the deep, they ran two, and now there was just one run to win.

To my great amusement I found a coaching book written by Trevor, in which he offered advice for such a situation: 'The one thing that the batsman must avoid is to lose his head. He must avoid having a death or glory swing.'

He was the ultimate thinking cricketer, always calculating the odds, and what did he do? He tried to hit another six and this time was caught. And there was Dickie, who believed in going with the spirit, shaking his head in despair. "I don't know why he did it. There were three to win off four balls. Why on earth did he keep trying to hit sixes? ... He claimed he didn't know what the score was. But Bailey who always knew everything about everything, forgotten what the score was, that was ridiculous."

There was so much that fascinated me in all this: the challenging distinctness of Dickie's message, the strange incongruity of Bailey's batting, the contradiction of the free-flowing Dodds, a vicar's son, being the professional and the ever-calculating Bailey, son of a minor civil servant, the supposed amateur.

I wrote up the game, calling it 'The Enigma of Bailey' and beginning with the quote about nobody knowing where he came from. As with all these interviews, I had promised Dickie that I would send it to him for his approval, and he rang me immediately, alarmed to discover that he had gone so far off message. "Tape recorders are dangerous things; I'm afraid I talked without thinking. Only I have never been interviewed like this before."

Could it really be true that Dickie had opened the batting for Essex for the first 14 summers after the war, come close to being picked for an MCC tour and had never given such an interview? What a different world that was! When in 2014 I was finishing a book about the county championship, I wanted to interview the last person to make their debut in that summer, and it turned out to be a 17-year-old 'A' level student from Swansea, Aneurin Donald, who had played in Glamorgan's last game. I asked Huw Morris, the county's Chief Executive, for his contact details, and he handed them over happily. "He'll be fine," he said. "He's had his media training."

In time Dickie and I got the piece right, to the satisfaction of both of us. There was something in what Dickie had said – about materialism not being an adequate motive in life, about needing to love what you were doing – that struck a chord with me, and I was especially moved by his affection for his opening partner Sonny Avery, a barber's son from the East End who had spent his later life as a coach at Monmouth School. "He loved seeing the craft, the skill, coming alive in a boy. I'm sure he was a wonderful coach. Sport was in him. He was impelled towards it. I really believe that almost everybody's got a destiny of one sort or another."

Monmouth was not far away so I telephoned Sonny Avery. His wife Marjorie answered, telling me that he was very poorly, close to death. But she suggested a time that I should come up. Twice he was too ill to see me, and after the second cancellation I suggested leaving it. I was making a nuisance of myself. "No, he does want to see you," she insisted, and finally there was an afternoon when he was well enough for a visit.

He sat in the armchair. He was one of those people whose face told you straightaway that he was a kind man, and he tried hard to answer my questions. He was clearly in pain but, speaking slowly, he recalled his days working as a young clerk at Essex's Leyton headquarters in the early 1930s, looking down at the great players and figuring out their styles.

He told me of his debut in 1935. "I was with Tom Wade at Chelmsford. The idea was to help the groundsman in the morning and to practise in the afternoon. But how could we practise? Tom was a wicket-keeper, and I was a batsman. This girl called me. 'Come along,' she said. 'You're playing at The Oval tomorrow.' I thought she was pulling my leg."

He scored 28 not out in the first innings, batting at number nine. But his memory was sharper when he recalled his second innings. "I didn't last very long. Alf Gover got me out for a duck, caught at the wicket. The following season I was promised I would play in every game. In actual fact I played none."

I made the mistake of butting in. I wanted to know if anything was said that summer, about his not playing. Did people in those days talk to you about such things? Or were you left to cope on your own?

He paused for an age. I had broken the flow of his thought, and he struggled to find some way of answering my question. Eventually he spoke: "It's such a long time ago to remember a detail like that."

"We always told him he should write a book," Marjorie said. "He had so many lovely stories."

The memories had already faded. Within weeks Sonny was dead.

I met Bernie Constable, the Surrey batsman, and he too died soon afterwards. He told me the story of his championship debut at the end of 1939. With war imminent, the match was re-routed from The Oval to Old Trafford. They arrived at 4 a.m., slept in the pavilion, and on the third morning, play was abandoned and they caught the train back to Euston. "Kids being evacuated were all over the station when we arrived."

Here was a glimpse of our history; with each death it was slipping further from view.

*

I had coffee in a hotel lounge near the M25 with Kent's Derek Ufton. The county was at its lowest ebb in the 1950s, and he chose a match at The Oval when against all the odds they beat the mighty Surrey. It had all the makings of a good story, but Derek's memories of the game were too fragmentary and, unlike all the other old cricketers, he did not shine a cheerful light on those years.

A Charlton Athletic footballer who played once for England, he wanted to be a winner, but he summed up his county's culture at that time as: "You're playing for Kent, enjoy your cricket, we're nice people, play the game and jolly good turnips." The mid-season arrival of amateurs, depriving professionals of their match fees, created a bad team spirit, he said, and, when I invited him to talk about the individuals in the Kent side, he was uncomplimentary about most of them.

"Who were the happy guys?" I asked, looking for some lightness.

"I don't know that any of us were. We were such a poor team. We had more friction than fun. Some of us wanted to do well but, if you wanted to do well, it got kicked out of you somehow."

On the journey home I decided to discard the match, and perhaps that was a mistake. My collection of pieces was a tapestry of voices, and his darker offering might have given the whole a richer mix.

He did tell me one tremendous story. As I drove home, I thought to myself, "The trip has been worth it if only for that." It involved a man called

Alec Debnam, a flight-lieutenant in the war who had switched from amateur to professional which, according to Derek, was especially disapproved of.

"I played a game for the second eleven at Bristol. In 1949. You can look it up in *Wisden*. A chap called Alec Debnam was playing. He scored 177 and took a lot of wickets, bowling leg-spinners. We won the game, and the skipper Gerry Simpson, lovely guy, well into his sixties by then, spoke to us. He had a stutter. 'U-ufton, you and D-d-debnam, go down to Weston-super-Mare. D-don't be late. You're both playing against S-somerset tomorrow.' I knew I would be playing. There was a Test match, and I'd deputised for Godfrey during the previous Test. It was going to be my second game in the first team. We got the train, and we turned up at the hotel. Didn't see a soul. Got to the ground the next morning. I stood to attention. 'I'm Ufton. This is Debnam.' David Clark was captain, and he read out the team. And he never mentioned Debnam. So Alec said, 'Excuse me. I've been told I was playing.' David Clark said, 'I've read out the team. What do you mean you were told you were playing?' He said, 'I got 177 at Bristol.'

"I can remember it like it was yesterday. In the tiny little pavilion at Weston. David Clark said, 'Mister Pryer has come all the way down from Cambridge especially to play. And you, Debnam, you can be twelfth man. Put your whites on if you like. Bring out the drinks.' Mister Pryer got nought and one, or something, and never played again. That used to happen all the time to us."

It was a wonderfully revealing story, and I chuckled about it all the way home. But, alas, I did look it up in *Wisden*, and it was not right. Yes, it was Weston. Yes, it was Derek's second game for Kent. And yes, Barry Pryer played. He got nought and seven and yes, he never played again. So far, so good. But Debnam's 177 at Bristol was a whole year earlier. And worse still, the Kent team at Weston included one A. Debnam.

Something along these lines must have happened somewhere, or Derek, who was no fool, would not have told the story. But I could not figure it out. With great reluctance I put it to one side. Cricket, with its every score recorded, can be the enemy of lively story-telling.

One who had no such concern for factual accuracy was 'Bomber' Wells, whose name had come up repeatedly on my travels. The funniest man on the circuit, the tales about him were many and, although I had already covered Gloucestershire with Arthur Milton, I decided to visit him. We agreed that I would arrive at his house in Gloucester at ten o'clock one Friday morning. I was due at Ken's net in Stroud at four so that would give me plenty of time.

Normally I set out for an interview with two 90-minute cassettes, but somehow, though I was yet to meet Bomber, I had an inkling of what was in store and I added a third.

"What do you want? Stories?" he asked when I settled on the sofa in his front room. He sat at right angles to me in a large armchair, looking out towards the Gloucester ring road, with an old cross-collie dog lying on a rug at his feet. His wife Mary brought me a cup of tea and disappeared out the back.

"Yes, stories would be good," I said, and off he went with a long yarn about his debut match, how one Friday evening he had been sitting on a bench in the park with his girl friend, eating fish and chips, when "this huge chap came across. I thought, 'I recognise him.' It was old Tom Goddard; his picture was in the paper every other day. He came up to me and he said, 'Are you Bomber Wells? ... Get down to Bristol tomorrow. You're playing against Sussex.'"

Arthur had already told me about this match, how none of them had ever seen Bomber before, how he strolled into the dressing room casually, a rough-and-ready character from the back streets of Gloucester. Then, coming in off a two-pace run, he took six wickets in the Sussex first innings. In all he bowled 61 overs in the match, at the end of which he is reported to have looked round the dressing room. "Well," he said, "if I'm going to be playing for this team, I can see that I'll be bowling a lot of overs. I shall have to cut down my run-up."

Bomber had only got a little way into this tale when he digressed into another story, then another. On and on he went, like a great Catherine wheel sending off sparks in every direction. Mary took the dog for a walk, we had some cheese-and-tomato rolls for lunch and, even with his mouth full, Bomber never stopped talking. Shortly after 2.30, with Mary out again with the dog, the third tape came to an end, and I took to scribbling notes as fast as I could. At 3.30, in a brief lull, I said that I needed to go, but Bomber ignored this and carried on. The dog went for a third walk, and just before half past four, conscious that Ken's net would be half-over by the time I got there, I stood up. "I really must go now," I said.

Bomber looked crestfallen: "But I haven't finished telling you about my debut match."

*

When I got to see Dennis Brookes in Northampton, I was near the end of my journey. With only Northamptonshire and Kent remaining of the 17 counties, I was hoping that Dennis would choose a thrilling game at Dover that I had spotted.

Instead, he opted for a match at Old Trafford in 1953. I turned to it in *Wisden*, and there were names in the Northamptonshire team that, even after months of immersion in 1950s cricket, I did not recognise – Greasley,

Pickering – and no sign of the larger-than-life characters Freddie Brown and Jock Livingston. I tried to steer him to the Dover game, but he was firm. He was a frail man, quietly spoken and very considerate, but he had been a justice of the peace and, even in his eighties, he retained an air of authority. So I settled back to hear his story of the Old Trafford game.

What a good story it was! Little Northants, who had never won at Old Trafford, scraping home by one wicket against a Lancashire side hoping to win the championship. On a dangerous pitch Frank Tyson, back in Lancashire for the first time since they had rejected him, bowled at his fastest; Geoff Edrich, hardened by years as a Japanese prisoner-of-war, with his wrist broken by a Tyson thunderbolt, hit a battling 81; and, best of all, the unknown Peter Pickering, summoned to Old Trafford on the morning of the match, hit crucial runs in both Northamptonshire innings.

"The trouble in cricket," Dennis said, "is that the professionals, they see something happening and they think, 'Oh you can't ... oh dear ...' But Pickering went in, he was an amateur cricketer, he just played as if he was playing against schoolboys. He was a professional footballer, he'd played for Chelsea, so his nerves were all right. He played a natural game. He wasn't waiting to see if the ball turned or popped. He just hit it."

I tracked down Peter Pickering in South Africa, and he replied with a long letter. As his only game of first-class cricket, it was still fresh in his memory, not confused with a host of other games. He recalled being at his desk at work when the public address system summoned him to the chairman's office, how he was lent a car to drive to Manchester, how he arrived after lunch and had difficulty persuading the gateman that he was playing.

It was the best story in the book, and Dennis, with a twinkle in his eye, enhanced it with some delightful observations. One tale I especially loved involved Freddie Brown and Wilf Wooller, two Cambridge University men who seemed to treat the contests between their Northants and Glamorgan teams as a private feud. At the end of one tedious draw, when neither captain gave the other a chance of victory, they met at the pavilion gate. "Thanks for fuck all, Wilf," Brown snapped, only to get the reply, "Bugger off, Freddie." Behind them Len Muncer, Glamorgan's senior professional, turned to Dennis, his counterpart: "Oh, I am glad I sent my children to elementary school."

*

By the end of April my travels were over. I had interviewed so many different characters: Bomber Wells was a comedian, Dickie Dodds an evangelist, Tom Cartwright a craftsman. There was John Pretlove, a Southern amateur, who had had a successful career in the construction industry, Ken Taylor, a

Northern professional, who had taught art in a public school. Martin Horton had been New Zealand's national coach, Dennis Brookes chairman of the magistrates' bench in Northampton. Terry Spencer ran a window-fitting business in Leicester, Harold Rhodes was a travel agent in Derby, and Arthur Milton cycled across the Bristol Downs with the morning papers.

They had gone their separate ways after cricket, each with his own memories. Yet there was a common picture that I had built up from listening to them all.

They had grown up in a world without television sets and home computers, with only a few motor cars. Most workers were in manual jobs, with just two or three weeks of paid holiday a year. They had all known war, and their values were permeated with ideals of public service, hard work and fair play, ideals that, by the time we were talking in 1997, had been eroded by affluence.

Inevitably there was an element of nostalgia in looking back to this lost world, and perhaps some of their testimony had acquired a rosier hue than it had at the time. In the final section, in which I rounded up the themes of the book, I quoted the Yorkshire slow bowler Arthur Booth who had played on either side of the Second World War:

> He often said that it was a better game when he started than when he finished. "Mind you," he would add, "my father said the same." His father's playing days began in the Golden Age before the first war. "And his father before him said the same as well. My word, it must have been a hell of a game when it started."

It was never my intention to say that life was better in the 1950s: the long hours of low-paid work, the diseases that had no cure, the widespread colour prejudice. But, at the end of the book, as I reflected on the memories I had gathered, there niggled in me a sense that something might have been lost:

> Perhaps the past is a foreign country that the old, who once inhabited it, will always see through rose-tinted spectacles. Or are their memories our last contact with a lost world of well-honed craft skills and shared good sportsmanship? Could it be that, in the drive for profit and prosperity, we have started to forget why we created such a wonderful game?

6

My back pages – the 1950s

When we look back to the 1950s, we tend to think of it as a drab, grey time, giving way in the 1960s to an explosion of life and colour. Maybe that is partly because the surviving film of the 1950s is mostly in monochrome. Yet undoubtedly, so soon after the war, life was harder. The last rationing restrictions were not lifted till 1954, there were uncleared bomb sites, and the consumer boom of motor cars, washing machines and cheap package holidays to the continent had not yet reached large parts of the population.

Britain was a conservative country, with a small and a large C. It was holding on to its traditional way of life, with a powerful Church and a strong belief in the family unit. People, for the most part, knew their place in the social order, and that bred a mixture of good manners and deference to authority.

We look back now, and we shake our heads at the pompous absurdities of the old class system, the talent that was wasted as a result. We are appalled by the cruel prejudice that greeted the post-war immigrants. We view with pity the low wages, the long working hours, the industrial accidents that blighted lives.

Yet it is never that easy, is it? There are down-sides to all change, and writing *Runs in the Memory* reminded me of aspects of the world of my childhood that were good and that were lost in the years that followed.

Perhaps that old world of county cricket was one. It had a summer-long rhythm, unchanging from year to year, and it held a central place in our nation's sporting consciousness. It was played with a strong sense of etiquette, and it embraced cricketers of all types from all backgrounds.

Soon enough, in the 1960s, English cricket's economic viability would reach crisis point, and it would succumb to an avalanche of reforms: one-day matches, Sunday play, commercial sponsorship, the introduction of overseas stars, the abolition of amateurs, a diminution of MCC's powers and the creation of a trade union-style Cricketers' Association.

In all this it held up a mirror to the wider society, where so many of the old ways had become unsustainable and were being reformed.

*

In the 1950s, when our father's timber business was still prospering, we lived a life of comfortable routine. We were day-boys at a prep school in Salisbury five miles from home, and every morning our mother drove us there. A stickler for time-keeping, she got us out of the house at ten past eight and delivered us fifteen minutes later.

With three boys to keep occupied in the car, she created a game of observation. She drew up a list of ten familar faces on the route, and we had to see how many we could spot. Among them were our village postlady, a milkman in Wilton, a moped rider with a yellow patch over his eye, an elderly man who sat on a bench outside the mental hospital gates, our dentist walking down Castle Street, a man with an umbrella striding down Wyndham Hill and, as our number ten, Mr Rigiani, a teacher who walked down Wain-A-Long Road to our school. We never got all ten, but we rarely got less than seven. At one stage, to our sorrow, 'Patch' disappeared for several months, but he came back and we all cheered when we saw him again.

As a young boy that was the world I knew. Everybody was going about their business at the same time every day, year after year. Nothing changed.

Our dentist, number six of our ten to spot, was a tall, middle-aged Scotsman, with a little moustache that was greying, always polite and correct in his manners. His two boys went to our prep school, where he came to watch the rugby matches, sitting throughout on a shooting stick.

Kind though he was in his formal way, I dreaded the visits we paid him each school holiday. I always needed fillings, and his old-style drill was an agony, grinding remorselessly on the nerve of the tooth. But we had confidence in him and, even into the 1970s, when I had left home and was living in London, I went back to see him twice a year. Our father had died and, with so little left of the childhood world I had known, he offered me a comforting point of connection with my pre-adolescent world.

"How are you doing, young Stephen? Do you get to play any cricket?"

He had left his surgery in the centre of town and was working from a room in his own home, a mile away in leafy Stratford-sub-Castle. For a while at this new address his waiting room would be busy, with a receptionist answering the phone. Then gradually, as he grew older, the waiting room became emptier and he was answering the phone himself. "Yes, when would you like to come? Today, tomorrow, next week? ... Morning or afternoon? ... Ten? Eleven? Twelve? ... Half past eleven. Right you are. Let me see ... Yes, you're in luck. I've got a cancellation. I could squeeze you in there, my boy." On one occasion, pinging the bell and wandering through the open front door, I sat for an hour in the upstairs waiting room, with the house in silence, before he realised I was there. By the end I was wondering if we were now his only patients.

He had time to talk. Once, when we got onto the subject of evolution, he pulled out of a cupboard a large jawbone that he had brought back from East

Africa during his wartime service in the Army Medical Corps. "Just look at it," he said. "What a wonderful specimen."

He left the jaw in my hands as he returned to the mixing tray. His voice was more hoarse each time I visited, and he had taken to wiping his cough on his trousers. "In a hundred years' time there won't be a jaw like that anywhere in the world. Not eating potato crisps and Instant Mash. Nature has got the message."

The last time I saw him, he said my fillings were all good. "I think you can relax and look forward to some settled years with your teeth." Unusually that day he accompanied me down to the front door and, as I left, he called a "God bless" after me. Soon afterwards my mother heard that he had died; he had had cancer of the throat.

Two or three months later I developed an excruciating toothache and, with some trepidation, I checked into a dentist in a seedy shopping street in Finsbury Park where my teeth were inspected by a hyper-macho Australian who declared them a complete mess. "What have you been doing, sucking yourself to sleep with sugar lumps?" He threw a copy of Reveille into my lap and bounded through swing doors where I heard him shouting at another patient. "Mr Ali, I'm not mending that denture again. I've told you, it's no good. You get yourself a new one, Mr Ali, or you clear off. Do you hear me? You clear off. Nurse, prepare an injection for Mr Whatsisname next door."

He had equipment I had never seen before – a near-painless needle for an injection, a high-speed drill, X-rays – and over several visits he replaced every filling in my mouth. And, though it was all on the National Health Service, he surprised me by asking for payment, something our Salisbury dentist had never got round to doing.

On one occasion, during a dustmen's strike, he filled my mouth with paraphernalia and launched into an angry tirade. "Did you see that Japanese film on television last night, Nurse?" He stepped back, kicked up his feet and, with an "Aaah-so", aimed a mock karate chop at my neck. "You've got to admire them, haven't you? They come over here with their watches and cameras, and we can't even get the rubbish off the street for bloody strikers. Trade unions, Jesus Christ! I'd shoot the lot of them. I would. I'm not joking. They've destroyed this country. People all over the world used to look up to England and ... Keep your mouth still, man."

I was lost in a big city, a long way from home, a long, long way from the certainties of my childhood.

*

My parents did not vote Conservative, but in many ways they were the most conservative of people, sticking loyally to what they knew.

Every year we took our family holiday in Eastbourne. Always the same fortnight, always the Burlington Hotel on Grand Parade. We booked early and asked for the same rooms, 206 and 207 with an inter-joining bathroom, looking out over the floral display to the pier. We even asked for the same table in the restaurant so that we could be served by the same waiter, a kindly old chap called Harry Ford. Every year without fail he recommended a trip to Alfriston. "It's a lovely village; you won't be disappointed." I am not sure we ever went, but he left his mark on Peter who chose it for his honeymoon.

In the mornings we went onto the beach with our buckets and spades and swimming trunks. In the afternoons we went on a cruise round the bay or a walk up to Beachy Head or a trip to Drusillas Zoo or Battle Abbey; there was so much to do. Then, if we were back in time, we had tea in the lounge of the hotel where a waitress came round with a trolley with a great spread of cakes to choose from. They were the best two weeks of the year.

Amidst the holiday-makers in the hotel were some elderly folk who lived there all the year round. They were mostly women, probably widows who had been left enough money to live this seaside life with no domestic chores and no cooking. One, who always sat on her own, had a strange mottled skin, perhaps from living abroad; she was heavily made up and smoked constantly through a long cigarette holder. Another, a woman of great mystery to us, had a screen drawn around her whenever she sat down for tea. She was always dressed in black and, if she rang her bell, the waitress dropped everything and hurried straight to her.

In the autumn of 1981, soon after Mum died, I took Sue to Eastbourne for the day, to show her the scenes of my childhood. It was cold and windy, with rain in the air, and everything seemed so shabby: the bandstand, the floral display, even the pier. None of it was as it had been in the 1950s when the whole seafront was packed with holiday-makers. To dispel my melancholy, I suggested that we go to the Burlington for afternoon tea. Cakes on a trolley. "Let's splash out."

The revolving door and the porter's kiosk were just the same, but there was a partition across where we used to walk through to the lounge. I enquired about tea, and my request was met with confusion. Eventually we were sat down awkwardly in front of the partition, and they brought us a pot of tea, made from teabags, and two small packets of biscuits wrapped in cellophane.

Seven years later the hotel featured in a BBC documentary. It was being refurbished, a £20 million uplift to create a new conference-and-banqueting complex. There were only seven long-term residents left, and they were reassured that all would be well when they were moved out of their prime seafront rooms for the duration of the works. Then, when it was all over, they found themselves in smaller rooms on the top floor at the back of the hotel, overlooking the fire escape.

The world had moved on. Business conferences were what made money now, not the holiday-makers of the 1950s and certainly not the old ladies living on family trusts and dwindling investments, each demanding to be served at a separate table in the restaurant. If the hotel was to survive, it needed to shake off the impression that it had seen better days.

I wonder. Is county cricket like that? Something that had its heyday long ago, that can only survive by being ruthlessly refurbished.

Perhaps. And perhaps that Burlington manager was right; the hotel could not afford to indulge those old women any longer. He was full of charm, with a twinkle in his eye when he told one of them, "I'm sure we'll come to an amicable arrangement."

7

Not financially viable

At Waterstones, working through the books in the cricket section, I drew up a list of all the possible publishers for my book. Then, after I had completed a few chapters, I wrote to them all, enclosing a brief synopsis and a sample of writing.

The replies came back, as many as twenty of them, and in their differing ways they all said the same thing: 'Your material fully deserves publication but would represent a risk to us ... I am sorry to say I am somewhat doubtful about being able to achieve sufficient sales to make it financially viable. We would need to sell at least 2,000 ... This proposal sounds wonderful. However, it's too specialised for our current list ... A lively and readable text. We just don't sense we could find a large enough market on 1950s county cricket ... Ideally I am looking for biographies fronted by well-known and established names.'

Each time I opened another of these letters, I felt a pang of hurt. My neighbour Adrian's words returned – "That's not a job, it's only a hobby" – and I wondered whether I had got lost down a cul-de-sac. My pot of redundancy money was emptying; I had a family to support.

Yet the mood rarely lasted long. I had to go on, not least for the men I had interviewed. Several of them, when I sent them their chapters, reacted with an intensity of emotion that suggested I had touched a deep chord.

"It's really smashing," Bryan Stott rang to tell me. "I've read the piece three times now, and I'm still finding new things in it."

"It's brilliant," Tom Cartwright said, and I was so relieved and so glowing with the warmth of his praise that I did not quite catch what he said about 'not since John Arlott'.

My fall-back position, to publish the pieces in *Cricket Lore*, no longer seemed adequate so I started to explore the idea of publishing it myself. Others had done it, I discovered, and the sums of money mentioned were not prohibitive. There was even a local printing firm, Antony Rowe in Chippenham, which structured its pricing to attract short print runs.

I struggled for a long time for a title. For a while it was *The Memory Be Green*, a line from *Hamlet*, but that seemed a bit contrived. Then it was *The Matches They Still Remember*, but that was lifeless. Ken Biddulph's suggestion

Memories Are Made Of This was too sentimental, and the same applied to *Roses In December*. Eventually, while watching Alan Bennett's *Forty Years On* at the theatre in Bath, I found *Runs in the Memory* popping into my head.

Then there were the illustrations. Expecting to find a publisher, I had given this no thought. I had no idea how to access old photographs or what they cost. Ken Taylor had shown me some crayon drawings he had done of his cricketing contemporaries, and one evening the thought occurred to me that I might use them instead of photographs. I would have liked Sue, a trained artist, to have looked at them, but that was not possible. So, with nothing more than the knowledge that Ken had studied at The Slade and a general sense of having liked what I saw, I rang him. We arranged to meet at the end of May when the Journeymen were on tour in Norfolk.

I knew from Sue how little publishers pay illustrators, and I was determined to be more generous. But what would Ken think a reasonable price? Sitting in his car outside Sainsbury's in Fakenham, I anxiously broached the subject, offering an advance payment and a royalty. I was trying hard to sound as if I knew what I was talking about, but I was unsure how convincing he found me. Maybe he expected nothing much to come of my book. "Whatever's reasonable," he said airily.

I decided that I needed a foreword. My first instinct was to go for a big name outside the world of cricket, somebody to catch the wavering buyer's eye, so I wrote to Harry Secombe's agent. "I'm afraid he's off to Australia in a few days," came the reply. Then I changed tack and thought about the cricketers I had interviewed. Tom Cartwright seemed the obvious choice; I knew he was on a wavelength with what I was trying to achieve.

He readily put pen to paper:

> It must be very difficult for the modern county cricketer to grasp just how much glamour there was being a player in those days. Saturday mornings – the first day of a Championship match – at Edgbaston you would see huge queues at every entrance. It was not unusual to see the gates closed before lunch ... The publication of *Runs In The Memory* will give insight and pleasure to those who didn't experience the fifties. To those who did, it will be a welcome reminder of a magic time.

The summer of 1997 was a strange one for me. I picked up three part-time lecturing posts at local universities, all to start in the autumn, and that gave me a sense that my time on my own was drawing to a close. The book would have to be taken through so many processes before then. But what were they? I knew almost nothing about any of them. I had read books all my life – I had an MA, with Distinction, in English Literature – but, when I took books down from the shelf, I found I knew nothing of the conventions of title pages and margins. Now it is the first thing I notice when I pick up a book.

Somehow I stumbled through it all and, for a while, the names that had filled my head for six months – Close and Cowdrey, Shepherd and Shackleton – were replaced by WinZip and Postscript, Chromalin and ISBN. I set up spreadsheets that calculated breakeven points for different print runs, settling on 1,500 copies, and I laboured my way through the tasks of indexing and proof-reading. I also wrote a blurb for the dust jacket, a strange out-of-body experience in which I had to look at my work as if I was somebody else:

> It is an original book, comic and serious, nostalgic and critical. The games themselves are all enthralling, and the players' voices combine to provide a portrait of a period of cricket that is rich in craft skills and camaraderie.

A broken thumb stopped me from playing cricket, though I went along to most of the Journeymen matches, as much for the camaraderie as for the cricket. There were three all-day games at Fenner's, and they named me Man of the Weekend for my scoring. For much of the time I was on my own on the side of the ground, perched on a chair on a narrow stone ledge where I had to cope with the twin demands of the scorebook and the antiquated board. Some of the numbers were on rollers, but others were on tin plates which had to be put up with a long pole, a perilous task on the ledge. It was often frantic work, not helped by the great staple-like contraption that was clamping my broken left thumb. But I loved the mad challenge of it. "There'd be five people on a county ground doing what you were doing," one team-mate said.

The Journeymen were less inclined to appreciate my book, taking great delight in repeating to everybody my encounter with the former Sussex captain Robin Marlar. Robin was the book reviewer for the magazine *The Cricketer*, probably the most important place for me to get a favourable write-up, and I was conscious that my last chapter, with its description of the Yorkshire victory at Hove in 1959, had had more than a little fun at his expense.

I was an outsider. I had no idea which jokes would cause offence and which would be taken in good spirit. So I thought I would do well to send him the chapter and invite his comments before I went to press. I posted it to the head-hunting agency he ran in central London. After two or three weeks when I had had no reply, I rang his secretary to check it had been received.

That evening, the longest day of the year, the last light was fading from the sky when the telephone rang. "Mr Chalke? This is Robin Marlar speaking."

My heart leapt up in anxiety; I was not sure I liked the tone of his voice. "I receive a great deal of correspondence in the course of a week, much of which I care not to answer, and yours most certainly came into that category. I have absolutely no comment to make, either now or at any time in the future, about any matter you raise in your letter." I was still quaking the next day.

I sought some advice from Vic Marks, cricket correspondent of *The Observer*, whom I had got to know from a fixture the Journeymen played against his brother's village team. "Oh well," he said cheerfully. "Maybe three or four paragraphs of Robin's bile will do more for your sales than some anodyne review."

I rang Jim Parks, who had contributed to the chapter, and he laughed. "It's a good job I didn't tell you about some of the more ridiculous things he did."

On reflection some of what I wrote about Robin was too facetious, and I regret that. It was not the purpose of the book to create bad feeling between former cricketers – though, of course, my Journeymen team-mates all thought it was hilarious.

We lived in Fairfield Park in Bath so we called ourselves Fairfield Books, just right for cricket, and I turned my mind to marketing. I priced the book at £15.95 and set up a special Family and Friends offer of £14 that brought in some early orders. "What are friends for," asked a former work colleague, "if not to buy one's books?" He was publishing a poetry collection to raise money for asthma research, and I bought five copies.

I designed a leaflet, stringing together as many positive comments about the book as I could, starting with Ken Biddulph – 'It's so refreshing to read a book about the fun in cricket' – and ending with Bomber Wells: 'My wife will definitely buy a copy.'

The printing did not go smoothly. Our account supervisor was a middle-aged woman who had recently returned to work after long years of bringing up children, and she assumed a convincing air of expertise that was, alas, not based on a working knowledge of the technical processes. She mislaid our cheque, setting the job back three weeks. Then, when I asked a technical question about the four-colour jacket, she sent us off to get the job done ourselves, recommending a local firm that, it turned out, was putting it through twice on a two-colour press. Ken's cricketers looked like they were batting and bowling in the middle of the night – and, when we sat down to negotiate a price for doing the job again, it transpired that, by being separated from the book, the jacket had become liable for VAT.

Finally in early October, with these problems surmounted, the floor of our main downstairs room filled up with boxes, an exhilarating moment that called for a celebratory glass of wine – but, with so many jiffy bags to pack and post, did not get one.

First to ring was Ken Taylor, delighted by the way his drawings were displayed on the cover; then Ken Biddulph, for once left lost for words by my dedicating the book to him. Then Martin Horton, who had planned to take it on holiday to Malta but, on opening it, found he could not put it down: "I can't remember when I last enjoyed a book so much." And our friend Pauline in Suffolk, opening the parcel and ringing straightaway: "Good heavens, it's a proper book!"

The editor of the *Cricket Society Journal*, Clive Porter, purred with compliments. "You must have shown great sensitivity and tact to get the players to open up so much to you", a point I had not considered. And Dennis Brookes wrote a lovely letter: "I don't often read cricket books, but your book gave me so much pleasure."

Then came disaster. On my way home from the post office I bumped into a chap from Hazel's evening class, and I told him about my book. "Come and have a look at it," I said proudly but, when we came through the front door, I was greeted by scowls from Sue and, behind the chap's back, frantic gestures along the lines of "Get him out of the house, we've got a problem."

Jeff Hancock, the librarian at The Oval, had rung to say that his copy had a whole section where half the pages had no print on them, and Sue, diving into the boxes, had unearthed another with the same fault and one with a section upside down. I had tried so hard to give the book a professional look, and in my despair I thought of all the people who could also have been sent defective copies, not least the potential reviewers: Christopher Martin-Jenkins, Frank Keating and, worst of all, Robin Marlar.

In the batch of 1,500 books we found twenty or so that had such faults, and we reported them to the printers. Our supervisor refunded us, saying something to the effect that "these things happen", which at the time I had no reason to doubt. It must have been three print jobs later, using a different firm, when I finally realised that these things were not something you should expect and that, when you sent out batches of books, you did not need to go through every one, checking that the pages were all present and correct.

There followed a long, agonising wait for the reactions that would make a difference. The first came one Saturday night. Halfway through *Casualty*. Frank Keating of the *Guardian* rang. "It's brilliant, absolutely brilliant. You've brought so many of these cricketers alive ... Why didn't I write this? ... I'm going to write a column, and I'm going to head it Book of the Year ... What a pity you're too late for the William Hill prize."

We were not *Guardian* readers so for three weeks I kept walking down to the newsagent to see if his piece had appeared. Then one day, when I had given up hope, I arrived home in mid-afternoon to find Sue beaming with delight. There were ten photocopies of his column on the table: Frank Keating's 'hooraying choice' for Book of the Year. 'Such cameos of recall are two-a-penny, ten-a-page in a quite riveting new book by a first-time author.' Now the orders started to cascade through the door.

I had spent months in front of a computer, just Sue and Martha for an audience. "There's only ever one topic of conversation when you're around," Martha would complain. Now the reactions were coming from all sides.

Letters arrived, extraordinary letters that left me feeling quite humble. Some were from the players themselves, others from readers I did not know at all. There were lots of them.

> A marvellous read in a field which is rapidly becoming stale and stereotyped ... A lot of insights you don't get anywhere else ... A superbly conceived book. Beautifully written. Very funny but also highly evocative and, at times, strangely sad and haunting ... I treat it like a fine single malt, to be read and savoured very slowly... John Arlott would have loved it ... I've read about a thousand cricket books, and quite frankly this is my favourite ... Thanks for switching on a light in a room that hadn't been visited for a while.

And one I especially liked:

> My husband's been driving me quite mad. He's spent the whole weekend sitting in the garden, chuckling away at your book.

One man in Portugal wanted the book posted to his mother in England, and he sent me a letter to insert in it:

> Start with the magnificent illustrations by Ken Taylor. The two I like best are of Hutton and Compton. If you look at the Hutton picture, you know for a fact that his eye was in a direct perpendicular line with the ball and the toe of his boot at the moment when he struck the ball. There was only one best way to play each ball, and Hutton knew what it was. Compton was almost certainly equally well positioned when he struck his ball, but his whole body was in movement. That gave a greater possible inventory of shots, a greater chance of a stunning shot, and a greater chance of being out. Compton was flowing, often improvised, grace and Hutton was elegant, iron-clad, authority.

Ken was dead chuffed. "I bet you wish you'd written that," he said.

Before publication I had sent a copy to a leading cricket writer, and he had written back to say he was not convinced that my use of the present tense worked. I was so sure that it was at the heart of what freshness I had achieved in the writing that I did not budge. So the letter that came from a reader in Aylesbury lifted my spirits greatly:

> I loved your use of the present tense and your references to items of contemporary news and social life. Above all, though, I was struck by the way you were able to make the past seem distinct and distant yet at the same time somehow part of the present.

There was also a letter from a man in North London:

> I am enjoying your book very much. Unfortunately it's taking a long time to read as I seem to drop off to sleep very easily.

Then came Robin Marlar in *The Cricketer*. Just two paragraphs in his round-up of the month's books. The second began, 'Chalke makes mistakes,' and he cited my muddling up of two secretaries at Old Trafford, Rupert and Geoffrey Howard. He went on, 'The definitive account of Yorkshire's championship winning match at Hove is yet to be written.'

My older brother Peter was most impressed. He had gone into local politics, with some success, and finally his under-achieving brother had done something he could be proud of. He arranged for me to be interviewed for the *Salisbury Journal* by a woman writing under the name of Hobnob. I got the feeling he was expecting it to do him some good in the next local elections. Her article concluded:

> Stephen plays down his own youthful sporting prowess. "My younger brother Andrew was a better cricketer than I was," he says. The odd one out is undoubtedly Peter. "I can't remember him bowling me a ball, even in the back garden."

Peter put a brave face on his disappointment when he rang. "Oh well," he said. "I suppose there must be some voters out there who hate cricket."

He sent my book to John Major who, as it happened, was Dickie Dodds' MP. At the local Conservative Association's Christmas reception the former prime minister came across to him. "Ah, Dickie, I've just been reading about you."

"He said it was the best book on cricket he'd read," Dickie told me.

"The best?"

"Or one of the best. I can't remember exactly what he said. Certainly the word 'best' came into it."

I was sitting in Bath, anxiously wondering what people were making of the book, and compliments reached me like this, second hand and slightly garbled.

I did not know how to get the book into the right hands for review. But things somehow happened, and at times they caught me by surprise.

One Saturday afternoon I was in the Peter Wight Indoor Cricket School in Bath. Peter, the old Somerset player, had a session for the junior members of the Somerset Wanderers Ladies Cricket Club, and I used to go down with Martha. It was a cold, shabby place, but Peter brought his own warmth to the girls' sessions. He had a high-pitched voice, with a strong trace still of his native Guyana, and he made us all muck in. "Come on, Dad, have a bowl," he would call out to me.

Ken Biddulph used to wax lyrical about his batting – he must have told me a dozen times about two innings Peter played against Laker and Lock on a spiteful Oval pitch – but Ken also told tales of his hypochondria. "I used to do twelfth man a lot. I got very good at carrying the drinks and very good at running down the chemist's shop for Peter Wight."

That Saturday I was waiting at the bowler's end when a mother told me in a casual way that she had seen my book mentioned in a magazine called *The Week*. "Some writer named it as one of his six best cricket books of all time."

"Really? Can you remember his name?"

"Um ... Samson ... or was it Swinson? ... Something like that."

"Swinson? Not EW Swanton?"

"Yes, that's right. Swanton."

I was beginning to realise that, if the book could get enough publicity, it could go further. The place I most wanted a review was the *Daily Telegraph*. At the time it was the paper with the best reputation for sports coverage, and many of the cricketers of the 1950s read it. I rang the sports desk three times, the last time suggesting that they ask John Major to review the book.

"Look, mind your own business," the man told me with obvious exasperation. "It's entirely up to us whether we review your book and, if we do, we'll decide who reviews it."

I thought I had blown my chance. Then, out of the blue, one Friday afternoon a few weeks later, somebody rang from the sports desk of the *Telegraph*. Michael Parkinson had submitted his column for Monday, it was all about my book and could I get a copy to them by tomorrow morning? In my excitement I left for London at 5 a.m.

Looking back from the late 1990s, it was not difficult to view the 1950s, as Michael Parkinson's piece did, as a golden age of English cricket. The county games attracted great crowds, and the England team were on top of the world, beating Australia three times in a row, not losing a series against anybody for over seven years. By contrast, in spring 1998, England had lost an unprecedented five series in a row to Australia – and, against all countries, they had won two and lost ten of their last fifteen series. At the end of the decade, when *Wisden Cricket Monthly* created a table based on recent results, England were in last place, below Sri Lanka, New Zealand and Zimbabwe.

Though I had not planned it this way, it was not a bad time to be bringing out a book that looked back with affection to the cricket of forty years earlier.

The *Daily Telegraph* put my phone number at the foot of the article, and on Monday morning I was answering calls almost non-stop. All manner of people ordered the book, many of them wanting to tell me about themselves and their own connections with the cricket of those years: "I was one of Trevor Bailey's colts at Essex ... I know Ken Taylor's brother ... I'm George Emmett's sister ... I knew Cliff Gladwin very well. He took a year off his age when he went to play for Derbyshire, you know. Then, when he tried to retire from the Coal Board at 65, they said he still had a year to go. I had to sort it out for him."

I had unearthed a forgotten world, a world that had become buried deep in people's memories. As the reader put it, I had shone a light on a room that had not been visited for a while.

The following week I ordered a reprint.

*

During the summer, while I was preparing the book for the printers, I had taken Martha to a women's cricket international at Bristol, where I had approached Mike Simpson, the chairman of the Gloucestershire Cricket Lovers. Desperate for any chance to promote my book, I asked if he could put aside a little time for me to talk at one of the meetings.

"Yes, that will be all right," he said a little suspiciously. "Perhaps the second one of the winter. Let's say five minutes."

Five minutes. What could I fit into five minutes? I wrote a formal letter, thanking him for offering me 'five or ten minutes', and I picked out some paragraphs from the Arthur Milton chapter to read.

> Cooky wasn't the worst with the bat. He made a hundred when he was in the raff. At a place called Bulawayo. He always used to talk about his hundred at Bulawayo.

What was it Hazel said? "You've got to hear a voice reading it. You've got to catch a rhythm."

Come the evening, I was finishing supper when the phone rang. "Stephen? It's Mike Simpson here. Our speaker has got held up on the M4. You couldn't manage half an hour, could you?"

I was in a state of panic. What on earth could I talk about for half an hour? I started with Arthur, then I went on to Bomber, then to Dickie Dodds. They seemed to be smiling and laughing but, as the minutes passed and there was still no sign of the speaker, I grew gradually more hysterical, even telling them about the phone call from Robin Marlar.

The scheduled speaker was David Rayvern Allen, a radio producer who was due to talk about John Arlott. Every time somebody appeared at the door, I asked in desperation, "You're not David Rayvern Allen, are you?" In all, I did 45 minutes, and I sold 15 books in the interval.

"I'll recommend you at the next meeting of the Council of Cricket Societies," Mike Simpson said, and another world opened up. Every month in winter, in venues from Southport to Southampton, Chelmsford to Chesterfield, cricket lovers gathered for such meetings. And they were all on the look-out for speakers. Especially cheap ones like me.

Cricket, I was fast discovering, was full of sub-worlds: associations of statisticians, of umpires, of memorabilia collectors. There were dining clubs and specialist book dealers, a Forty Club for older players and several counties with societies for exiled members, some of them with regular journals. Twelve months earlier I had known almost nothing of this.

In my pre-publication spreadsheet I had calculated that the shops on the county grounds would be my main sales outlet. but that was wildly off the mark. "Fifteen pounds?" the woman at Derby repeated sceptically. "Most of the people who come in here wouldn't spend fifteen pounds on a second-hand suit in Oxfam."

I took to ringing high-street bookshops, a task which did not come naturally to me. I acquired a list of all the branches of Waterstones and worked through it. If the first calls of the day came up trumps – "Send us four ... We'll try six" – the whole session seemed to go well. But if I got off to a bad start – "No, not for us ... Thanks for trying" – I found it hard to keep the sparkle in my voice, to convey that crucial sense that I *expected* them to say yes. At times the responses seemed frustratingly random. "Leamington Spa have sold fifteen already," I pleaded with the man at Stratford-upon-Avon, but he was not to be moved. "Well, good for them," he said.

We typed the best book reviews – Michael Parkinson, EW Swanton and especially Frank Keating ('Unquestionably the Book of the Year') – and pasted them onto strips of stiff coloured paper that we wrapped around the books, and that helped sales. One day Ken Biddulph rang with exciting news for me: "Waterstones in Cheltenham are saying your book is their Book of the Year." I did not have the heart to tell him that the wrap-around was our work.

What was clear was that, when we got the book onto the shelves, it did sell. County cricket in the 1950s: despite what the publishers had all said, there was a market for it.

*

We kept *Runs in the Memory* in print for twelve years, through four editions of the hardback and one of a softback. In all, we sold 4,500 copies. If we had had a mainstream publisher, with high-powered publicity and distribution systems, I am certain we could have sold a lot more. Not long ago, in *The Times*, *Runs in the Memory* was the cricket book featured on a page with the headline 'The best sports books that you've never heard of'.

That delighted me, but better still was the paragraph Paul Coupar wrote when it was chosen in the magazine *The Wisden Cricketer* as one of the best fifty cricket books of all time:

> In the 1930s Alan Lomax travelled America recording obscure Blues artists before their stories were lost. In the 1990s Chalke did the same with county cricketers. The result is a masterpiece: affectionate yet honest, with the bittersweet flavour of real life.

I have always been a great lover of folk and blues music, the authenticity of the songs handed down in the oral tradition. To have my humble visits to the homes of long-ago county cricketers mentioned in the same breath as the man who discovered Robert Johnson and Woody Guthrie, Leadbelly and Mississippi John Hurt, I was walking on air for weeks.

Then one morning there arrived an e-mail from Andy Irvine, an Irish folk singer who had played with Christy Moore in the group Planxty. He was not somebody I would have expected to like cricket, but it turned out that he had grown up in St John's Wood and had spent many happy childhood hours at Lord's. His e-mail began:

> Dear Stephen,
> Forgive me for writing a fan letter! I haven't actually done this since 1959 when I tried to contact Woody Guthrie.

Oh the joy!

There was skill in what I did – the teasing out of the memories and the way I shaped them into stories – but let me not get too full of myself. Alan Lomax would have been nobody if it had not been for the music he discovered. And *Runs in the Memory* would have been nothing if it had not been for Ken Biddulph and Arthur Milton; Dennis Brookes and Dickie Dodds; Martin Horton, Tom Cartwright and all the others. So many of them are dead now. It was my privilege to preserve their voices.

8

The second book

They say the second book is the hardest.

In town one morning I met a fellow student from Hazel's writing class, and I asked how he was getting on. At the end of the course he had told us how he planned to become a journalist, but he seemed in low spirits now. I sensed that nothing much had come of his aspiration.

"And you?" he said. "Have you managed to get anything published?"

So much was happening for *Runs in the Memory*, and I was trying hard not to get carried away with it all. Given his despondency, I knew it would be better if I did not tell him too much. Yet somehow I could not contain myself, and it all gushed out, even about John Major and Michael Parkinson. I must have really got up his nose.

He listened to me for a while, the wind blowing through his hair. "Oh well," he said eventually. "They say we've all got one book inside us." And he walked away without another word.

So that was it. There was nothing special about writing a book. Anybody could do that. But could I write another one? That was the real test.

*

Part of me wanted to leave cricket and to try out my technique on another subject. Repertory theatre, another of the passions of my formative years, appealed to me. I visited the archivist at the Salisbury Playhouse, and he recommended an old actor, Derek Smee. I wrote him a letter but I got no reply, and somehow the idea died a death. For years afterwards Frank Keating kept asking me, "What happened to that book about repertory theatre?"

My redundancy money had gone, I was working again, and I settled for the low-risk option: a sequel on county cricket in the 1960s. Same format, same style. Twelve games, twelve illustrations by Ken Taylor. Whether it was the right decision in creative terms, I shall never know, but it made sense financially.

My first phone call was to Martin Horton. Who would he recommend from Worcestershire in the 1960s? "Roy Booth," he answered immediately, and a few days later I was sitting with Roy in his main room. He took me back thirty years to a game in 1968 – yet for me, coming out of my first book, it was not thirty years back but ten years forward. I had left my childhood behind; I was a university student trying to make sense of the tumultuous events of that summer. The assassinations of Martin Luther King and Robert Kennedy, the escalating Vietnam War, the student riots in Paris and, in the week of the game that Roy described to me, Russian tanks in the streets of Prague. It was a time when the last certainties of my childhood world seemed to be collapsing.

I am not sure that I properly started again with that second book. With *Runs in the Memory* I had been exploring unknown territory, both in my journeys into the dimly-lit world of my childhood and in my attempts to shape the stories in the way I wrote them. The sense of a lost age emerged, a world of county cricket in a last period of stability before everything changed.

This time I was looking to repeat the formula of that book, and I did not quite capture the zeitgeist of the 1960s. My short-story format worked well with the ebb and flow of the three-day games and, sticking too much to that, I did not encourage the cricketers to choose any of the one-day matches that were such an important part of the story of county cricket in the 1960s.

For all that, there were some wonderful matches among those recalled and, with the narrators a little younger and the distance of time shorter, there was a greater freshness in some of the material.

Roy Booth's game was the best in the book. It was back to 'The Day We Beat Yorkshire', this time with the added twist that Roy was a Yorkshireman himself. Indeed, he had kept wicket for them in the early 1950s before moving to Worcester. He knew Brian Close and Fred Trueman all too well, and he had a wry sense of humour about the pair of them.

Close and Trueman, I loved writing about them. They were two of the great cricketers and great characters of the '50s and '60s. They both pushed beyond the constraints of the time, and they had boundless self-confidence. They had started in May 1949, in the same match at Fenner's, and they were still here at Worcester in August 1968. For twenty years they had played together, always with that peculiar mix of mutual respect and exasperation.

Fred was near the end of his days. He was 37 years old; he still had the heart and the self-belief, but he had lost his great pace. When the two teams had met earlier that summer, at Sheffield, Close had caused a sensation by leaving Fred out of the side, and Roy told me how "Fred spent most of the time in our dressing room, chatting away. 'A right prat is Closey,' that sort of thing."

On the last morning at Worcester, with Fred once more sitting with the Worcestershire players, the door burst open and Close hurled Fred's leather bag into the room. "You've been in there for two bloody days. You can change with the buggers today."

Cricket at its best is a beautiful game to watch. It has rhythm and elegance; at times it is almost balletic. But it has this other side: the players interacting with each other, the passions simmering beneath the surface.

Around that time the Journeymen played a game in Devon where our hosts included in their eleven a fast bowler who had had a shoulder injury and was using our friendly game as a first step towards recovery. He was a well-built man, who had played rugby for Harlequins, and he started his spell well below full pace. Normally our opener David looked to play classically through mid-on and mid-off – as a boy he had been coached at Monmouth School by Sonny Avery – but that day, sensing something in the bowler's personality, he took guard further down the track, trying without great success to hook every ball that was short of a length. The atmosphere was soon crackling with electricity. The bowler muttered and growled, he got faster and faster, his deliveries shorter and shorter, until suddenly his shoulder went and he had to leave the field. It was only a friendly game but, my word, it mattered.

We won by one wicket off the penultimate ball, a misfield by mid-on. You should have heard the language as bowler and fielder walked off.

That is what you cannot experience when you sit in the crowd and watch other people's cricket. But it was what Roy, sitting in his armchair and chuckling, was giving me. "Fred was fielding down at long leg at some point in that match. He'd bowled, and I don't think he'd had much success. Then a wicket or two went, and he was signalling he'd like to come back on. And Brian was ignoring him. In his heart Fred thought he could still bowl us out, but he'd lost the nip and movement that he'd had. I can still see him waving to Closey from the bottom end, to say 'I'm ready for coming back on.' And Closey was walking backwards so as not to look at him."

The other key character was the umpire George Pope, whose career in the game went back to the 1930s. After an injury to his fellow umpire, he had had to take the lead at both ends for almost three full days. The match was played in a heat-wave, and he was struggling by the last afternoon. "The game was always going to be dwelling on a few runs, and there were a few lbws. Towards the end it got keen, and a few words were being said amongst us. It was getting a bit uptight, and George was really trying to control it. 'Come on, come along.'"

Yorkshire needed 139 for victory, for the championship. When their ninth wicket fell, they only had 123 of them. It was left to Tony Nicholson, the number eleven, and who else but Fred to score the last 16.

"On the second evening George and Fred had been having a drink, and George said, 'Which way are you going back, Fred? ... Will you give me a lift?' So Fred is giving George a lift."

There was an appeal for lbw against Fred, and George said 'not out'. Then another, and it was the same reply. Then a run out, and that was not out too. Slowly the score rose to 137. One to tie, two to win. And wonderfully it ended with George Pope giving Fred lbw. "It looks as though my lift's gone," he said disconsolately in the pavilion.

As a short story, it had everything: plot and sub-plot, characters and a magnificent ending. It could not have been better if it had been made up.

"Oh dear," Roy said rather forebodingly when I sent him the chapter. "I don't know what Fred's going to say."

He was less worried what Brian Close might say: "He's a good lad, Brian. As good as gold. He's uncomplicated in his way. There's no malice in him."

Then, with a chuckle, he repeated the last conversation he had had with Brian, on the subject of Lord MacLaurin who had just taken over as the supremo of English cricket.

"What do you think of Ian MacLaurin taking over, Brian?"

"I don't know. He's been a good business man and that. I've written him a letter. I've said, you'd do well to meet me so I can put you wise to a few things."

"Has he arranged a meeting with you yet?"

"No. I've had a letter back, saying he's pretty busy but he hopes to see me some time in the future."

Something about the way Roy told the tale, I think he knew that Ian MacLaurin was not looking to be made wise by Brian Close.

*

Close and Trueman reappeared in the Hampshire chapter. A reader of my first book had suggested that Alan Castell might be a good choice of subject, and so he proved. Born in 1943, Alan was much the youngest person I had interviewed, and he reflected that in his chirpy, irreverent approach to life. A car upholsterer's son from Oxford, he wanted to tell me about his debut match against Yorkshire at Dean Park, Bournemouth, where we met.

By this time Dean Park was no longer staging county cricket, another of the casualties of centralisation. Yet it was still a beautiful ground, with houses and trees circled all round it, and it had special memories for me, the place where Andrew and I had come for Easter coaching with Peter Sainsbury.

Alan took me out to the middle, to the pitch, and we drifted back in time to August 1962, to relive the scene when he walked out to bat, at number ten, in the first innings. "Don Wilson was bowling from that end. Without exaggeration, Stephen, I'd taken guard, and Brian Close was there." He pointed to a spot only feet away. "As I'm playing forward, he's trying to catch it off the blade of the bat. He's actually diving in front of me. I'm not used to this. I'm just a boy from Oxford."

Bournemouth. 24 August 1962
A.T. Castell c Close b Wilson 0

61

It was tougher still in the second innings. With Yorkshire pushing to win the championship, Hampshire were hanging on desperately for a draw. Most of the large crowd were Yorkshire folk, taking their summer holidays to coincide with their county's southern tour.

Alan told me about the first morning, when Fred Trueman had come into their dressing room. He had Fred's accent to perfection: "Who are you, sunshine, what do you do?"

"I'm Alan Castell. I bowl a few leg-spinners, try to bat a bit."

"Bat a bit, bat a bit. Think you can bat, do you? Can you hook? Can you hook? If not, you'll have to learn. I'm sorry, you'll have to learn."

On the final evening, half an hour before close of play, with the new ball almost due, Don Wilson trapped Derek Shackleton lbw, and Alan made for the dressing-room door. Now it was his Old Etonian skipper Colin Ingleby-Mackenzie's turn to be imitated. "Cassers, stay there. You don't go until I tell you to go." "So I waited for Shack to come up the steps, along and into the room. Because there's no twenty overs in the last hour. It's kill as much time as you can." "Cassers, good luck to you, my beauty, in you go."

"And I'm booed all the way to the wicket. Here I am. I'm playing in my first game, I'm on a pair, on a Hampshire ground, and I'm booed to the wicket. The atmosphere was electric."

Almost immediately he was facing Fred Trueman with the new ball, knowing that soon enough a bumper would be coming – and it did. "I thought as he came up, 'This is it, he's stretching a bit.' And I ducked under it. But I'd got the bat up, and it hit the top of the bat and flew down to fine leg where Padgett was fielding. And it went through his hands for four. So, of course, there was a confrontation between Trueman and Padgett. Then one of the Hampshire supporters picked up the ball, and he didn't throw it back straightaway. It was like a scene from Hull Kingston Rovers down there."

A wicket fell, and in came the number eleven who insisted on leaving Alan to face Fred. They both survived, and Alan showed me the scrapbook his mother had kept. Amid the glowing headlines – 'Courageous Castell ... The kid defies Tykes' – was a cartoon from the *Southampton Echo*. In it a tiny husband was squaring up to his ferocious wife, with the caption: 'Since I saw Alan Castell face up to Freddie Trueman, I'm not frightened of you anymore.'

One reviewer of the book said that the players 'all manage to repeat 30-year-old conversations with a clarity which suggests that no self-respecting player of the '60s ever took the field without a tape recorder in the pocket of his flannels.'

The book was called *Caught in the Memory*. That is where those conversations were. In the memory. You could take Alan's snatches of conversation in whatever way you liked. The literal truth. The approximate truth. An emotional truth. A psychological distortion. Or just a story egged up after many retellings.

Some people do have good memories, and Alan struck me as one such. When he looked at the scorecard of his game, he could not believe what he read. "My memory must be going. I could have sworn Ken Taylor was playing for Yorkshire." He had a picture in his mind's eye of all the fielders gathered around him, and Ken was among them. "And Mel Ryan, wasn't he playing?"

I went to the newspaper library and, hey presto, in the *Yorkshire Post* I found a sentence: 'Ryan and Taylor were on for Stott (tooth extraction) and Hampshire (stomach ailment).' If Alan could remember that, why should he not remember the gist of what Fred or Ingleby said to him? It was his first match. The match he remembered better than any other he ever played. And cricket does have that hold on you when you play it.

The morning with Alan was great fun. His lively irreverence reflected much of the mood of the Sixties, and there were others I interviewed who had a similar sense of fun, among them Essex's Robin Hobbs, Glamorgan's Peter Walker and Somerset's Peter Robinson, nephew of Roly Jenkins and just as loquacious.

I loved listening to their stories. Yet, as with my previous book, I was also fascinated by the sense of its being another world: Keith Andrew, winning a crucial match at Cardiff and ringing the result back to Northampton from a public call box; the Essex players in pre-season nets at Fairlop, clambering over a wire fence to retrieve the balls from an adjoining chicken run; the basic catering at Taunton: "We just had Bill Moor," Peter Robinson said. "'Another horse died in Blagdon,' he'd say as he served up steak and kidney pie. The potatoes would all be in dishes in water, with the eyes left in them. We always reckoned the pies had done at least two race meetings."

The reviewer who had come up with the line about the tape recorders also wrote how he felt 'yesteryear's players talk pityingly rather than enviously about the better-paid, heavily sponsored, highly-stressed men of the '90s.'

"It was fabulous fun," Yorkshire's Don Wilson said. "We were a community of men. We were there to play cricket, we were there to enjoy it, and we were there to entertain. The players of that era, we have all got good memories."

"I was born in 1933," Brian Jackson of Derbyshire said. "We were different from young people today. We were much harder. We didn't expect as much as they do now. The game today, they want much more out of it."

Much harder but not expecting as much from their lives, that is a quote as good as any in my books, an insight that you can apply to a lot of things.

Then and now: I raised the comparison in my introduction:

> The memory is not a reliable lens, but often it is our only lens. 'The game today comes second to the money that's made from it' ... 'For all the gimmes and the cars, they don't really look very happy' ... 'I don't think they have the fun we had.'
>
> Is it old men romanticising the past? A case of 'the older I get, the better a player I was'? Or do their memories remind us of qualities of life that we have been too careless to preserve as we enjoy the fruits of affluence, the benefits of new technology?

Peter Wilby, the editor of the *New Statesman*, was clear which side he came down on. He wrote of 'the irritating glow' in which, he said, I had bathed the past. Everything that was wrong with English cricket was in the pages of my two books: the camaraderie of the players, the way they call each other 'lovely blokes' and 'look out for each other', an acceptance of mediocrity, a failure to meet the increased international competitiveness.

> Read Stephen Chalke, enjoy his lyrical accounts of long-forgotten summer days and treasure this unique heritage. But don't look further for an explanation of why England can't win a Test series.

I had set out to capture the fun of county cricket, back in the 1950s and 1960s, when England did win Test matches, and I had finished up here: being told that I had described the whole circuit, from Tom Cartwright to Brian Close, as happy to be second-rate; the way of life, with its comradeship and its 'looking out for each other', as too easy-going.

He was politically on the Left, and John Major on the Right. Yet, straying into this world of county cricket, John Major saw the camaraderie as admirable. And this chap despised it, seeing only the need to weed out the workforce, increase their productivity and, as Mrs Thatcher might have put it, make our cricket leaner and more competitive.

*

On reflection I realise that this second book did dwell too much on the fun. There was more decay in the 1960s than it conveyed. Nevertheless the memories it captured gave pleasure, not least to the comic writer Peter Tinniswood whose *Wisden* review gave a much-needed lift to my spirits:

> Read the book. Read the book, I beg you. I commend it wholeheartedly – and not least for the splendid illustrations by Mr Ken Taylor. He won't remember, but once he trod on my toe in the tea interval at Bramall Lane. He could grind my whole body into the ground without trace if he compels Mr Chalke to produce another volume.

Maybe, but it was time to move on.

9

Laughter in his soul

"Have a chocolate digestive, my friend."

I was back in Bomber Wells' front room. The dog had died, the furniture had been moved around, but Bomber was still sitting in prime position, looking towards the window, across the ring road and away into his memory. We were nearing the end of the century, but he was back in the 1940s. In the early years of the war. In New Street, Gloucester, among the boys playing cricket.

"If we got hold of a bat, we'd drop it handle first onto the pavement, see how many times it bounced. Boom-boom, that's a two-springer. Boom-boom-boom, that's a three-springer. 'That's a better bat, that's a three-springer.' They were all things that kids did in those days. You lived in a world free of all this intense commercialism. You lived in your own little world, and you were satisfied with your lot."

I had done that myself as a boy, but I had not remembered it.

I had not long brought out my first book, and Bomber had rung me. He wondered if I would go fifty-fifty with him on publishing his novel, a Dick Francis-style thriller set in 1950s county cricket. I met him and Mary in Easton-in-Gordano service station, west of Bristol, and he passed me a supermarket carrier bag with the script in it. There were 800 pages; the thought of publishing it scared the life out of me.

I rang him some weeks later with my verdict. "Why don't you do a book of stories about your own playing days?"

"Right, we'll do that then," he said.

So suddenly, without ever quite agreeing to it, I was 'doing that'.

We had two sessions in March 1998, and they were as magical as any two sessions I have ever had as a writer. Bomber had a pulsating life-force, and he talked on and on, almost without pause, one thing leading to another, with none of that veneer of middle-aged respectability or acquired language that would have distanced the world he was describing. Somehow, sitting in that armchair, he was happy to be once more that boy in New Street.

"I can see them now, my dad and his brothers. Sitting around the coal fire. Our dad sat there in his grandfather chair, flanked by my uncles. And there I was on the lino floor, listening."

Bomber had never had children, but he managed to be both the child he had once been and his father holding forth from the grandfather chair.

"I listened to them talking about Charlie Parker, Wally Hammond, Tom Goddard, all those great Gloucestershire cricketers. My uncles would come round in the winter, and I would sit by the fire and visualise these great gods. Charlie Parker: if he couldn't bowl them out with his spinners, he could bowl them out with his seam. Wally Hammond, so brilliant he could play the ball with just the edge of his bat. Tom Goddard, he could spin it from one side of the pitch to the other."

I was transported to that lino floor, listening to his every word.

"They'd have a crate of beer on the table, a couple of dozen bottles, and they'd down the lot. And all the time they'd be talking about cricket. Picking their best England team, that sort of thing. And the more they had to drink, the more Gloucestershire players there'd be in the side. And I just listened. I never realised it, the actual effect it was having on me at the time. When you're young, you don't realise you're taking it in, do you? You don't realise what you're storing away in your cranium."

He was a free spirit, letting himself go, and I was enchanted.

Our next meeting came during Ken Biddulph's annual coaching weekend in the Cotswolds. Ken advertised the course in *The Cricketer* magazine, and a dozen or so club cricketers from all around England gathered from Friday teatime to Sunday afternoon to prepare for the coming summer. The weekly nets in Stroud had died a death so it was a good chance for me to fine-tune my game, ready for another campaign.

Ken was not happy when we gathered. At the last minute he had been let down by his batting coach, and during the morning he had tweaked his back bending to take a bottle of milk out of the fridge. He had asked Bomber and me to speak after the meal on that Friday evening, and he was anxious that we should give good value.

It was a little guest house on the outskirts of Cheltenham. At the table I sat next to Bomber, who was on top form during the meal. Ken was at the other end. He loved Bomber, but he was on edge, wanting everything to go smoothly. As we ate, Bomber, a lifelong Labour Party member, got into a line of stories that all had something of an anti-establishment flavour to them. The chap across the table from me, a lad from Derbyshire, thought him wonderful.

"Tell me," he said. "Why has Fred Trueman never got a knighthood? Is it because he's too left wing?"

"Left wing," Bomber boomed. A couple of peas shot out of his mouth across the table. "Fred? Left wing? He's a bloody fascist."

I glanced towards Ken, who was staring down our end with a look of complete panic. "I think it's time to hear Stephen speak," he said hurriedly.

The next day Ken took us to a country pub for lunch. It was the height of the BSE crisis, and he had ordered minced beef all round. Next to me was a charming Anglicised Indian called Francis, an accountancy lecturer, and he expressed to me his concern about eating beef, a concern that I shared.

"Excuse me," he said, pulling across the waitress. "Would you mind if I don't have the beef?" She offered him an omelette.

"Could I have one too?" I chipped in, and she rounded on me.

"Don't be such a bloody nuisance. He's got his religious reasons. You're just causing trouble."

Once more Ken looked down the table in alarm. Then, after she had left the room, Francis turned to me with a grin. "I hit the four," he said, "and you got the bouncer next ball."

I turned fifty that summer, and my cricket was a mixed bag, right from the outset. My neighbour Adrian was always trying to get me to play at his club, Hampset, and one Saturday in May I turned out for their second eleven, bowling a match-winning spell and coming home full of early-season confidence. Then at lunchtime the next day he turned up on my doorstep, saying the third team were one short. They were playing at the Purnells ground in Somerset; would I mind making up numbers? I had planned a day with the family, but Purnells Sunday third eleven did not sound much good and, fancying some easy wickets, I agreed.

Unfortunately Purnells were also a man short, and their solution was to draft in their overseas professional, Irfan-ul-Haq, whose tall, athletic frame and Pakistan state under-19 jersey stood out amid the various shapes and scruffy clothes of the rest of them. It was my ill fortune to come on to bowl when he was starting to cut loose. He treated my gentle away swingers with disdain, moving early to the pitch of them and sending three in a row out of the field. Each boundary was accompanied by drunken cheers from the footballers having an end-of-season do in the clubhouse and a loud, tinny shout on the tannoy of "Great shot, Irfan."

After one six over mid-wicket, our captain left the field to collect the ball. He lobbed it over a hedge and, without realising he had not yet returned, I bowled the next ball of the over. "Hey, wait for me," he called from the gate. "There's no need to come back in," I shouted back. "The ball's over the road at long off."

Purnells, 17 May 1998.
Chalke, two overs, no wickets for 37 runs.

Five years later Adrian went up to Lord's to watch Bath in the final of the National Club Championship, and they lost by one run to Sandiacre in Derbyshire. He told me all about it and how Sandiacre had a very good Pakistani all-rounder. I looked at his programme. It was Irfan-ul-Haq.

*

Bomber and Mary came down to our house one day. A man who had helped with preparing my first book was involved with Marshfield Cricket Club, just north of Bath, and he asked me if I could suggest a speaker for an early-season get-together in their pavilion. So I put him in touch with Bomber.

Mary and Bomber ate with us and, as we talked, I grew confident for the first time about what I had undertaken. Then I drove Bomber to Marshfield where sadly I did not stay for his talk. In his day, they say, Bomber was the funniest speaker on the circuit. He would tell long and hilarious stories about his bowling without a run-up, all delivered in his broad 'Glorster' accent, and he would have the audience in stitches.

My all-time favourite involved a club match back in the 1940s when, coming in off his non-run-up, he bowled out a top batsman who was not ready. The batsman was called back by their captain – "We played all away matches, you see, we didn't like to offend anyone" – and the same thing happened a second time. Then, when the captain went to call him back again, the batsman swung round: "If you think I'm staying here for him to get his bloody hat-trick ..."

Another tale involved an occasion at Worcester when he was starting an over to Roly Jenkins just as the cathedral clock started to strike twelve. Between them they contrived to complete the six balls by the twelfth strike. a performance which did not amuse his amateur captain, Sir Derrick Bailey, who accused him of 'making the game look stupid'. He ordered Bomber to come in from further back.

"I thought to myself, I can do better than that. I can bowl it from there. Because that's what he actually said. 'Come in from further back.' So I stood still, and I bowled it from there ... And I landed it on the spot."

There was much laughter, but Sir Derrick was not amused. "He dropped me for two matches, but it was worth it."

Would the stories work as well when printed on the page? That was my problem. They needed to be credible, and I was not sure that even I believed them. Yet other cricketers came forward, and their memories were all of a piece with Bomber's.

Frank McHugh described what it was like to be a fast bowler at the other end. "One time I was walking down to third man at the end of my over, and

68

I heard this shout. And the ball whistled past me for four. Then I found out it was the second ball of the over. I'd hardly have my sweater on, and in no time I'd be taking it off for the next over."

I hope the Marshfield folk enjoyed it. When I went to collect Bomber, there was a glow on the faces of the older men gathered around him.

"I'll be in touch," I said as he and Mary left for home. "I'm going to leave things till later in the summer. Then I'll get down to the book in earnest."

*

Bomber never gave another speech.

In June Mary rang. Bomber had had a bad stroke. He was in the Gloucestershire Royal Hospital, and he would not be out for quite some time. "I'll understand, Stephen, if you don't want to go on."

It was devastating news. We had hardly started, and he was lying in a hospital bed with little power of coherent speech. I knew from my father's strokes that he would get better, but how much better?

"I do want to go on if I can," I said, and she agreed to keep in touch and to tell me when he was ready to start again.

That was June 1998, and we did not pick it up till May 1999. By then I had written and published *Caught in the Memory*, and I set up a routine of driving up to Gloucester every Wednesday morning. The visits went on for several months, and I lost all sense of what the book was going to be.

"Have a ginger nut," he would say. "Go on, take several." Alas, he was on a strict diet, and Mary did not offer him the plate.

He had lost most of the use of his legs and was always in a wheelchair when he was out. But at home his greater immobility was not that noticeable, given how he had always sat there in the chair.

He did not have the speed of speech that he had before. His brain could not jump about so anarchically, and he would sometimes forget a word. Nevertheless he still had a relish for words, like this description of Harry White the Gloucestershire masseur:

> He had hands like gorilla's. He was an ex-matelot. Always smoking. He had the filthiest bloody pipe in Gloucestershire. He came with us because he was cheap. Everything had to be cheap in those days. Just the bare necessities. Big bottle of embrocation, a few plasters, and that was Harry.

He was from the roughest of backgrounds, he poked fun at the old amateurs and voted Labour, but at heart he loved the way things were in his youth. He was full of funny stories, but he wanted always to make it clear that the cricket of that time was not soft.

We weren't light-hearted. Far from it. No one ever gave you anything. It was played harder then than it is now. But you appreciated each other's skills. When I played, it was a much gentler society. People had time. They'd sit and watch the game and appreciate it. Now, with these Sunday matches, it's like a football crowd, isn't it?

It was this juxtaposition, harder and gentler, that intrigued me. For Bomber the modern game had not been made more competitive; it had been commercialised.

> I remember speaking at a dinner for Neville Cardus. The limited-over game had been going for two or three years. Millions of words had been written by every Tom, Dick and Harry, trying to describe it. And I said to him, 'Right then, Neville, what do you think of the limited-over game?' He thought for a few seconds, then he said, 'It's like trying to play Beethoven on a banjo.'

My father had a series of aphorisms which he would come out with regularly and which he always delivered to us in the same words with the same slow emphasis. "Cricket," he would say, "is not the game that is played at The Oval and Lord's but *on the village green*." And Bomber thought much the same. He was as happy at the Spa, watching his beloved Gloucester City, as he was at any county match. Cricket, wherever it was played, was all the same to him.

"Club cricket is stronger now," he said. "But it's nowhere near as interesting. You've got more players who've been coached and can play with a straight bat. And they look players, they dress immaculately. In the '40s and '50s, they came out in old grey flannels and striped gear – not for Gloucester City, they were strict, but for clubs we were playing. And they all had strong personalities. A chap would come in with his sleeves rolled up, he'd have a nickname, like Basher Brain of Lydney, and he played as he was nicknamed. It's another world now. Everything's got to be done according to the book."

Bomber had such a sense of audience, of being a story teller, of being an old man passing it all on. Many of my generation would not have taken to him as I did, they would have thought it all far-fetched, but that would be because they were taking it too literally.

"When I started at Bristol," he said one day, "there was this old boy on the committee, Teddy Spry. As a young man he'd played with WG Grace. I used to sit with him. I think I was the only one who did. I loved listening to all his stories. You can learn a lot from old men, you know. They're the obvious people to ask. They might exaggerate things, but it doesn't matter. You get the gist of what they're trying to say."

Bomber set me up with two speaking engagements: the Nottinghamshire Cricket Lovers at Trent Bridge, a group he had started during his years there, and the Gloucestershire Exiles at their lunch during the Cheltenham Festival.

The Notts secretary, sensing my anxiety, offered some advice: "Try to work in Derek Randall, he's a great favourite up here." That was not easy. Derek had made his debut in 1972, and I was talking about county cricket in the 1950s. But at least I could pass on some of the stories Bomber had told me about his time at Trent Bridge in the 1960s. An especial favourite involved a team-mate Roger Vowles in a match at Bath. At one stage in the tale he was unable to field a ball for an Alsatian dog standing over it and snarling. "After that, the crowd really took to Roger. Whenever the ball came near him, they all started barking."

At Cheltenham, at the end of the Exiles lunch, I told them the story of a match Bomber had played there against Yorkshire in 1957, the game that Arthur Milton had tried to choose when I was starting out on *Runs in the Memory*. Bomber watched encouragingly from his wheelchair and, despite my nerves, the speech got off to a good start. Then, outside the marquee, the match resumed and suddenly wickets were falling. 'Hick's out,' I heard someone say. Then 'Solanki's out.' There was a buzz in the tent, and the audience started to come and go, torn between two climaxes: one in 1957, the other in 1999. It was hard to tell which world they wanted more to be in.

I always enjoyed the weekly trips to Gloucester, but I was putting off and putting off the task of making something of it all. Then one morning in February, after nine months of our weeekly meetings, Bomber broke off at the end of a story and looked across at me. "Are we doing a book or what?"

It gave me the jolt I needed. I came up with the idea that the book would be set at Cheltenham in 1999, with Bomber on the boundary telling the story of the 1957 match. It would read as if we were sitting there, talking away as one does at cricket, with each interval in play providing a self-contained digression. Bomber's stories would be just that – stories.

"What a lovely, simple way to write a book," one reader said, thinking that all I had done was turn up at the ground with a tape recorder and type out the conversation. I did not have the heart to tell him of all the hours I had spent in Bomber's front room, wondering how on earth I would ever make any shape of it all.

With at least 120 sides of A4 paper filled with my small handwriting, I had no shortage of Bomberisms to play with, and I rounded out his stories by talking to several of his Gloucester team-mates, including Arthur Milton and Tom Graveney.

Best of all was Charlie Light, the father of the Gloucestershire Exiles chairman. He was an 87-year-old retired forester, a cousin of Laurie Lee, and his memories of the Cheltenham Festival went back to 1926.

"The village cricketers all used to go there. Some years the local fixtures had to be cancelled. And the beer tent did good business. Flowers Bitter was seven pence. Six pence was the price of beer for years. But Flowers was better than Stroud or Ciren Beer. It was worth the extra penny."

It was always a joy when somebody took me beyond the boundary like this. "Back in the '20s the villages had a different way of talking from each other. Chedworth had a lovely drawl. North Nibley swore; they put a swear word between syllables. If anybody from Chedworth went to North Nibley to buy a dog, they had to take somebody from Birdlip as an interpreter. And they all looked alike from inter-marriage."

He had spent his life as little more than a serf, a sensitive man whose intelligence had found its outlet in the craft of forestry, and he was saddened at the way his craft was no longer being followed. He told me of a day, long after he retired, when he had gone on a conducted tour of some local woods, and for a while he found himself taking over from the guide:

"Ash wants a fur coat and a bare head," he told them. "Ash on its own is hopeless. You have to put broad leaf, like beech or sycamore, with ash. Ash likes a shaded floor ... There are so many places on the Cotswolds where ash seed blows in, and it comes up like winter wheat ... You need to start with fifty per cent larch. Larch, you see, nurses. It draws the ash and the beech up. Then you take out all the larch."

Surrounded by so many strange faces, he soon stopped talking but, at the end of the walk, a man came up to him. "Charlie, why did you stop? I could have listened to you all day. These young people are all piss and wind."

"I go by local woods now and, dammit, it upsets me. Ash has to be tough. They used it in the First World War for aircraft, didn't they? If you thin it out, it will be beautiful fifty years later. I seem to be the only one now who knows, the only one who bothers."

A couple of years later a reader in Cumbria told me his amateur dramatic society was staging *Cider with Rosie* and they were struggling with the accents. So I sent him my tape of Charlie talking. I still get goose pimples when I listen to it.

For Bomber and Mary, the chapter with Charlie was the best in the book, and we invited him to the launch in a marquee at the Cheltenham Festival. To Bomber and to me he was one of the star guests, a man of inestimable worth, but for Charlie, brought up in an age when he had to know his place, the whole experience was overwhelming.

"He's in seventh heaven," his son said. "He'll be talking about it all winter."

Also at the launch were the sister and daughter of George Emmett, the Gloucestershire captain who had died more than twenty years earlier. Bomber told plenty of stories about "old Emmett", many of them portraying him as a would-be Napoleon, a little man strutting about and standing for no nonsense. He was the kind of man I would have rebelled against as a teenager, in those years in the 1960s when we all thought we knew more than our elders.

"We won a game," Bomber recalled, "and in the dressing room somebody said, 'It's good to win.' Old Emmett got up. 'It's good to lose, too,' he said. 'It keeps your feet on the ground. You should never gloat over winning.' He went on for about ten minutes about playing in the right spirit. People in Gloucestershire now don't realise how much he did for the county when he was captain. He was magnificent."

Whenever Bomber talked of Emmett's batting, he glowed. The little maestro, he called him. A wonderful player to watch, he would have had a far better record if he had not been out in the nineties so often. "He deserved so many more hundreds than he got. Other batsmen played for them, but he didn't. He played exactly the same from start to finish, and they're the kind of people you remember, aren't they? The Boycotts of this game are non-entities. They've given nothing to cricket except facts and figures."

Emmett's sister Joyce lived in Torquay. She had not been to Cheltenham for more than forty years, and she had a golden day. "It's so nice to bathe in the reflected glory of being George's sister. I'd forgotten what that felt like."

Bomber drew his wheelchair alongside her. "Now then," he said with a twinkle. "Are you the sister or the daughter?" It was the perfect start, and it got better. "There's never a day goes by at Cheltenham when you can't walk round the ground and hear somebody talking about some innings by your brother."

Bomber had persuaded me, good socialist that he was, that we should price the book at eight pounds. He did not think people would be able to afford ten. Then at Cheltenham he sat in his wheelchair, and each time he sold a copy he was offered a ten-pound note. "I'll tell you what," he would say, reaching into his top pocket, "I won't give you change. I'll give you two pounds worth of these raffle tickets for Gloucester City Cricket Club."

"I wasn't even going to buy a copy," one woman complained. "And he was sitting there, telling me he'd written me a dedication." Heaven knows how many books we would have sold if he had been able to walk round the ground.

We had a glowing review in the *Daily Telegraph* from Michael Parkinson: 'Bomber Wells, there was a summer's day in his face and laughter in his soul.'

The book also caught the imagination of Frank Keating in the *Guardian*: 'It is as precise and formulated as a Pinter reunion on the stage. Romantic, dangerous, even subversive.'

Frank had grown up in the Cotswolds and, like Bomber, he loved the romance of cricket, hating the way it was being taken over by marketing men and supermarket bosses, what Bomber called 'all this intense commercialism'. 'Had M'Lord Tesco served another term,' Frank wrote the following year, when Ian MacLaurin stepped down as ECB Chairman, 'domestic cricket might have transmuted into Inter-City 10-over rounders matches under floodlights.'

We had a less glowing review from Robin Marlar in *The Cricketer*: 'Chalke is so starry-eyed that he is prone to believe every word the old players tell him!' was the thrust of his put-down, a sentence that enraged Ken Biddulph. "What's he mean by that? Why shouldn't you believe everything old cricketers tell you? Is he saying we're all liars?"

Robin drew attention to a mistake in the book. I had said that a 1957 MCC sub-committee on amateur status had been chaired by the Duke of Norfolk where, in fact, the chairman had been Viscount Cobham. It was a tiny colouring detail, but I beat myself up over getting it wrong. Knowing little of MCC's inner workings, I had clearly misunderstood the entry in *Wisden*. It was a bad mistake, revealing once more that I was writing about matters about which I knew very little.

In a subsequent issue Robin returned to the subject. A reader had written to him to say that I was right, quoting Tony Lewis's history of MCC. But he stuck to his guns. "I was there, I know," was the essence of his argument. So, suitably chastened, when the book went off for a reprint, I corrected my error, changing the chairman to Viscount Cobham.

It was only when I started on my next book with Geoffrey Howard, who had served on the sub-committee, that I discovered that I had been right in the first place. It was the Duke of Norfolk. Geoffrey remembered him arriving late for a meeting because he had been involved in the planning of Winston Churchill's funeral, seven years before the great man died.

Of course, if you think about it, that proved that Robin had been right with his primary criticism of me. I was indeed too prone to believe every word the old players told me – in this case, him.

There was an extraordinary review in a little publication called *The Cricket Statistician*. The reviewer, Robert Brooke, called the book 'the monumental, unforgettable book all writers hope they have within them'. Then he went on: 'Chalke will never find another Wells. Whatever the future holds for him, it will inevitably be something of an anticlimax.'

That made me laugh. If I am honest, it was what I myself felt at the time.

George Emmett's sister Joyce took a more positive view of my future, taking me by the arm before she left the launch. "God bless you. Whatever you do with your life, I hope you have great success. I'm sure you will have."

I stood on my own after she walked away, trying not to be overwhelmed. It is a cliché to say it, I know, but I felt very humble. If I could re-live one moment from the story of this book, I think it would be that. I had such a glow inside me.

This forgotten world of 1950s cricket had all manner of emotions swirling around it. All I had done was to bring it back to life for people, turning on a light in 'a room that had not been visited for a while'.

*

One day Bomber talked to me about the decline of spin bowling, how nobody in English cricket understood any longer how devastating a good spin bowler could be. It is a complex subject, about playing surfaces and modern bat technology, and people can become quite boring talking about it. But for Bomber it was simple. The game of cricket was losing one of its most magical ingredients. "Soon," he said, "the generation will be gone who remember any different."

I have always used an inner ear when writing – trying, as Hazel put it, to catch the rhythm – and, when I sat in my room at home, I found the words swimming round my head:

> Soon the generation will be gone who remember any different ... I seem to be the only one now who knows, the only one who bothers ... You lived in a world free of all this intense commercialism ... Charlie, why did you stop? ... You can learn a lot from old men, you know. They might exaggerate things, but it doesn't matter. You get the gist ... Have a fig roll, Stephen. Go on, take several.

I had built this constant offering of food as a kind of comic chorus into the book and, when I next went for a check-up on my teeth, my dentist told me he had been to Cheltenham with his son and had bought my book. He repeated with delight the exchanges about food: "Have an apple, Stephen ... No thank you, Bomber ... Go on, take it."

"We're saying it to each other all the time at home now."

There was a filling to be done, and my mouth became cluttered with a suction tube and cotton wool around the gums.

"I met your friend Mr Wells," he continued. "He said the next time I had you in the chair and you couldn't answer back, I was to tell you not to give up writing about cricket."

10

My back pages – the 1960s

I was born in 1948, part of that post-war generation brought up by parents who wanted to create a better world, to save their children from the horrors of war and the hardships they had experienced. By the start of the 1960s the economy was once more growing, and young people had money to spend. National Service was abolished, higher education expanded, and everywhere there was a sense of progress: from city centre developments to large housing schemes, from the welter of new household appliances to the landing of men on the moon. And, for soundtrack to it all, there was the cheerful energy of the Beatles.

Cricket found it hard to keep up with all that, but it did its best, initiating a multitude of reforms and remaining the nation's principal summer sport. In comparison the popularity of football grew, especially after England's victory in the 1966 World Cup, but the two seasons were still largely separated.

*

For six months in the summer of 1966, between school and university, I worked as a Community Service Volunteer at Harperbury Hospital near Radlett, an institution for 'the severely mentally subnormal' with 1,700 patients.

CSV had been set up by Alec Dickson, a visionary who had also set up VSO, Voluntary Service Overseas. He had left VSO when it insisted on a selection system for applicants. In his view everybody who wanted to give should be given the chance to do so, and at CSV he found placements for all, even the blind and the severely disabled. There was one scheme in Bradford in which a volunteer, placed in a school with a high number of Pakistani children, got a list of old people who were living on their own and persuaded some of them to entertain the children, to help them to speak better English. Then he told the children that the old people were lonely and needed company. So both sides were giving. That had Alec Dickson written all over it. He was a strong believer in loving and giving and, like many in the 1960s, he saw the great potential for good in the idealism of the young.

I knew nothing of 'mental subnormality' when I arrived at the hospital. There was another CSV there, a girl called Jocelyn who was nearing the end of her stay. On the evening before I started, she described the various conditions I would encounter on the children's ward where I was being placed: mongols, spastics, epileptics and, most frightening, hydrocephalics with large heads and microcephalics with small ones. That night I had disturbing dreams.

The next morning, on the dot of nine, smart in my tweed jacket and woollen Woolworths tie, I pressed the bell of Children's Ward 6, to be greeted by a sister who was flummoxed by my arrival. Nobody had mentioned me; she had no idea what I was supposed to be doing on the ward. They had never had a man working there before.

For the next two months I went there every weekday, helping out as best I could, trying to play with those children who could manage anything. The nurses were mostly from Mauritius, brought in not long before in plane loads; their English was poor, and they were at full stretch coping with the essential tasks: the meals, the baths, the laundry, the cleaning.

One boy David, a 'mongol', was brighter than the rest. Untypically he had parents who visited, and they had given him a little cricket set with a soft ball. I set up games with him on the grass at the back of the ward, but other children got in the way and wandered off with the ball. The same happened when I bought him a jigsaw; two of the pieces got chewed by another child. "Mad," he would say to me, twisting his finger against the side of his head. Alone in this strange world, my Christianity was tested.

Then one evening, when I was mending a puncture on my bike, Matron stopped to talk to me. When she found out that I had three 'A' levels, two of them in Maths, and was off to university, she was shocked. "We must put you to better use," she declared.

She was a fierce woman; her staff were terrified of her. "Matron's coming," they would say, and she would sweep onto the ward, running her finger along a dusty window sill and giving them all a fearful bollocking. It was worse than the prefects at my public school. Unfortunately for her this approach went down less well with the Area Health Authority where her demands for more staff, accompanied by fist-banging and shouting, got her nowhere. So she took me into her office and gave me all the facts: the numbers on the staff, their hours, the annual leave, the training days, the ratios required for different patients. Then she gave me an A1 sheet of stiff paper and some coloured pens and told me to prepare charts that she could present to them. It took me three hours that afternoon in my bedroom, and at the next meeting she got everything she asked for.

I was now her golden boy, and she promptly sent me off to the Psychology Unit to undertake a project with them. I watched them conducting IQ tests which consisted of asking the patients to fit different shapes into the spaces on a wooden board. Half of them failed to understand what they were being asked, and the results, on a scale with an average of 100, ranged from 40 down to about 5. I accompanied the psychiatric social worker in her fast sports car down to Notting Hill to visit a young couple, with a baby, who were being reintegrated into society; they were living in a large, bare room with not an item of food in any cupboard, and they were soon back in the hospital.

The staff in the Unit were most friendly to me, all except a young psychologist who had that earnest, radical look, with a crewneck black jersey and steel-rimmed glasses, that was starting to become fashionable. He asked me where I came from – "Salisbury" – and ignored me for the rest of my stay. Only on the last day did I discover the reason for his unfriendliness; he had assumed I was Rhodesian and hence some kind of white supremacist.

On Saturdays I caught a bus to London, going to the theatre or to a day's cricket at Lord's. My father gave me a ticket for the FA Cup Final, and I also attended a Billy Graham religious rally at Earl's Court. I was a lost soul searching for something.

My project was back on the children's wards. I conducted ten-minute observations of the behaviour of each child who was not attending the hospital school. Then, when the hospital school was closed for its summer holiday, I used the main schoolroom for a playgroup that I supervised, picking a group of children who were not attending the school.

Two friends from my old school came to see me at work, and on that day a bug had gone round the children's wards. When they arrived, I was on my hands and knees, mopping up liquid shit. By then it was all in a day's work to me, but they were horrified.

Towards the end of the weeks allotted to the play group, I conducted fresh observations of the children. In most cases, given structured activity, they had shown significant improvement, and I presented a paper to this effect. I had to learn the passive language of such reports – "It was observed that" rather than "I observed" – but I had the analytical brain to process the findings and to make well-structured recommendations.

In the background there was a tension about whose project it was, Matron's or the Psychology Unit's, but I tiptoed as carefully as I could through that. The children's wards had almost no playthings or soft dolls so I was horrified when, late in my stay, I discovered a locked cupboard, along the corridor from Matron's office, packed with toys that had been donated to the hospital. They were only put out on the rare visitors' days, in case they got damaged.

Alas, my two successors were less prepared to humour Matron, there was an almighty blow-up, and CSV had no more to do with the hospital. It was a full seven years before I found out the end of this story.

I was teaching English in a comprehensive school in North London where one day I read to a class of 15-year-olds Jon Silkin's poem 'Death of a Son (who died in a mental hospital aged one)'. In rapt attention they listened to my description of the children at Harperbury, and they asked if I could arrange a visit. I found the telephone number of the Psychology Unit and rang from the phone in the staff room, getting through to the Head of the Unit. "My name's Stephen Chalke," I said. "You won't remember me."

"Won't remember you?" he repeated with incredulity. "Of course I remember you. We built our Activity Centre on the strength of your report. It's been a major success, so much so that we've just expanded it."

Years later, when Martha was small, I was talking to a fellow father whose job was to empty out Harperbury Hospital, to rehouse all the patients in society. There were barely a hundred left there by then. It sounded such a kind policy, 'Care in the Community', but I had my doubts.

*

That summer of 1966 the West Indian cricketers were in England. I was too far back in the queue to get into the Saturday of the Lord's Test so I never saw the 96 that Tom Graveney scored. But my father got tickets for the Saturday at The Oval, and we sat together in the East Stand, watching the last stages of a magnificent 165 by Tom, followed by a most unlikely last-wicket stand of 128 by John Snow and Ken Higgs. My hero by then was Garry Sobers. In every Test that summer he had turned the game with his magnificent batting, and I was certain that he was going to do the same again. At close of play West Indies were 135 for four in their second innings, still 124 runs short of making England bat again, and Sobers was next man in.

Full of anticipation I switched my Monday work to Sunday and arranged to meet a school friend at the ground. The day's play had barely begun when there was a run out, and Sobers strode in. A thrill ran through me, then oh horror! he was caught first ball at short leg by Brian Close. The match was all over soon after lunch.

We joined the crowd in front of the pavilion, then took the tube to Oxford Street, where we watched Olivier's *Hamlet* in the Academy Cinema. It is a very good film, but I would rather have seen Sobers score a century.

*

CSV were delighted with the success of my project. They put me forward to be part of a feature about voluntary service in the *Observer Colour Supplement*, and two years later they invited me to join the national committee.

In the spring of 1967 I wrote to Alec Dickson, asking if he had anything for me to do during the summer vacation, and he offered me a place on a project about racial discrimination in Birmingham.

As with mental handicap, the experience of black people in England was a subject about which I knew nothing at all, but I knew where my sympathies lay. I had my Bob Dylan LPs – "How many years can some people exist before they're allowed to be free?" – and I loved Martin Luther King's 'I Have A Dream' speech, with its heady mixture of idealism and Christianity.

Under the supervision of Dipak Nandy, a university lecturer in English, we spent that summer knocking on doors up and down the streets of Handsworth. We had two tasks, to collect evidence of racial discrimination and to identify people who would take the lead in forming a local branch of the Campaign Against Racial Discrimination, CARD as it was known.

Whether I was an appropriate person to be doing this, I am not sure. The Black Power group who took over CARD at that autumn's AGM thought not; they derided the use of white volunteers. Whether we achieved much, I am not sure, either. Dipak said our fieldwork was crucial in persuading Roy Jenkins, the Home Secretary, to introduce fresh legislation but, if it was, he must have added a great deal from other sources.

What I do know is that the experience had a profound effect on me. Growing up in rural Wiltshire, I had never witnessed urban poverty, and it shocked me. I returned to Bristol, to my studies, and I threw myself into community work in the St Paul's district.

*

I had less opportunity to watch cricket in that summer of 1967, though I do recall how my Handsworth companion and I used to stop outside the television rental shop to catch the latest score in the Test match. I can remember our disbelief when Asif Iqbal, batting at number nine, and Intikhab Alam, at number ten, added over 200 runs together at The Oval. Every time we looked, they were still batting.

When the next year the MCC selectors did not pick Basil D'Oliveira for the South African tour, I was outraged. My young mind was in turmoil. Martin Luther King and Robert Kennedy, two beacons of hope, had been shot dead in America, Enoch Powell had delivered a speech that had stirred up ugly sentiments, and now my beloved cricket had given in to the wicked apartheid policy of South Africa.

In recent years I have met some of those involved in what we now call the D'Oliveira Affair, and I have come to realise that the people at Lord's were placed in a near-impossible position. At the time it seemed to me that a great wrong had been done. And, though I am now more sympathetic to some of those MCC people, that is still what I think.

11

Spreading my wings

After the success of *Runs in the Memory*, I suppose I might have found a publisher to take me on, to relieve me of all the routine chores, but that never appealed to me. I liked the fact that I had complete control: from the words in the book through the layout of the pages to the cover design and the publicity. I liked it that readers rang up and chatted to me. In a strange way, after a lifetime of intellectual work, I even enjoyed the manual tasks, the humping up and down stairs of boxes and the packing of parcels.

Sue shared the adventure and the hard work, which helped greatly, and soon enough we realised that it was our lack of overheads – no hired premises, no paid staff – that enabled us to get the books into profit. If I had calculated the hourly rate of pay, it would have been nowhere near the minimum wage but, with our simple lifestyle, that never seemed to bother us. The romance of it appealed so much, being the little guy holding his own against the corporate giants, doing it all with an idiosyncratic personal touch.

My brother Peter had taken on the family timber business at the age of 23, when it had been at its lowest ebb, and he had made a great success of it. So he thoroughly approved of my life change. "You've become a good capitalist at last," he said several times. Though my bank balance showed no sign of any accumulation of capital, I knew what he meant. After years of working in the public sector, I was giving expression to our father's entrepreneurial genes and I was enjoying it.

When I look back now, I struggle to understand how I found time for it all. Martha was still at home, studying for her 'A' levels, I was lecturing part-time at three universities, and I was playing 30 or 40 games of cricket each summer. Yet not only was I researching, writing and publishing my own books but, in my determination to make a success of my new life, I started spreading my wings into new ventures: publishing books by other writers, writing a regular column for *Wisden Cricket Monthly* and touring the length and breadth of England giving talks.

The talks gave an outlet for the actor manqué in me. As a troubled adolescent I had fallen in love with the theatre, taking part in all the school productions. I had won a major scholarship to a public school on account of my mathematical ability, and I was being trained to sit the scholarship papers for Cambridge, but I turned my back on that and studied Drama, English and Philosophy at Bristol. Once there, alongside Tim Pigott-Smith, I soon realised that I was not even in the second division of talent, and I gave up acting in favour of writing theatre reviews. One of my lecturers – Laurence Kitchin, once of *The Times* – encouraged me, but my burning social conscience, wanting to make the world a better place, led me into teaching. Could I have been a successful theatre critic, as Laurence Kitchin believed? I am not so sure. In one review of a play set in the southern states of America I criticised the unconvincing accent of an actress; it turned out that she was the only American in the cast.

Could I have been a successful actor? Almost certainly not. My greatest weakness, among many, was a lack of self-awareness. What little talent I had was comic, and I did not value that, yearning to play serious roles. Making people laugh was easy and trivial, I thought – and, of course, as I now realise, it is no such thing. Thirty years on, when I started talking to cricket lovers' societies, I loved nothing more than making them laugh.

One of my first talks was at Waterstones in Bath where the man in charge of the sports section set up a small launch event for *Caught in the Memory*. There was an audience of forty, the majority of them friends, and I spoke for an hour. Ignoring a quote from Benjamin Disraeli that was printed in my diary for that week – 'An author who speaks about his books is almost as bad as a mother who talks about her own children' – I described the process by which I had created the book, and I read some extracts. There was plenty of laughter, which was interspersed with some serious reflections about cricket and about life. Afterwards Hazel, who had sat in the middle of the front row taking notes, took me aside. "You must take this talk around the country," she said. "This is how you will sell the book."

As always, she was right. Yet in those early days I was riddled with anxieties about doing it. I felt I was an impostor, holding forth on a subject, county cricket in the 1950s and 1960s, about which I knew very little, just the stories the old players had told me. Many in my audiences had watched far more county cricket, both in those years and since, than I had. I needed to promote my books, yes, but why would anybody want to listen to me?

At Bristol, returning for a full evening with the Gloucestershire Cricket Lovers, I got them laughing. Then, without planning it, I finished the evening by becoming philosophical about the social changes of the past forty years. Had the pursuit of affluence led to a decline in our sense of public service? Did the generation brought up in the war have a greater sense of right and wrong? Was there a down-side to social mobility? I asked the questions, leaving people room to think for themselves, and I left, feeling it had gone down well enough.

The following night I was speaking to a bigger audience, maybe one hundred, in Leeds. The chairman, Tony Vann, gave me a terrific introduction, praising my books to the skies, and the audience exuded a lovely north-country warmth that, together with the confidence I had gained the previous night in Bristol, brought the best out of me. I intermingled the stories and the philosophising, so that laughter and rapt silence alternated, and the adrenaline ran so fast inside me that I never seemed lost for the next thing to say. I sensed it had gone well, though it shocked me when the woman on the door said that several people, when leaving, had said "Best ever".

No other evening in those early years was as good as that. It gave me such a strong sense of what I was trying to achieve.

The hardest evenings were when the audience was small, as they sometimes were for me, an unknown name. When, on an evening on which there was a one-day match on television, Hertfordshire Cricket Society made a last-minute switch of venue from Shenley to Sawbridgeworth thirty miles away, I found myself speaking to seven. "Shall I sit and chat to you, or would you like my normal speech?" I asked, and they opted for the normal speech. I stood up, and it was down to me to generate the adrenaline that an audience of seventy would have produced. My word, it was hard. I was so exhausted that, when I was leaving town, I came close to crashing into another car on a dual carriageway.

Being a nobody had its moments. I went to the County Ground in Chelmsford where I was greeted at the door by one of the society's committee. He offered to buy me a drink and, as we walked towards the bar, I asked him how many he was expecting. "Maybe forty or fifty," he said. "We used to get a lot more, but the numbers have gone right down. And the trouble is, once the numbers go down, you can't afford good speakers."

At Stourbridge I had Martin Horton sitting in the front row. His Roly Jenkins stories, complete with the Worcester accent, were part of my usual repertoire, and with some misgivings I told them in front of Martin. At the end of the evening I asked him how I had done. "You were very good," he said. "But I was trying to work out where that Roly Jenkins came from. Was it Birmingham or Pakistan?"

Far worse was agreeing to speak at the Arundel Castle Cricket Foundation Spring Lunch, on the subject of county cricket in the 1950s, when I found myself sitting on the top table between Hubert Doggart, former Sussex captain and MCC President, and Colin Cowdrey. The only thing that saved me from total panic was the man across the table. Sensing my difficulty, he tried with great charm to put me at my ease. Somehow I survived, and I drove home, wondering if it had been a mistake to accept the invitation. I had no inkling of what was to follow from the conversation with the man across the table.

With the right audience I was fine, but I soon realised that that audience did not extend to club dinners. I spoke to a group of thirty umpires in Nottinghamshire, and they laughed repeatedly, an afternoon that led to their booking me for their league's annual dinner. "Just give the same speech," the chairman advised me at the start of the meal. But, in front of four hundred people, many of them young lads who had been drinking all evening, even my best Bomber Wells story was met with bemused silence. After a few minutes a voice at the back of my head was shouting at me: "It's not working, Stephen, you can't go on like this." I ended up giving a short headmasterly peroration about looking after the game.

At least they heard me in silence, which was more than I was expecting when I got up to speak at a Forty Club dinner in York, an assignment that involved a 500-mile round trip which I completed that night. The audience had been playing an inter-regional tournament during the day, and all meal they were drinking heavily. At one point during the main course, sitting on the top table, I was approached by a glassy-eyed Scotsman with a lump of Yorkshire pudding in his hand. "Are you the speaker?" he asked, swaying on his feet. "Three minutes. Any more, and I'm throwing this at you."

The cricket societies were my natural habitat, none better than High Peak in North Derbyshire. Organised by the tireless Bob Wood, they had a hot-pot supper in the interval of the meeting, and such was their efficiency that they knew in advance exactly how many meals were required. The first time I spoke there, it was more than 140.

There was still a part of me feeling I was an impostor. I knew I had a good speaking voice and good comic timing, but it took me a while to realise that my material had a specialness about it. A few years ago I had to speak at The Oval, to a lunch of executives in the oil business, and one of them was in raptures afterwards. "I go to so many of these dinners," he said, "and you get to hear the same stories over and over again. But your stories, they're all so fresh. I've never heard any of them before."

That, of course, was the up-side of being an unknown nobody.

*

It was on a whim one day that I wrote to Stephen Fay. He had just been appointed editor of *Wisden Cricket Monthly*, and I asked him if he would like a regular column from me, interviewing old cricketers about special moments in county cricket's past. 'From my experience, county cricket is full of material that hasn't been properly recorded,' I wrote. 'Believe me, there are lots of people out there who would love it.'

He had a long think about it, then asked me to submit a piece about one of my suggestions, the resumption of cricket after World War Two. It was not ideal territory for me, with too much of the material coming from books and newspapers, but he liked it enough to ask for two more.

This time I was left to choose my own topics. I picked an extraordinary innings by Don Wilson, when he went in at number eleven with an arm in plaster and brought off a last-minute one-wicket victory with a flailing 29 not out, and an even more extraordinary bowling spell by Leicestershire's Charles Palmer when, as a part-time seamer with a bad back, he put himself on for one over against the mighty Surrey, took a wicket, carried on and, after 12 overs, found himself with figures of eight wickets for no runs.

Stephen was convinced. "You can do one every month from now on," he said breezily. "And when you've done a hundred, you can put them in a book." The column was called 'Only Yesterday', and it appeared alongside one by Angus Fraser. County cricket past and county cricket present, side by side.

Over the next years the column was an excellent opportunity for me to explore new topics, but it was hard work. It seemed that no sooner had I finished one – phew! – than I was being chased up for the next. Each time I had to think of a subject, and usually, believing that the best interviews are done face to face, this would entail me in a long day out, followed by two or three days of research and writing.

Somebody told me that Rupert Webb, the former Sussex wicket-keeper, was good fun so I arranged to meet up with him at a suitable halfway point, the café at Southampton Airport. On the phone he alerted me to a good story about the Reverend David Sheppard in his year as captain of Sussex, and it was my intention to focus on that. The story had a nice mix of material: a great innings by Sheppard, a light shone on the nature of his leadership and some unexpected humour in a pivotal moment. Rupert duly gave me everything I needed for my 800-word piece.

What he also gave me, returning to the subject repeatedly, was a great number of stories about Robin Marlar, who had taken on the Sussex captaincy two years after David Sheppard. Robin had been responsible for ending Rupert's career, giving the wicket-keeping gloves to Jim Parks who till then had been a specialist batsman. In wanting to have a keeper who could bat, Robin was years ahead of his time, but Rupert had never forgiven him, neither for the decision nor for the manner in which it took place.

Rupert was one who could bring the past alive when he spoke, and he knew how to tell a story to maximum effect. In that respect he was perfect for me. But, beneath the humour of his stories, I could sense the anger in his obsession with Robin Marlar. With no wish to inflame the ill-will between the two of them, and certainly no wish to get into a fresh tangle with Robin,

I stuck to writing up the story about David Sheppard. Alas, it did not prove to be my last involvement with their feud.

*

One day at Cheltenham, when I was with Bomber promoting his book, I got talking with David Foot, the West Country journalist and cricket writer.

So many of the cricket books I read before I took up writing about the game were dull. I remember a family holiday in Devon when I borrowed from the local library a biography of Maurice Tate, the old Sussex and England bowler. I was in the mood to lose myself in the 1920s, a period of cricket about which I knew little, but the characters and the games did not come alive for me. There were passages that were little more than scorecards turned into words.

By contrast, the prose in David Foot's books hypnotised me. There was a richness of language, a fascination with human frailty and, in his West Country subjects, a deep understanding of the soil out of which they had sprung. He was writing about cricket, but always he was writing about so much more than cricket. At times there was a mistiness in the prose, a sense of blur akin to an impressionist painting, and that added to the mesmerising effect of it all, the inner self of each character always just out of reach in a past that we could never quite get back to. I was spell-bound.

I read *Beyond Bat and Ball*, his set of 'eleven intimate portraits', not long before I set to work on *Runs in the Memory*, and it inspired me. I was also inspired by a 15-minute radio feature by Harold Pinter, about the old Somerset cricketer Arthur Wellard. I taped it and listened to it regularly, enchanted by the way he counterpointed the voices of the narrator and of Wellard, together with an occasional brief statement of cricketing fact. Pinter had a brilliant ear, and he carried it off to perfection.

That counterpointing was something I played with in *Runs in the Memory*, but there was nothing in David Foot's prose that I could copy nor did I want to. It was special to him and to the way he saw the world.

At Cheltenham he told me he was working on a sequel to *Beyond Bat and Ball*, a second set of studies of men who fascinated him, this time including some from other sports. He was still looking for a publisher, and without a thought I said, "Oh, I'll do that."

"You couldn't, could you?"

"Why not?"

"Well, can you afford an advance?"

"I expect so."

Beyond Bat and Ball had been privately published and, before I had put *Runs in the Memory* into print, I had picked David's brains at length about the finances of self-publishing so I had some idea what sort of money we might be talking about, though we still managed to argue about it.

After agreeing the advance, we discussed the royalty per book. The normal arrangement in the trade is for the publisher to pay a percentage of the money they take from book sales, say 10%. So, if a book retails at £15 and the shops pay the publisher half that, the author will get 10% of £7.50. To keep matters simple, I decided to cut out the percentages, and that is where the argument started.

"I'll pay you two pounds a book."

"No, no, no. You can't pay me that much."

"Yes, I can. And I will."

"No, you certainly won't. I won't accept it."

In the end I bullied him into agreeing my terms, and we signed a contract.

The book was called *Fragments of Idolatry*, a title I was happy with, though Frank Keating said it was 'poncy'. It certainly proved too complicated for one customer who rang up for *Fragments of Adultery*; I hope he was not disappointed.

There were twelve studies in the book. The first two, on Raymond Robertson-Glasgow the cricket writer and Carwyn James the rugby player, were typical David subjects: Robertson-Glasgow was a manic depressive who made several attempts on his life before succeeding with a massive overdose, while James died 'with cruel, mystifying suddenness in a nondescript Amsterdam hotel'. A little later in the book he profiled the writer Alan Gibson, whose life had spiralled downwards, a mix of alcohol and depression, and ended in a residential home. It was quite a relief amid such gloom to discover Tom Cartwright and his combative views on how cricket should be played and coached.

Tom was flattered to be included in the collection but also a little disturbed. "David's a strange writer," he said to me. "I seem to be the only person in the book who hasn't committed suicide."

But that was David. 'In the midst of life we are in death,' the Bible says, and David's writing never lost touch with that.

I have no idea what David had said to him but, when I took Bomber a copy of *Fragments of Idolatry*, he passed me a handbill. "Here," he said with a grin. "Give this to your friend David. He might like to go along." It was an advertisement for an open day at the local funeral directors.

I loved my visits to Bomber and Mary, as did Ken Biddulph who became a close friend of theirs. The following year, when Ken turned 70, I made him a special birthday card. I went through my *Wisdens*, finding all the times he had dismissed great batsmen cheaply, and I arranged ten of them into a pretend scorecard: Cowdrey b Biddulph 6, Graveney c & b Biddulph 7, May c Atkinson b Biddulph 5 and so on. It added up to 67, and I headed it 'BATTING GREATS CRASH TO 67 ALL OUT – BIDDULPH TAKES ALL TEN.' Inside the card I wrote, 'K.D. Biddulph not out 70.'

He rang as soon as he had read it, purring with pleasure and reliving every wicket in detail. "I'm going to take it up to Gloucester to show Bomber," he said. Then the tone of triumph disappeared out of his voice. "I know what will happen. He'll read the names, and he'll say, 'I got every one of those first ball.'"

David Foot's world was darker than this but, to be fair, there were several essays in *Fragments of Idolatry* that had a lighter touch. They were all beautifully written, like this description of the young Maurice Tremlett who was briefly the great hope for English fast bowling after the Second World War:

> Tremlett was well-built and blond, someone who stood out, an effect he never tried to cultivate. He walked with big strides and a movement that was apt to appear a little stiff-jointed, as if he were wandering along a side street in Taunton on market day rather than shaping like a 23-year-old recently in khaki.

If the biography of Maurice Tate had had paragraphs like that, I would not have taken it back to the library unfinished.

David was a joy to work with, but it was not as easy a book to sell as I expected. Its mix of sports, including football, boxing and rugby, meant that it was hard to place on the bookshop shelves, and such subjects as Reg Sinfield and 'Kid' Berg were not household names. Nor, outside the West Country, was David Foot. "Is he that chap from the *Socialist Worker*?" one bookshop asked me.

On the plus side *The Observer* ran an extensive extract from the profile of Robertson-Glasgow, and the *Guardian* did the same with Carwyn James, though they insisted on directing sales to a book distributor in North London. It took 40 copies and went bankrupt before paying for them.

The book sold well enough, making a decent profit for David and me, so I was not put off the idea of publishing other people's work.

Taking responsibility for putting another author's book into print created its share of anxiety, but it set me free from the awkwardness I often felt when I had to promote my own books. I could describe the essays in *Fragments of Idolatry* as 'a beautifully written collection' and David as 'a widely acclaimed author', phrases I would never have used about my own books or myself. Without self-consciousness I could contact potential reviewers or ring bookshops, and I enjoyed that. It made me feel like a proper publisher.

There is a romance about self-publishing, holding your own as the little man, but there are times when you yearn for that other person to believe in you and to promote your book. David was a far more experienced writer than me, but deep down, for all his success, he had a strong streak of self-doubt. I knew that doubt for myself, and I enjoyed being his publisher, providing him with the reassurance and the praise. I could even cope with the reviews, not that they were anything other than glowing. The best came from Robin Marlar who was at his most perceptive:

> The real attraction of David Foot's writing is that he is attracted to the loveable without being alarmed by the mysterious. Both he chronicles faithfully as essential features of the whole man.

*

Other writers started to approach me with ideas for books. One which I took on, from a journalist on *The Independent*, involved a series of profiles of England Test cricketers who had started their playing days with village sides, but in the end, like so many ideas, nothing came of it.

Then, just before Christmas 2001, there was a phone call from John Barclay, the man who had been sitting opposite me during my ordeal at the Arundel Castle Spring Lunch. That summer he had written a series of articles for *The Times*, looking back twenty years to his first season as captain of Sussex, when they came so agonisingly close to winning the county championship for the first time. He wondered if it would make a book and if I would publish it.

Sue and I read the manuscript and, once we had tuned into his distinctive style, we were captivated. The writing had an elegant, almost old-fashioned simplicity, but beneath the surface there was so much more going on. Against a background of Ian Botham's derring-do against the Australians and the wedding of Charles and Di, the Sussex team spent a long, high-energy summer in search of their own glory. "Jeez, you must all be on pills," the umpire Bill Alley told them. In the end they did not make it, but they were not down: 'Our abiding feeling was that we would win the championship the next year.' They never did, and it was still gnawing away inside John: 'It is only with the passing of time that the disappointment of not winning the prize has grown. I can never quite put it to the back of my mind.'

The characters of the team were brought alive, the rhythm of their summer fondly captured, yet beneath this there was a meditative, almost spiritual quality to his recall of the summer and all its 'what if's. Life does not always work out how you want it to, but it is still to be cherished.

That summer of 1981 was his first as a father, when family life was young and full of joy. And the summer of 2001, when he was looking back, was his first after his wife had died of cancer. He did not write about that, but I could feel it beneath the surface, how the coming to terms with the disappointment of the cricket sprang from a deeper well.

Sue had contributed some pen-and-ink drawings to Bomber's book, and this time we built her drawings more centrally into the book, with one in each chapter. She picked out references away from the cricket itself, including one of four dead wasps on a window sill that remains an especial favourite.

John was delighted by them, likening them to EH Shepard's drawings for *Winnie The Pooh*: "I get more compliments about Sue's drawings than I do about my writing," he told me once, though I suspect that was not true.

The series in *The Times* had been called *That Summer* but, with the pivotal moment – the greatest 'what if' – being an unsuccessful lbw appeal at Trent Bridge, we opted to call the book *The Appeal of the Championship*.

We asked David Sheppard, another captain who had taken Sussex to second place, to write a foreword. I am not a great believer in forewords; half the time it is obvious that their writers have not read the book and are just having their names added as a marketing ploy. But David was quite the opposite. He rang to say how much he had loved the book and apologised that he had far exceeded my suggested word count. In his foreword he praised the book lavishly, saying how it had made him laugh out loud 'more than any book has achieved for years', and he compared his own summer of captaincy with John's: 'I could feel all those hopes and fears again, as I read John Barclay's lively account of Sussex 1981. Enter into it with him!' I could not have asked for more.

As a great admirer of David's life's work, I was nervous about the financial arrangements for this foreword. I drafted a letter, offering him a fee and suggesting that he might prefer me to give it to a charity of his choice. I showed it to Sue, who was withering in her response: "I don't think you need to be suggesting to a bishop that he gives his money to charity."

The success of the book reinforced my naïve belief that publishing was not that difficult – little did I know – and, as with *Fragments of Idolatry*, it brought out the best in Robin Marlar, who once more saw to the heart of the writing:

> A gentle passion shines from every description of incident and every glimpse of character. Beautifully produced, with delightful drawings by Susanna Kendall, the book is dedicated to Mary-Lou, his wife, who died tragically young. A finer tribute is hard to imagine.

11

Milked by an amanuensis

"I went with my grandfather, my father and my brother. Four of us went. I think we sat at the Vauxhall end. I'm pretty sure, because I can see the players coming from the pavilion. And if you were at that end, you would see them. Yes, we were at the Vauxhall end. It was pretty rough in those days. Uncomfortable and scruffy."

I was sitting in front of a gas fire, in a converted cow barn, up a narrow, winding lane in Nailsworth in the Cotswolds. My host was Geoffrey Howard, the former Secretary of Lancashire and Surrey. He was one week short of his 92nd birthday, and he was trying to find in his mind's eye the answers to my questions about his first visit to The Oval in August 1919. Eighty-two years earlier.

"Was there a big crowd?"

"Yes," he said emphatically. "In the same way that there was in 1946, '47. Just after the war. Deprived of cricket, deprived of entertainment."

"And do you have any memories of what you saw?"

"It may be incorrect, but quite clearly in my mind Yorkshire fielded. The Surrey innings was opened by Hobbs and Donald Knight, and Jack Hobbs certainly made fifty. I saw him out. Donald Knight, I didn't see out because he went on and made a hundred. I watched for what seemed like a long time Wilfred Rhodes and Rockley Wilson bowling endlessly, or so it seemed, with enormous accuracy."

"And at lunchtime you walked round the ground?"

"Yes. As most people do. Because they've been sitting uncomfortably. They walk around the perimeter behind the seats. And we walked round behind the pavilion. And it just so happened, as we went round past the players' entrance, Jack Hobbs was standing outside. He always wore his MCC touring cap and blazer. And I got as near to him as I could, because he was obviously going to be a hero, and I just touched him."

The touch of the blazer. The ten-year-old boy in 1919 felt the thrill of it, and here he was in 2001, passing that magic on to me, to put it in a book and to pass it on still further down the line of time.

I was going back way beyond where I had ever before been as a writer, back to a time when so much of our modern way of life was in its infancy.

"I remember my father telling me about wireless telegraphy and particularly Marconi. His was the great name at the time of the *Titanic*. And I started myself: making wireless sets with crystals, coils, bits of cardboard. I was picking up signals on a little thing called a cat's whisker, a tiny coil of wire, finding a spot on it. I can remember sitting at home and shhh-ing the family because I could get this faint sound of a human voice. 'Two L.O. calling.' From the BBC at 22 Savoy Hill. It was so exciting."

I was enchanted. I was being transported back most of a century in the company of a man who still exuded so many of the best qualities of that long-lost time. He was an old-fashioned Englishman, courteous and kind, taking his time and doing things properly.

His own grandfather had been an early Fabian, a pioneer of the garden city movement and the driving force behind the creation of Letchworth. When Geoffrey had first gone to school there, he had been picked up from the railway station by the headmaster's wife in a pony and trap.

His first employment was to cut up and make ready advertisements for the British Journal of Dermatology and Syphilis. "I shall never forget the phone ringing one day when I was on my own in the office. It was the first time I had ever answered a telephone, and I was trembling with fear."

A position in Martins Bank led to cricket with the Private Banks club. It was a time when the best of amateur cricketers would go off and play in their holidays for the county sides. "At one time people used to say, 'Have you played for Essex this year?'"

Geoffrey's chance came with three games for Middlesex in 1930. In the first against Gloucestershire at Lord's, he went out to bat on the first afternoon. The Gloucestershire captain was Bev Lyon, Wally Hammond was at slip and, after a few minutes of Geoffrey's innings, Lyon turned to Hammond: "Take over for half an hour, will you, Wally? I'm going for a haircut."

Oh, how I was enchanted.

I had come to be with Geoffrey as the result of a telephone call from Scyld Berry, the cricket correspondent of the *Sunday Telegraph*. For some years, I later discovered, Geoffrey had wanted to record his memories before he died, and various attempts to do this had ended in failure. Derek Newton, a former chairman of Surrey County Cricket Club, had decided to make one last effort on Geoffrey's behalf, and Scyld was ringing round cricket writers. When he rang me, I got the distinct impression, though he did not quite say it, that several other people had turned down the assignment.

Geoffrey had been Secretary at Old Trafford and at The Oval. He had managed three England tours, notably the one of Australia in 1954/55 when Len Hutton's team, spearheaded by the pace of Tyson and Statham, dramatically won the Ashes. Geoffrey, Scyld told me, had moved in the inner corridors of cricket; he knew so much that should not be lost when he died.

My first instinct was to turn it down. Geoffrey was a cricket administrator, not a player; in any case he only wanted somebody to do some tape recordings with him, and my great pleasure came from writing. But I have never been very good at saying no. The book with Bomber had happened by accident, and so would this one with Geoffrey. Scyld suggested an exploratory conversation, and I agreed to go with him to Nailsworth.

"But if I do take it on," I said, "I will want to write it up as a book."

He drove me up the A46. Even by my standards Scyld had a real old banger, which was full of the muck and muddle of his rural life with three small children. His father had been an eccentric, a professor of Middle English, hence the name Scyld from a character in *Beowulf*, and there was something similarly other-worldly at times about Scyld.

We had hardly sat down with Geoffrey before Scyld was firing questions at him one after another, questions that left me wondering quite where the project was leading. "Was Rockley Wilson gay? ... Which cricketers were gay? ... Was freemasonry rife at Lord's? ... Is that why Doug Insole got the job? ... Was Gubby Allen the illegitimate son of Plum Warner?"

With immense courtesy Geoffrey failed to offer any illumination on these subjects. Yet in my diary that evening I wrote, 'Geoffrey seems to like me and his power of recall is exceptional – so this may prove to be an excellent assignment for me.' He said he had read and enjoyed *Runs in the Memory*.

During the car journey home Scyld was still thinking laterally, suggesting that somebody should fund a centre for the oral history of cricket with a job for me. I thought, 'What a lovely idea – but I'm enjoying working on my own, away from all the politics of institutions.'

Scyld flew off to Sri Lanka, to cover England's tour, and I got to work, arranging to visit Geoffrey each Tuesday morning. At our first session he talked about his early life, and the next week I took him a draft of a chapter based on what he had told me. We sat in front of his fire, and I read him the pages slowly and carefully. I needed him to be comfortable with my way of writing.

"Three matches, six innings," I concluded. "This was his full first-class career. The little round of applause at Lord's never grew louder, and he returned to the bank, to many happy years of club cricket, with never a thought in his head that twenty-five years later he would be at the very heart of one of English cricket's greatest triumphs."

Geoffrey sat in silence for what seemed like an age. I did not feel confident. I do not know why, but I can never shake off this sense that the way I write is a bit quirky, not to everybody's taste.

Geoffrey had a habit of composing his thoughts into sentences before he spoke; he felt no pressure ever to speak hastily. "I have only two things to say," he said finally. "First, that it is wonderful. And second, that having read your other work I'm not surprised." He went into the galley kitchen to make us each a coffee and, when I followed him in, I found him dabbing his eyes with a handkerchief.

He was living on his own. His wife had died five years previously and, though he had family nearby, if he went long without company, he became achingly lonely and was not afraid to say so. He certainly found no comfort in the television; it often irritated him greatly. "Why can't they just read the news? Why do they have to sit on these sofas, giggling away at each other?"

We always sat in the two chairs by the gas fire in the house he had converted from a cow barn. "We must get a move on," he would say. "The clock is ticking." I juggled my commitment to him around my lecturing, and the chapters started to mount up.

In my previous books I had seen the game through the eyes of the players, almost all of them professionals. Now I was looking at it from another angle in the company of a man with a clear grasp of social history and no sentimental nostalgia colouring his vision. For two years in the late 1940s he had been Assistant to the Surrey Secretary, Brian Castor, who had spent much of the war as a prisoner of the Japanese. A High Tory, Castor yearned to get things back to where they had been in the 1930s, which Geoffrey, as a younger man with progressive views, knew could not happen.

> He wasn't looking forward at all. He was just upholding the traditions he'd grown up with. And he suffered, as a lot of people did in those days, from the indignity of being governed by the Labour Party ... He called me a Communist. Anybody who wasn't a Tory was a Communist. We worked in the same office, and one day he got irritated with me to the extent that he swept his glasses off and threw them at me. It was near the end of the day, and before long we were both on our hands and knees in the half-light, searching for the glasses and laughing at ourselves.

Their argument went to the heart of the choice that not just cricket but all of Britain had to make in the years following the war, between upholding the old way of life, the old England that Castor had yearned for in his prisoner-of-war camp, and recognising and adapting to the demands of the new.

When Scyld returned from Sri Lanka, I sent him the first three chapters: Geoffrey's early life, his war and his two years at The Oval. It ran to forty pages, and there was not much cricket.

"Why don't you leave out the war chapter?" Scyld suggested, but I was reluctant to do that. Most war memoirs tell of dramatic conflicts and great bravery, and Geoffrey's experience – desperate to play a part, yet wherever he went finding himself far from the action – was a fascinating insight into the war that so many people must have had. "Can you imagine the life of an anti-aircraft gunman when there's nothing to shoot at, or any likelihood?" he asked me. "Gunners used to say, 'What are the three most useless things in the world? Men's tits, the Pope's balls and anti-aircraft guns.'"

After Scyld's call, I sat down with a blank sheet of paper and I thought for a while. It was like trying to solve a logical puzzle. 'How about starting the book at Brisbane in November 1954?' I thought, and I wrote out an order of chapters, alternating the Australian Tests with sections of Geoffrey's life.

Looking back from the summer of 2001, when England were losing their seventh successive series against Australia, it was hard not to see that tour of Australia as a distant peak, towering above all around it. So many of the great names of post-war English cricket were there, the heroes of my childhood. There were the survivors of the hard years of the 1940s – Hutton, Compton, Bedser, Edrich, Evans – and the rising stars of the 1950s: May, Cowdrey, Graveney, Statham, Tyson. Add in Bailey and Wardle, and you had almost all the great names of those years, all except Trueman and Laker who had been left at home. So many of them were dead. Yet here was their manager, their father figure in those six golden months, talking about them all, bringing them alive.

Three winters earlier, in 1951/52, Geoffrey had managed a trip to India and Pakistan. He had never been to India, he had never managed a tour, he had no support staff, not even a scorer, yet, with just two journalists for company, he was sent off with 17 players. What another world it was from modern tours, when the support staff outnumber the players and the journalists outnumber both combined.

"What sort of briefing did you get from the MCC?" I asked him.

"Briefing," he repeated, looking pensively at the gas fire. "Briefing?" Eventually he found in his memory something that might come in the broad category of a briefing. "The Secretary of MCC, Colonel Rait Kerr, was a Sapper; he knew India, he'd served there. He came down to St Pancras to see us off for Tilbury and, as we parted, he said to me, 'Well, good luck, old boy, rather you than me. I can't stand educated Indians.'"

Geoffrey fell in love with newly independent India and even more with Pakistan. After we had finished the book, when he had a spell in the Gloucestershire Royal Hospital, he found himself in the next bed to a Pakistani. "He knows more about my country than I do," the man told me.

For the tour of Australia things were a little better than for India in that he had George Duckworth as baggage man and scorer. "Dear old George. He couldn't face telling his wife he was going on the trip. He told me on the boat that he'd left a note on the table, saying 'I'm going to Australia. I'll be back in April.'"

I drove Geoffrey to Lord's one day, to watch MCC play the visiting Melbourne Cricket Club, and we were in a box with Chris Cowdrey, who had heard all about Geoffrey from his father. "Tell me," he asked, "who exactly did you have in your management team in Australia?" Geoffrey pondered. "Management team?" He had a lovely way of drawing attention to words as he spoke them. "Management team? Well, I had George Duckworth."

When they disembarked at Fremantle, he discovered that MCC had forgotten to arrange the international transfer of any money. So he ran the whole tour on a personal overdraft negotiated with a local bank. Somehow, from the way he spoke, I got the impression that it was not untypical of the way MCC ran things in those years. He summed it up quite simply one day: "How much easier I would have found it to manage the tour if MCC had provided me with the two things I didn't have: help and money."

Yet the tour was a great success, on the field and off. When the book was published, Frank Tyson wrote in a review that English cricket would have dominated the world for longer if Geoffrey had managed the next tours as well. But Geoffrey had four young daughters, and he was unhappy about spending so long away from home.

Geoffrey worked hard to find what he could in his memory, but he was 92 years old and often he struggled to get beyond a few pictures and scraps of conversation. After my visits he would retire to bed exhausted, quoting John Milton: "My brain has been milked by my amanuensis."

Then one morning we had a breakthrough. He knew he had some photographs somewhere, snaps that he and the Middlesex batsman Jack Robertson had taken in India, and he went into his bedroom to see if he could find them. He came across a long-unopened box, a box that belonged to his late wife Nora. He opened it, and there inside it were all the letters he had written home each day from the three tours, tidily folded together in chronological order. "Take them away," he suggested. "You might find something of use in them."

I started with the ones from his tour of Australia, and quickly I found myself experiencing the rhythm of his six months away. There was the voyage out, with his first attempts to form a relationship with Len Hutton: 'He is easy and difficult, chatty and reserved – a whole host of opposites. An enigma in fact.' Then his early attempts to master the local dialect: 'A great Aussie expression is "I beg yours?" All the emphasis being on the <u>yours</u> which comes down the nose ... Another picturesque Aussie expression, "I am dragging my fur." Not feeling too good: not quite "feeling crook" but not "good thanks".'

A sequence of bad luck led to disastrous defeat in the First Test at Brisbane: 'Why do these things have to happen to touring cricket teams? You will all be so horribly fed up and disappointed – I could weep for you all – all of England.' Then in the Fourth Test at Adelaide the Ashes were won: 'I feel like the fellow who could not refrain from shouting, "Beaten the schoolmaster!" Beaten the Aussies – and what a win. No bodyline, nothing but playing better cricket than they have.' Here were the emotions of 1954, spoken in the language of 1954.

As I sat at home in fascinated absorption of these Australian letters, Geoffrey read through the pile from his Indian tour, and my telephone rang. "Stephen, there's something here that I seem to have forgotten."

"Oh? What's that, Geoffrey?"

"Well, it seems that sometimes, when we flew, I took the controls of the aircraft."

Ten years later, after the Munich disaster, MCC insisted on dividing their tour parties into two planes, but here was the whole England team in a twin-engine Dakota with their manager as pilot, a manager whose only flying experience had been as a trainee navigator in the war, a traineeship that was ended when they decided he was 'slow on the uptake'.

Amritsar, 18 October
We arrived here yesterday after landing at Delhi for breakfast and to refuel. An all round trip of about 700 miles or so. I flew the old Dakota nearly all the way from Indore to Delhi (about 3 hours) and thoroughly enjoyed it.

"You know, I can't recall that at all," he admitted. He said the same when he read his description of a group of boys playing an exhibition football match on stilts. "I would have thought that I would have remembered a thing like that."

I drove him to Radlett to see Donald Carr, who had been with him on two tours to the Indian sub-continent. I drove him to Edgbaston to meet Rose FitzGibbon and Sheila Delve, who had worked in the office at Old Trafford when he had been Secretary there. To Longparish to reminisce about Australia with John Woodcock, the *Times* correspondent. And to The Oval, where Micky Stewart, Derek Newton and Bernie Coleman recalled his days as Secretary.

Although the book was less about Geoffrey than about what he had witnessed in his long life in cricket, it was obvious wherever I took him that he was held in the highest regard. It did not need me to underline this. His qualities shone through every time he spoke in the book.

After the Australian tour, on his first day back at Old Trafford, rather than sit at his desk, he cycled round the ground, speaking at length to the ground staff, the painter, the carpenter, the sign writer. Undoubtedly he would have asked them about their families; almost fifty years on he still remembered all their names.

I could not help but contrast that with the senior managers in my last years at the college in Bristol: their mission statements and wildly impractical initiatives, their constant desire to reorganise and replace the staff they had, their inability to get the best out of people. After publication Ursula, Geoffrey's third daughter, picked up this theme. "You can read the book as a manual of good management," she said.

At Geoffrey's progressive school in Letchworth he had been in a form called The Go-Aheads, and he had stayed true to that tag all his life. In his years of cricket administration he had tried to find ways of bringing fresh life and money to the game when its audience was drifting away. He organised pop concerts at The Oval and brought in advertising; he even turned up at a committee meeting wearing a coloured shirt: "Why don't we wear these for our Sunday matches?"

I called the book *At The Heart Of English Cricket*, and I inserted a dedication – 'in memory of Nora Howard' – which brought a tear to Geoffrey's eye when he read it. "It's so long now since I've seen those two words."

On the same page I printed a sentence by Alan Bennett that I had read in the *London Review of Books*. It seemed to be so much in keeping with the project I had undertaken with Geoffrey:

> Anyone of any distinction should, on reaching a certain age, be taken away for a weekend at the state's expense, formally interviewed and stripped of all their recollections.

The book ended with a short chapter on Geoffrey's years of retirement, with one story that especially caught my fancy. It was about a balloon flight his youngest daughter Rosalind had given him for his eightieth birthday.

> We probably shouldn't have gone up. The wind was quite strong. I said to the chap, 'Are you looking for somewhere to land?' And he said, 'I'm always looking for somewhere to land.' 'Where are you making for then?' 'I'm making for that field over there.' And I watched as the field went away in the other direction. We finished up with the balloon hanging off some telegraph wires and us in the basket in a ditch. It was a rough old landing. My last balloon flight.

I loved to read him the chapters, and for this final one his eldest daughter Frances was sitting with us. Normally when I read, Geoffrey sat in silence with his eyes closed but, on hearing the words 'my last balloon flight', he looked up with a smile and offered a correction: "My last so far." Frances looked horrified.

The book went off to the printer. "I've spent so much of the last few months thinking about the past," he said. "It's quite a relief to get back to the present and the future."

When I took it up to him, however, and he sat signing some copies, he was going strong again. "I was lying in bed last night, and another memory came back. After I had seen Jack Hobbs, we walked round to the Vauxhall End. Where the stands are now, there was a stable for the horse that pulled the roller. I remember stretching up and stroking the horse's head. It was probably a big Clydesdale horse. They were commonplace, doing the work of the world. They wore big leather over-shoes, covering their hooves, to make sure they didn't leave any marks. It was one of the items in the annual expenditure: 'repair of, or purchase of, new shoes for horse.' Four substantial, hand-made over-shoes. They wouldn't have been cheap."

'Doing the work of the world', what a lovely expression! Geoffrey had left school at sixteen, but his language had a richness, born of reading good literature, that seemed of another age by the start of the 21st century.

The horse had gone by the time he became Surrey's Assistant Secretary in 1947, but the roller was still there. "It was called The Bomber. It was six foot or more in diameter, with great shafts, and it needed a whole gang to pull it. I can see the wonderful wave of water it pushed in front of it as the liquid top dressing was rolled in."

"I'd have put that in the book," I told him.

"Never mind," he said. "We can always do a second volume."

The book had a big launch at The Oval, organised by his friends there: Derek Newton, Bernie Coleman and Raman Subba Row. Geoffrey arranged a minivan to take up a party from Nailsworth, including his car mechanic who offered to bring his guitar and entertain them en route. "Knowing Geoffrey," Raman said, "it wouldn't surprise me to hear he was playing the guitar himself."

It was a grand day out. The Long Room was packed with all manner of people, much more of a cross-section of English life than most such functions. Amid the throng was Ken Biddulph, who radiated joy as he met once more contemporaries such as Alec Bedser and Doug Insole. "Is that Donald Carr?" And off he would go to relive another cricket match of long ago.

For years Geoffrey had been out of it all, living in his cow barn in Nailsworth and suffering from loneliness, and he loved the attention.

It went on for weeks. First, there were the phone calls. Once he had been a junior office boy, almost too frightened to pick up the receiver. Now he rang me regularly – "You'll never guess who's just rung me" – and it would be David Sheppard, Mike Brearley, Bob Appleyard, Geoff Edrich, men who had long disappeared out of his life.

Then the letters. "I've had the most extraordinary letter from Mike Vockins in Worcester," he rang to tell me. "I've never had a letter like it. If it were to somebody else, I'd say it was the most wonderful letter you could get."

I also had wonderful letters, including one from David Sheppard: 'The book is a delight, cleverly organised and beautifully written. I am praising it on all sides.' Unlike David I did not know Geoffrey in his working life, but I was not surprised when he added, 'Geoffrey's memories are shrewd and, I am glad to say, at times slightly indiscreet, as he would not have been years ago!'

Geoffrey had made at least three previous attempts to set down his memories, by tape or in a book, and he had not gelled with any of his collaborators. In one case he had answered an advertisement, something along the lines of 'For the price of a fortnight's holiday, let me write up your life story'. The first I learned of this was shortly after Geoffrey's death when the author rang, with menace in his tone, to accuse me of plagiarising his earlier work.

The matter rumbled on unpleasantly for several months. Even when he accepted with reluctance that I knew nothing of his 'book', he argued that Geoffrey must have been refreshing his memory by reading it before each of my visits. He offered to settle the matter by selling me the copyright of his volume for £350. When a copy of his typed pages eventually reached me via a third party, they took barely half an hour to read. Where my book had devoted 60 pages to the Australian tour, his contained two short paragraphs, with some of the players' names misspelt. Ursula said that her father had been so appalled by this first draft that the man had been paid off.

For Geoffrey, after such an experience and so late in his life, there must have been something special in my coming along. I found his Fabianism attractive, and I was beguiled by the charm with which he told his story to me, with a thread of humour running through so many of his observations. From my perspective I could not imagine how anybody would not fall in love with him.

The reviews were all superb, none more complimentary than Robin Marlar's in *The Cricketer*: 'This is Chalke's best so far, lovingly and beautifully crafted from recorded conversations.' In my first encounters with Robin, I had experienced only his waspish side, the razor-sharp pen that could cut a foe to shreds. Now, I was realising, there was another, much warmer side to him. He was a good friend of Derek Newton – he had been exceptionally kind to Derek after his wife had died – and he also admired Geoffrey greatly. So, to my great relief, our silly spat was finally put to rest.

Geoffrey had opened his heart to me, and it created a closeness that endured after the impact of the book began to die down. I took him to Alf Gover's memorial service at the church along the road from The Oval. I thought we had started out from Nailsworth in good time, but it did not work out that way. Half an hour before the start of the service, we were stationary on the A40 outside the Hoover factory, miles from The Oval.

I was distraught. He was nearly 93. I had promised to drive him to the service, and I had let him down. "I'm so sorry, Geoffrey. I don't think we'll even make the end of the service." But Geoffrey had such a way of saying the right thing. "Let's look at it this way," he said after a silence. "I don't suppose, if it were my memorial service, that Alf would be making all this effort."

Then by a seeming miracle the traffic cleared in front of us, and we were walking through the door of the church, Geoffrey pushing forward on his stick as fast as he could, just as the congregation rose to start the service.

Our next, and last, trip to London was on happier business. The book was on the shortlist for the Cricket Society Book of the Year, and the winner was to be announced one lunch-time in March at the Royal Overseas League off Piccadilly. These prize-giving ceremonies can be an ordeal. I try not to think about the possibility of winning, but on this occasion I felt so strongly that it would be such a magical moment at the end of Geoffrey's life that I could not stop myself lying awake the night before, imagining him at the front of the room with the members of the Cricket Society all applauding.

It would have been safer to have gone on my own, not to have exposed him to the long day with its high chance of disappointment, but Geoffrey was not one to miss out on an occasion such as this. And I felt a rising optimism when one of the judges greeted me: "Are you Stephen Chalke? How nice to meet you. I can't say too much at the moment, but I did so enjoy your book."

The chairman was David Rayvern Allen, the man whose delay on the M4 had left me talking for 45 minutes to the Gloucestershire Cricket Lovers. At the end of his speech he passed a sealed envelope to Simon Briggs, a young journalist on the *Daily Telegraph*, sponsors of the prize. He opened it and read out: "The winner is *At The Heart of English Cricket* by Stephen Chalke."

As I reached the platform, I saw Derek Newton and Bernie Coleman at the back of the room, beaming, and I urged Geoffrey to come and join me. With his stick going at the double, he charged forward as if he had shed forty years from his ancient frame. He had spent so much of his life behind the scenes, receiving little public recognition, and now, with almost all his peers dead, the applause was ringing out.

The book would not have happened without my enthusiasm and energy, but I knew that Geoffrey was the one, with his great service to the game, who was bringing the real warmth to the clapping.

It was the last act of a project that had given him such enormous pleasure at the end of his life. Soon afterwards he was admitted to hospital, then he went into a nursing home.

Sometimes I would arrive at the home to find him brimming with ideas. "Why are there no amateurs now? The reason they were abolished was that fathers could no longer afford to pay for their sons to play cricket all summer. Now young people have gap years, travelling round the world. Surely some of them could afford to play cricket as amateurs." He would get me writing notes.

Sometimes I would find him miserable. "I'm in pretty low water," he would say. "I'm waiting my turn now." He read Cicero on old age, and he took to quoting the song in Shakespeare's *Cymbeline*.

> *Fear no more the heat o' th' sun,*
> *Nor the furious winter's rages.*
> *Thou thy worldly task hast done,*
> *Home art gone and ta'en thy wages.*
> *Golden lads and girls all must,*
> *As chimney-sweepers, come to dust.*

One day in late summer I took him for a drive around the lanes of the Cotswolds. We stopped for lunch at a café in a garden centre. The place was full, and we carried our trays to a table where we could hardly hear ourselves speak. So we went outside, where there were only two free seats, at a table where two young women were talking rather earnestly.

"Excuse me," the ever-courteous Geoffrey said, "would you mind if we joined you at your table?"

"Not at all," one of them said, though she clearly did not mean it. "As long as you're not shocked by our conversation."

We sat and ate in silence. They dropped their voices, and Geoffrey looked across at them, then at me. "I'm sorry," he said to them finally, "but, if we are to be shocked by your conversation, you are going to have to speak up a bit."

Oh how I loved Geoffrey – and how I missed him as soon as he died that November. Scyld missed him, too. He rang from Australia, where England were on tour. "I'm already thinking of things I want to ask him," he told me mournfully, and I thanked him for browbeating me into taking on the task.

I pulled the book down off the shelf and, as I turned over the pages, I could hear Geoffrey once more telling me the stories, passing on the voices:

Have you played for Essex this year? ... Take over for half an hour, Wally. I'm going for a haircut ... Well, good luck, old boy. Rather you than me. I can't stand educated Indians ... He just left a note on the table, saying 'I'm going to Australia. I'll be back in April.'

They asked me to speak at the funeral in Minchinhampton. The family had their own memories to share, and I was to cover his public life. I had never done such a thing before, and I was unsure how to approach the task. I felt I was such an insignificant person in the context of Geoffrey's whole life and that it was a bit of a cheek for me to be addressing people who had known Geoffrey for so much longer.

"We've given you five minutes," the vicar said. "Under no circumstances are you to go on longer." I opted for summarising Geoffrey's career, quoting a few tributes to him that others had paid.

Rose FitzGibbon at Old Trafford: "He worked so hard, and he would never ask anybody to do anything that he wouldn't do himself. They were wonderful days. Everybody on the staff was devoted to him." Derek Newton, recalling Geoffrey's response to his first suggestion as a young committeeman at The Oval: "'Marvellous, we're looking for new ideas.' "In all my years in cricket," Derek said, "Geoffrey was the only older person who said that.'" Frank Tyson: "A tour with Geoffrey as manager was certain to be enjoyable. He had in abundance that great quality of taking the trouble to do things well."

They were appropriate words but, when I stepped down from the lectern, I sensed that my address had lacked intimacy. I had not felt Geoffrey's spirit as I spoke. I had not brought him alive as I should have done.

*

Two months later, only a mile away in Amberley, I was speaking at another funeral, this time for Ken Biddulph who had died suddenly of a heart attack. He had been rushing about, worrying about everybody else: his wife in hospital, his mother in care, a coaching group he did not want to let down. It had all got too much for him.

A shudder went through me when I heard the news. Geoffrey had done his worldly task, but Ken was in the midst of life, still coaching, talking about writing a book.

From time to time we would meet for a drink, and I would get him talking. The last time I saw him, I was writing an article on the jobs the cricketers took in winter, and he told me about the time he and Malcolm Heath had felled trees on Stuart Surridge's willow plantations.

"It was the best thing that ever happened to me. It made me very fit and strong. After that I never once had a problem with my back, not even bowling on that concrete thing at Taunton. All that hard work, all that good food, at the end of the day a couple of pints of good old English ale, that's what you need to be a good fast bowler." But Ken, being Ken, could not resist ending this with a putdown. "It's a pity I didn't become much of a fast bowler."

I can still recall his words when we parted that day. "You always get me remembering so much. I'm going to cut down on the coaching and get going on that book."

His daughter Kim rang me. "I was wondering if I could possibly ask you something," she said. "Do say no if you don't want to. I'll quite understand. But would you be prepared to say a few words at the funeral? He always spoke so much about your writing."

It was funny. Ken had never told me he liked my writing.

"Of course I will," I said through my tears. "It will be an honour."

We sang 'All Things Bright and Beautiful', just the right hymn for Ken, though the tune was completely unfamiliar to me and, by the sound of it, to most of the congregation. Then I stood up to tell them about the Ken I knew, starting with the story of our first meeting: "Stephen? We're in luck. There's nobody in after us till six o'clock."

Then I told them some of the stories that Ken had told me, back on that balcony at the leisure centre. I stood at the lectern, and there were so many glowing faces looking up. Bomber and Mary, Alastair from our nets at Stroud, Malcolm Heath, Bill Alley, Tom Graveney. I wished I could have been down with them, listening to Ken himself talking. Instead, I had to hear his voice inside my head and to catch his inflections as I spoke:

> By the way, old boy, the batsman you didn't want to bowl at, his name's Peter May ... And, when they have seen you play, I don't suppose they'll want your autograph ... I've come all the way from Southampton to see Marshall bat, and some stupid bugger's got him out ... Another ball? What have you been doing to it? You've only had that this summer.

David Foot captured the occasion in the *Western Daily Press*:

> In a village church high in the Cotswolds they crowded into the pews, more than 40 years after he'd played his last match for the county ... Ken had dozens of stories about his chums. Now cricket writer and one-time bowling pupil Stephen Chalke told the best of them ... A congregation, all caught up in the mood of nostalgic affection, rocked with hearty, not irreverent laughter. As one, they were dreaming again of past summers and shared friendships.

*

Two months later, learning my lesson from this, I spoke at Geoffrey's memorial service at St Mark's in Kennington, the same church near The Oval where I had driven him to remember Alf Gover. Mike Vockins, who had sent 'the most extraordinary letter', officiated, and there were two pairs of speakers: his daughter Ursula for the family and Rose FitzGibbon for Lancashire, then Tom Graveney for the tours and me for his Surrey years.

I started by recalling the day of Alf Gover's service, when we had been stuck in traffic outside the Hoover factory: "Let's look at it this way. I don't suppose, if it were my memorial service, that Alf would be making all this effort." Then came the touch of Jack Hobbs' blazer: "He was obviously going to be a great hero of mine." Some stories from his days at The Oval. Then one about his retirement: "'You want to find yourself a nice quiet golf club," Alf Gover told him. "Become their secretary." Can you imagine it? Geoffrey passing his time in a quiet golf club? "I'd rather have slit my throat," he told me.'

I finished by reflecting on the book I had written for him:

> It hardly took one morning in his company to fall under the spell of his charm, his humanity, his humour – and his integrity. He was a man for whom I wanted to give my very best. I said at the book launch that I thought Geoffrey represented the very best of England, the very best of English cricket. Whatever magic was transmitted to him that day at The Oval in August 1919, when he touched Jack Hobbs' blazer, it stayed with him for the rest of his life, a life lived to the full, a life of great service, a life in which he too passed on countless times that magic.

Back at the reception in the Long Room Robin Marlar sought me out.

"Well done," he said. "That was very well spoken."

"Geoffrey was such a special person," I replied. "It wasn't difficult to say warm things about him."

"I know. But it still had to be said."

*

Many years later I received an e-mail from a man compiling a book about cricketers' memorials: burial sites, blue plaques and the like. He wanted to know if there was anything for Geoffrey.

I put the man in touch with Geoffrey's daughter Ursula, and he forwarded her reply. Geoffrey, who had been cremated, had expressed a wish for no memorial: 'Dad said often that the book on which Stephen Chalke worked so carefully with him was his memorial.'

13

An afternoon of madness

One afternoon in February 2002, three months after Geoffrey's book had been published, I went a little mad.

I had written four books, and I had published David Foot's *Fragments of Idolatry*, all of which had been well received and made a reasonable profit. I was writing a regular column for *Wisden Cricket Monthly*, I was speaking all over England and, in an exciting new development, I was in discussions with Faber & Faber about their representing and distributing my books. So much was happening, and that afternoon I got a bit carried away.

On and off I had been working on a book about county cricket in the 1940s, to make a trilogy of my *In the Memory* books. I did not fancy revisiting the 1970s, a difficult time in my life, so, with the first game of *Runs in the Memory* set in 1952, I opted for a book about the years from 1946 to 1951, the six summers before the accession of Queen Elizabeth, when Clement Attlee's Labour government began the post-war reconstruction.

Looking back from the turn of the century, from the vantage point of our more sophisticated lives, those years of make-do-and-mend seemed far away and rather quaint: the Oval groundstaff employing shilling-an-hour volunteers from the local flats to lay turf across the whole field, the county captains plucked from obscurity to maintain the tradition of amateur leadership, the struggle to find new players after so many years without cricket. Yet there was great idealism at work, a determination to rebuild, and the crowds flocked into the grounds. It was in these years that the seeds of English cricket's success in the 1950s were sown, and I wanted to tell the story while there were still witnesses alive.

I started well, spending a fascinating day with Somerset's Eric Hill in his cottage, 'Pennypiece', in the little village of Sampford Brett, just inland from Bridgwater Bay. He had written to me, full of admiration for my first two books, and he got fully into the spirit of the occasion, reliving several incidents from his chosen game and bringing alive the characters of the Somerset team with a down-to-earth truthfulness that I found most appealing.

As an RAF navigator, he had had an eventful war, being decorated twice. He told me of one mission, to photograph German ships off the coast of Norway when they were fired on, lost the aircraft's perspex bubble and, with their identification code and their maps gone, could not get radio assistance to guide them home. In silence they watched their fuel gauge drop nearer and nearer to empty till a brief break in the clouds revealed land below them.

The match he chose was a fabulously dramatic one, a one-wicket victory over Middlesex at Lord's. It even had the lovely detail, confirmed by the score in *Wisden*, that, needing one run to win, Eric's fellow debutant Maurice Tremlett made his partner run three: "just to make sure, as you do in village matches."

Eric caught the drama of it, even having memories of the train journey back to Taunton and of his team-mate Arthur Wellard telling the story of the game to the regulars in the Crown and Sceptre. But, however exciting it had been, he knew that it was as nothing compared with what they had been through in the war. "I think we all felt, 'Thank God we got away with the War and we're able to do this.'"

The summer of 1946 had been a damp, somewhat half-cock affair. But the sun came out for this game at Lord's at the start of 1947, heralding a golden summer, and for me the match was richly symbolic. I inserted the story of Eric's Mosquito trip into the chapter and called it 'A Break in the Clouds'.

I had read and been moved by David Foot's biography of Harold Gimblett, the Somerset and England batsman who had committed suicide in later life. It was perhaps the first book to explore the darker side of cricket's mental challenges. 'No one else has ever gone down into the pit with a cricketer,' John Arlott wrote. Yet Eric, who had opened the batting with Gimblett, offered a different perspective, one that reminded me of the attitudes prevalent in my childhood, in those years when the war was still close.

"There were two things which influenced Harold. There'd been a lot of people saying, 'Bad luck, Harold, you ought to be in the England team.' And that got to him. And he married a woman, Rita, who had pretensions to being a bit posh; she felt that she was a cut above us cricket crowd. So these two things reacted on Harold. And of course he was a prize hypochondriac. I remember one game. I stopped in longer than him and, when I got back to the pavilion, there were five doctors in there. Five of them!"

At another point, straying far from the acceptable language of the twenty-first century, he said that Gimblett "exploited this stress thing; he got into it when they first invented it." David Foot's book was based on tapes Gimblett had left before committing suicide: "Gimmo droning on and on about how awful life is. It nearly drove Footy daft."

I have suffered from depression myself; I know how debilitating it can be. I had three years of psychotherapy on the NHS after our first child died in infancy. Yet, when I replay these words of Eric in my head, hear again his no-nonsense Somerset accent, I find them strangely life-affirming. Eric knew about darkness, but he also knew that he did not want to give in to it. At one point in our conversation he started to lament the state of county cricket – "In my worst moments I wish it would stop; that's when I'm really down" – but he snapped out of it. "Let's not be downhearted," he said, and he switched to singing the praises of Marcus Trescothick's batting.

Unfortunately none of my five further interviews yielded material of the same quality. There were fewer cricketers left to choose from, and their memories had faded. Some of them, reflecting the values of an older generation, were more reticent when talking about their team-mates, and the newspapers of the time, with print rationed, carried much shorter, less colourful reports of the matches. Reluctantly I abandoned the project.

Before that mad afternoon in February 2002, I had also started on a book with Keith Andrew, the Northamptonshire and England wicket-keeper who went on to be Chief Executive of the NCA, the National Cricket Association, the body that supported the game below first-class level.

I had interviewed him for *Caught in the Memory*, when we hit it off straightaway. We spent the afternoon drinking coffee outside a hotel, where he relived a game at Cardiff in 1965, the summer when he came so close to leading Northamptonshire, the ultimate Cinderella county, to the championship title. He had written two well-regarded coaching books and, before I left, I gave him a copy of *Runs in the Memory*. For two or three minutes he sat turning over the pages, then he looked up. "I don't think I'll write another book now but, if I did, I'd ask you to do it."

"Well, you may not like my book."

"Oh, I will. I know I will. I can tell that already."

He had played army cricket with Bomber, and he had been on Geoffrey Howard's tour of Australia, so each of my books increased his enthusiasm. Four years after our meeting he rang to say that he would like to do a book with me. I agreed to give it a go, and I began a succession of 230-mile round trips to his village beyond Milton Keynes. It was a much greater undertaking than my journeys up the A46 to visit Bomber and Geoffrey, but there was always a warm welcome when I arrived.

As a writer looking to record and shape memories, I faced a fresh challenge with Keith. He was the kindest of men and he had an intelligence that was refreshingly unconventional but, when he talked, there were times when I had to concentrate hard to understand and join up the things he was saying.

We started in earnest on the book in January 2002, with a session in which he talked to me about his childhood in Oldham. Much of it was poignant; his mother, a mill-worker, had been abandoned by a husband from a wealthier family, and Keith recalled an occasion when, in a desperate state, she had trekked across town to appeal to his family for help. "They kept her standing at the door. That was enough. She never went again."

Would his story make a full-length book, and would it sell? A wicket-keeper, Northamptonshire, two Tests for England, the NCA? Much as I warmed to Keith, I was worried whether I had done the right thing in taking on the project. Geoffrey Howard's book had been underwritten by the people at Surrey, but this time I was on my own.

That afternoon in February 2002 I had a brainwave, and I did not stop to think it through. Talking with Sue in the kitchen, I came up with the idea that Keith's book could be part of a series of short books on old cricketers: 'not tedious recitations of facts and figures but affectionate portraits of human character – plenty of atmospheres and insights.' I could get a set of good writers to choose subjects, and we could launch the first six in twelve months' time. Some people would buy individual volumes, but many would treat them as a series to be collected.

A round of phone calls began. David Foot on Bill Alley, that was a distinct possibility. Derek Hodgson, the Yorkshire-based journalist, on Bob Appleyard, that was a project that had got stuck and could certainly be revived. Frank Keating on Arthur Milton. "My memories are my own," Arthur always said, but Frank seemed to think he could overcome that and, if not, he might take on Brian Close. I put Keith Andrew into the mix, and I rang Douglas Miller, a retired market researcher who had written an impressive booklet about Gloucestershire's cricket grounds. He knew Don Shepherd, and I asked if he would be interested if I had a space for a book about Don. Then I wrote to Michael Parkinson, asking him to join in: 'Your writing would fit beautifully into this project and add an extra sharpness.'

What a madness it was. It never happened, of course. One by one the books melted away – and quite fast, too. Arthur's memories were still his own, Bill Alley was ill, Frank made it clear that he had not been talking about the immediate future, and Michael Parkinson was far too busy.

I was left with a faltering book about Bob Appleyard, my Keith Andrew and the possibility of Don Shepherd, written by a new writer who would be taking an enormous step up from a factual booklet about cricket grounds. Shortly afterwards, knowing that he had disappointed me, David Foot asked me to publish a new edition of his Harold Gimblett book. So the upshot of that afternoon was not a self-contained project, six short books in a series, but four full-length books to supervise into print and sell – as well as John Barclay's book, to which I had already made a commitment.

The link-up with Faber & Faber promised to ease the pressure. Brian Simmons, who had recently retired as one of their editors, loved my books, both their content and the way they were written, and he would ring up from time to time, interspersing practical advice about the book trade with stories of car journeys with Stephen Spender and Philip Larkin. I was in seventh heaven, rubbing imaginary shoulders with these literary giants.

By then he was working part-time for Faber, placing their books in shops in the south-east, and as a sideline, without payment, he started doing the same for our books. Then he rang with the exciting news that there was a vacancy for Fairfield Books to be taken on by Faber, as one of the three specially selected small publishers that they represented all over the country; they would even take care of the stock and invoicing. They were ditching a firm that produced coffee-table books on heavy metal music, and he saw us as a perfect fit for the vacancy. All I had to do was to send them a submission, with our sales figures and our plans for the future. "Keep the numbers low," he advised. "They don't want anybody that's too big." Alas, he had a sudden heart attack and died. The person making the decision changed and was unaware of Brian's recommendation, and we were rejected. They said our numbers were too low.

I have few regrets about my years of publishing, but I do regret that the link did not happen. If we had had the support of Faber, and the continuing interest of Brian, I think we could have taken Fairfield Books up half a level. We would certainly have had more time for the creative side of our work.

*

I was still playing all the cricket I could, travelling far and wide with the Journeymen, including in 2002 a trip to Menorca where the small crowd included a Surrey member who had been at Geoffrey Howard's book launch. Much to my embarrassment, he insisted on introducing me to our hosts as a celebrity. Leaving aside that he was greatly over-egging my status, I preferred to play my own modest cricket without that baggage.

One of the joys of the team was playing with my brother Andrew, keeping that link with our childhood games. Though younger than me, he was always the better cricketer, and that remained so with the Journeymen, even when I was playing much more regularly. On the one occasion when I had the joy of 'sharing' all ten wickets with him, he took eight of them.

Perhaps for this reason one of my happiest memories of cricket was of a game that summer at Newdigate in Surrey. Batting at number seven, I joined Andrew in the middle with 45 runs wanted off six overs. The pitch was not easy and there was not much in the way of batting to come, so I told Andrew that I would keep up an end for him, let him have as much strike as possible. Then, in a rush of blood, I walloped my first ball over mid-off's head. Later I hit three successive balls for four, four and six, and I came off with 29 not out. It was a famous victory, and I felt in a bubble of elation as I walked alongside Andrew. We were 54 and 51 years old, 45 years on from our first back-garden cricket, and there was heartfelt applause all around us, much of it directed towards me. I felt so young and full of the joy of life. Then, as we went through the low gate to the pavilion, I overheard their scorer asking ours, "Are they father and son?"

That same summer, at the pretty National Trust ground at Buscot Park in Oxfordshire, with its thatched pavilion and ring of heavily-scented lime trees, I went out in the near-dark with six runs to score off 14 balls. My partner and I made such a mess of it that we still wanted one off the last delivery and, when his desperate poke at the ball missed, I was run out by about six yards. Back in the pavilion our captain pitched into me for not backing up properly, and we had a set-to that rumbled on for days. Oh the joys of an afternoon with the Journeymen! We were only a friendly side, and I can laugh about it now, but by heck it could get serious at times.

Keith Andrew recognised that. "I don't think he's a very good cricketer," he said one day of a well-known cricket writer.

"Well, I'm certainly not," I replied. The pathetic duck at Warley, the sixes hit by Irfan-ul-Haq for Purnells third eleven. On the way home from a match I would happily spend a two-hour car journey going over it all, but I did not want him thinking it was top club cricket or that I was a regular match-winner.

"But you're a serious cricketer," he said. "I can tell."

*

Fairfield Books soon had another venture on its hands. While writing *Runs in the Memory* I had been in the habit of looking into public libraries to inspect their cricket book section, and I drove one day to Chippenham where I could find nothing on 796.358 between athletics and golf.

"Do you not have any cricket books?" I asked the librarian.

"They're over there," she said, pointing to the far wall, and I walked across to find twenty shelves, tightly packed with everything from Arlott to *Wisden*. There was Percy Fender's 'Defending The Ashes' beside 'The Zen of Cricket', Ken Farnes' 'Tours and Tests' beside 'The World's Best Cricket Jokes'.

"Good heavens," I exclaimed. "Some of these books are quite valuable."

"Oh, that's not the half of them. You should see what we've got in store."

She led me into a back room where she rolled open several more cases. Thirty years earlier they had been donated to the library by the town's former mayor, and since then every new cricket book had been purchased.

I asked for a print-out of all the titles. "It will cost ten pence a sheet," she said, guessing that it would run to 15 sheets. In fact, it was 92 pages long. With about 20 books per page, that worked out at nearly 2,000 titles. From then on, Chippenham Library became the central point of reference for all my research.

Then the library decided to sell them. They were taking up too much room, and I was the only person reading them. Within weeks a lorry was outside our front door, and the living room was so full of boxes and books that we could hardly move. I put to one side the duplicates and the ones I did not want; then, for a crazy month, I became a second-hand book dealer.

There were phone calls galore and visits to the house. I set the prices to make sure I shifted everything I did not want, and they all went. I was surprised how much I enjoyed the buzz of it, the manic hard work. Later I had further forays into selling old books, once for a man who drove down from Birmingham with a large trailer with 1,200 books on it.

Each time was harder than the time before. The demand for old cricket books has dropped, with fewer collectors and many of the books easy to find on the internet. Even the *Wisden* almanacks are not snapped up as they used to be. For me it was fun as a novelty sideline but only once every three or four years, only after I had had time to forget how much hard work was involved.

Much more importantly, what I kept of the Chippenham collection gave me a first-class working library. I could stay at home to do my research.

*

The book with Keith Andrew took shape over a year, involving fifteen visits to Aspley Guise. I would get to his house for 10.30, and we would talk till lunchtime when he would take me either to the café at the local garden centre or to his golf club. Then we would carry on for a while back at his house, and I would leave for home before the rush-hour built up around Milton Keynes. In addition to these sessions, I returned to Dennis Brookes, who had been so good in *Runs in the Memory*, and he filled me in on the earlier history of Northamptonshire and, at Keith's suggestion, I visited Brian Crump and Malcolm Scott, two of the team he captained. It is always tricky to work out how many other voices to introduce; I did not want a book such as this to stray far from the testimony of the subject. With Keith, however, there were passages where I sensed that the text needed something more.

Occasionally his wife Joyce whom he married just before leaving for Australia in 1954, would join our conversation. Almost my favourite line in the book came from a moment when they were talking about her mother, a down-to-earth Lancastrian like Keith's mother. They had bought a television set which, when she visited them, they watched together on Saturday night. She gave her verdict over Sunday lunch. "It's all got up to be exciting," she said, "and that's a fact."

'All got up to be exciting'? On the face of it, it is a silly, little line, but it goes right to the heart of so much that has changed in my lifetime, what Bomber called 'all this intense commercialism'.

Keith was always on the vague side and, though I only half-suspected it at the time, he was in the early stages of Alzheimer's disease. So teasing memories out of him was not always easy. Yet, from his point of view, my visits were massively beneficial, keeping his brain active in the best of ways, and he looked forward to them greatly.

He was especially good at expressing his opinions, and I built this into the book as a feature. He was strong on wicket-keeping, how it was a skill understood by few. He was strong on the spirit in which sport should be played, views that chimed exactly with my own. And he was strong on the English class system, having only scorn for the culture of Gentlemen and Players.

When he was selected to tour Australia, he appeared on a television show, 'Guess My Story', where a panel had to work out why he was in the news. So I called the book *Guess My Story – The Life and Opinions of Keith Andrew, Cricketer*. For those of a literary bent, it was supposed to be a reference to *The Life and Opinions of Tristram Shandy, Gentleman*. Not that, to the best of my knowledge, anybody noticed.

I read him quotes from the *Daily Telegraph* and *The Times*, written after Warwickshire's Alan Smith, an amateur, had been selected ahead of him for the tour of Australia in 1962/3. One justified the choice by saying that Alan Smith was 'a great trier who really enjoys his cricket'; the other cited his 'character as a man'. It hurt Keith, and in his own quiet way he said so forcefully. "What are they saying about my character, my enjoyment of cricket, or any of the other professionals? They're astonishing remarks to put into print. In fact, these sentences say more about English cricket than any I've ever read.'

Alan and he rose to be important men at Lord's, Alan as Chief Executive of the Test and County Cricket Board, Keith as Chief Executive of the NCA, looking after the game at its grass roots. Once, when they were in conversation, Alan used the word 'we' about the Conservative Party. I have no idea how Keith voted, but he made a point of telling me this, as if it represented something within cricket that he did not like. "Why do you assume that I'm a Conservative?" he challenged Alan. The consciousness of that class divide never left him.

Keith made me look at cricket for the first time through the eyes of the man behind the stumps, the busiest man on the field but the one whom very few people seem to understand or are able to assess.

As a keeper he was of the quiet, unnoticed type, relying on soft hands and a perfect technique, and he knew that in many quarters that quietness counted against him. He explained how keeping was mostly about anticipation, how spectacular diving often resulted from late movement. If he played an exhibition match on a Sunday, he would wait a second and dive, and the crowd would love it.

By the time we were working together, the game was prioritising keepers who not only could bat but could also be the centre of all the noise the fielders made. And that made Keith angry. "We're reducing the wicket-keeper to a nonentity, a man who stands next to the slips with gloves on. Is that what we really want? It's like assembling an orchestra and getting some bloke to fill in on the first violin."

Above all, he was passionate about upholding the spirit of cricket. "Cricket is a game," he said. "You play to win. But that's not *why* you play cricket." It was a simple sentence, but I found myself thinking about it a lot. More and more of the club cricketers I met seemed only to enjoy their afternoon when they won. That was something that had changed during my lifetime.

"I wish we could put a greater warmth back into it," Keith said.

My tape of Roly Jenkins, speaking on BBC Hereford and Worcester, has him reciting the words of Lord Harris's letter to *The Times* in 1931:

> Cricket. It is freer from anything sordid, anything dishonest, than any other game in the world. To play it keenly, generously, honestly, is a moral lesson in itself, and the classroom is God's air and sunshine. Foster it, my brothers, protect it from anything that will sully it, so that it will be in favour with all men.

If we spoke like that now, we would be laughed out of the room. But increasingly I found myself wondering if, in all the improvements we had made to cricket – the better remuneration of players, the well-equipped grounds, the brilliant camera work on television – we were losing touch with the game's most special ingredient, its reputation for good manners and fair play.

I interviewed Doug Insole. He had been at the centre of English cricket and its administration for half a century, and his words fitted with Keith's:

> I've been in the middle of a lot of change, and I've supported it, even promoted it. But the main things I don't like are the social changes. When I think back to the 1940s, some of those buggers were extremely hard, but they didn't indulge in any practice that might be called dodgy. I don't suppose there's been anybody in the history of the game harder than Douglas Jardine, but he didn't go around sledging or trying to cheat people out. That's the aspect of it all that narks me now. It diminishes the game.

For Brian Close, coming into county cricket in 1949, it was not the amateurs who were the principal upholders of the game's values: "The professionals' attitude was absolutely first-class at that time. If any of your own side tried to cheat, like hit the ball and not walk, your own players would set about them. There was such a high moral standard in the game."

In our more cynical times we tend to debunk such talk, citing examples of batsmen who did not always walk, but I am convinced from my conversations that such instances were the rare exception.

Peter Walker, who is no strait-laced traditionalist in his outlook on life, talked to me about an evening at Leicester when Glamorgan had slumped to 11 for eight. He was at the crease, knowing that if they did not score another run they would set a new record for the lowest score in the whole history of the first-class game. "I've never told this to anyone before," he confessed. "Terry Spencer bowled this ball, and it just brushed my glove. Terry didn't appeal, but behind the wicket they did. The umpire said 'not out', but I knew that I'd gloved it. And I couldn't look anybody in the face. I shall carry that to my grave with me. I feel I let everything down."

Ken Biddulph had a different offence on his conscience, about a game at Trowbridge when, bowling for Somerset 2nd XI, he had wasted time in the final minutes to prevent Wiltshire winning. It was in August 1956, yet forty-five years later, after unburdening himself to me about it, he went off to write a letter of apology to Wiltshire.

"Being successful is one thing," Keith Andrew said, "but we want to enjoy our lives as well – and part of that enjoyment is friendship between sportsmen. If people are cheating, they don't respect one another, and the feeling for the game disappears. You don't go home at night feeling half so well."

*

Charlie Light, the Cotswold forester, died. At his funeral we sang 'Lord of all hopefulness'.

> *Lord of all eagerness, Lord of all faith,*
> *Whose strong hands were skilled at the plane and the lathe,*
> *Be there at our labours and give us, we pray,*
> *Your strength in our hearts, Lord, at the noon of the day.*

A grand-daughter read the lines in *Cider with Rosie* about Charlie's father:

> The new woods rising in Horsley now, in Sheepscombe, in Rendcombe and Colne, are the forests my Uncle Charlie planted on thirty-five shillings a week. His are the mansions of summer shade, lifting skylines of leaves and birds, those blocks of green now climbing our hills.

"I should have liked to have done some writing or painting," Charlie had told me. "But I had to leave school to bring home some money. And for years work in the countryside was slave labour."

He knew how much things had improved in his lifetime – "I mislaid my pension book, and they sent me four weeks' worth of giros. Two hundred and eighty pounds. I wish I'd had some of that to give my mother when she was alive" – but he also felt the pain of what had been lost: "I haven't seen a lark for years, or a house sparrow. There used to be peewits on top of the Cotswolds, and the hares have got fewer."

A world had passed, and I was brimming with melancholy.

*

The join between past and present fascinated me. I was watching Channel 4 in August 2001. The Fourth Test between England and Australia was about to start at Headingley, and the Australian Simon Katich was making his debut. On the outfield he stood in a semi-circle with all his team-mates, and he was presented with his baggy green cap by Richie Benaud.

Benaud spoke about Bradman and Lillee and about himself, about the long line of cricketers who had worn the baggy green, what pleasure he had had as an Australian cricketer and what pride he had wearing the cap. Now it was the newcomer's turn to put it on, and he hoped that he would have the same pleasure and feel the same pride. There were tears in my eyes at the end of the ceremony. I could feel the power that was passing from one generation to another. There was a history that gave it all a richness and a sense of importance.

At the start of that 2001 Ashes series, when the captains went out to toss at Edgbaston, Steve Waugh was proud in his Australian blazer and baggy green cap; Nasser Hussein was in a shell suit with a Vodafone cap. One reporter suggested that England were one game down before a ball had been bowled.

In England, certainly at that time, there was a disconnection between generations. Maybe it was because we had come to feel guilty about our imperial history, or maybe our culture had been Americanised, fast-moving and quickly thrown away. Whatever the reason, so many of the players I interviewed felt cut off from the game, being told it had changed and their experiences were no longer relevant. "They don't let me near the batsmen at Worcester," Tom Graveney said.

I was stumbling about with my own little projects, just about keeping my head above water, but inadvertently I was putting my finger on something much deeper, something that shone a light across so many walks of life.

*

Keith was a delightful companion. His memory was foggy at times, and he rarely focused long on a subject. When I sent him the pages of the book, he got them all in a muddle. I would ask him to ring me with corrections on a section, and he would ring back about another section we had already corrected. To an impatient journalist, wanting a three-minute interview, he

116

would have been a nightmare. But over several months, sitting together and circling round and round his life, I came to realise how articulate he was.

From my experiences with Geoffrey and now with Keith I was beginning to understand what a great responsibility it is to receive somebody's life and thoughts, to work them into a shape and to give them back in a book. It does have some parallels with the world of psychotherapy, as Mike Brearley spotted straightaway when first I talked to him about my work. Unlike therapy, however, there is a tangible endpoint when the book is written and published, and on the day we launched Keith's book at Northampton he made me glow with the praise he showered on me.

"There's so much warmth in what you've written," he said. "This book says everything I want to say. I really don't mind if I don't say another word now. You've put it all so well."

"But it's mostly your words, Keith."

"You're going to be famous one day. I may be gone, but you've still got so much more in you. And you'll keep getting better."

I wrote the words in my diary that night. The fame did not interest me. But he had made me realise that he had passed me something precious and that it was so important that I received it properly, shaped it and passed it on.

'Andrew is one of the game's nice guys,' Robin Marlar wrote in *The Cricketer*. 'None nicer, in my book. What he was and is, what he stands for and what he values, can be found in the pages of this splendid book.'

Early in his playing career, Keith had been on a Cricket Society panel in Oxford, answering questions from an audience, and he had spoken out strongly about the amateurs of the day, how they were all professionals really, just being paid in less obvious ways. Douglas Jardine, the stern Wykehamist who had caused such controversy as England captain, was a fellow panellist, and he was shocked by Keith's outspoken contribution. He invited Keith for a coffee afterwards.

"We talked for ages, with this silver coffee pot between us. 'Young man,' he said. 'Always speak and believe as you do now.' His finger wagged at me. I can see him now. 'Speak with conviction and honesty.' And we shook hands. 'I'm very pleased to have met you,' he said. I was astonished."

Almost fifty years had passed, and I sat enthralled, as I always did when Keith talked. I pictured Jardine's long, severe face staring at me from the other side of a coffee pot.

Keith's face was kinder and rounder, and he did not wag his finger. But he was staying true to the old man's instruction, speaking with conviction and honesty: "We have to play cricket and to foster its playing everywhere. And we have to look after what is special about it, what makes people love it.'

14

No coward soul

"I bowled a lot of overs in that match. I was on my knees. I really was tired then."

It was September 1951, Yorkshire against MCC at the Scarborough Festival. The great discovery of the summer, the Bradford-born Bob Appleyard, was on the verge of a unique achievement: 200 wickets in his first full season. More than half a century on, he sat in his living room in Ilkley, taking me through the match.

It was a quarter to nine at night, and I was shattered. I had left home at 7 a.m., and this interview with Bob had been going on since soon after two. And we had talked about nothing but that one summer of 1951. Together we had turned over the pages of *Wisden*, I had read out the *Yorkshire Post* reports, and Bob had recalled what he could about every match. His stamina was astonishing for a 78-year-old; after six and a half hours, with my body slumping lower and lower in the chair, he was showing no sign of flagging.

We had reached the last day of his long summer. He had taken 197 wickets, and he described in detail his 198th, brought about by a suggestion from Len Hutton.

"It was a fine, warm day, and Bill Edrich was not out overnight. As we took the field, Leonard said to me, 'The third ball of the over, bowl it a foot outside his off stump, fairly well up' – which I did. Len positioned himself at long on, in front of the scoreboard, and the ball went straight down his throat. I don't think he'd to move a yard. There aren't too many occasions when you put a man in a certain place, and the ball goes down his throat like that. It was definitely Len's wicket. He knew Bill. He knew his style."

After that, success did not come for several hours. 'His run-up was a dark and curving pathway across the green,' I read aloud from my *Yorkshire Post* notes. 'His leg trap crouched in co-operation, and occasionally the bat was beaten but when wickets fell they fell to other bowlers.'

The previous summer Bob had been a Saturday afternoon bowler in the Bradford League, with a full-time job as a salesman for a lift-making company. He had had three games in the Yorkshire first team, but he would probably not have bowled more than 500 overs in all cricket that year. Yet now, at the age of 27, with nearly 40 overs on this one day, he took his summer's tally to 1,323. His stamina was prodigious.

"200 wickets. Why should it mean so much more than 199 or 198? At one point I asked Norman Yardley to take me off. 'It's spoiling the game, skipper,' I said. And he just smiled. 'Keep going,' he said."

Finally, after a break for rain in late afternoon, the last two wickets of the innings fell to Bob, and our session was almost done. It only remained for me to ask him about the celebrations.

"Did you have a drink?"

"No, I was teetotal at the time."

"What about dinner? Was there any kind of meal?"

"No. Connie and I drove straight home. We stopped and had a meal somewhere between York and Tadcaster. At a café. Beans on toast or something. There was still rationing. People didn't go out for meals like they do now."

"And did you have a holiday afterwards?"

"No, that was our holiday. We'd been to the Festival."

We called it a day and watched television for a while. Then Bob showed me up to the spare bedroom.

"Leonard slept in that bed once," he told me proudly.

As soon as my head hit the pillow, I fell asleep – though, as the night progressed, I found myself waking with all the wickets of 1951 swirling round my head. It had been the most intense interview I had ever done, and we had only just started.

"Come on now, we need to get going. We're wasting time."

The chatter over breakfast was brought to an abrupt halt, and he took me up to his study where he showed me all the memorabilia of that summer: the photograph of him leaving the field at Scarborough, the telegram from Wilfred Rhodes, the menu of a meal at the Café Royal, the letter dictated by George Hirst – and a letter from the Secretary, outlining the club's proposed payments for the next year. All capped Yorkshire players would be on a basic salary of £500. In modern money, I calculated, the great Len Hutton would have been earning about £10,000 a year.

Bob was no starry-eyed romantic when it came to financial matters, but he was clear. "Money didn't come into consideration. You'd have given your eye-teeth to play for Yorkshire. You thought you were privileged to be playing."

My following visits to Ilkley were just as intense. Bob took the view that, if I was only with him for 24 hours, then we needed to use them fully. After a six-hour journey I would get about ten minutes to rest in a chair before he would draw the small talk to a halt. He had been on a naval training ship during the war, and he had clearly taken to heart the lines from Kipling's 'If' inscribed on the panels beside the stage where their Sunday services took place.

> If you can fill the unforgiving minute
> With sixty seconds' worth of distance run
> Yours is the earth and everything that's in it
> And – which is more – you'll be a Man, my son.

*

I had been intrigued by the story of Bob's career since I had worked with Geoffrey Howard on the Australian tour of 1954/55. It had been a tour written up in countless books by the journalists and the players. Yet there was this one name, Appleyard, at the top of the bowling averages, and he seemed to have escaped everybody's attention. Then, when I looked closely at his career, it was an astonishing story, quite unlike any other in cricket.

He was 26 years old before he made his second-team debut for Yorkshire, 27 during the summer when he took 200 wickets and topped the national bowling averages. He missed the next two years with illness, then came back with 154 wickets in 1954. There followed the triumphant tour of Australia, then another summer when he topped the averages. After that a swift decline set in, and he was gone by the end of 1958. In all first-class cricket since the First World War, only Hedley Verity had a better bowling average. It was a remarkable career, yet nobody had written anything of substance about him.

I heard that the journalist Derek Hodgson had started on a book with Bob and that it had got stuck. The journeys from Derek's home in the Cotswolds were arduous, especially after Derek developed a serious illness. When he could not interest a publisher, he lost enthusiasm.

Bob had been offered a lot of money by publishers in the spring of 1955, when he returned from Australia, but he explained, "At the time I didn't feel I knew enough about anything."

My shelves of cricket books would be half-empty if everybody thought like that. But, as I soon discovered, that was typical of Bob, wanting always to do things to the highest standard.

It is the main problem with sporting biographies. They sell best when the sportsman is at the peak of his game. Yet he becomes a much more interesting person when life has moved on and he has had time to reflect on his experience. What he has lost in immediacy, he has gained in perspective – though perhaps, in his case, Bob had left it rather longer than necessary. "Who's Bob Appleyard?" had been the response of most of the publishers Derek had approached.

In my mad afternoon in February 2002 I had reactivated Derek's book by offering to publish it. Derek had moved back to Yorkshire, five miles from Ilkley, and he resumed their meetings. By late in the year the chapters were arriving in my inbox.

I am not sure what went wrong. Derek was a good writer, but these chapters were a long way short of what I had been expecting. Perhaps the start-stop nature of the project had not helped, perhaps Derek's illness had taken too much out of him, and perhaps – most crucially – he and Bob had not gelled. I was disappointed and, more crucially, so was Bob. He summoned me to a meeting at his house in Ilkley, where his friend Ron Deaton and he sat across the table from me. "How are we going to add to Derek's work?" he asked.

It was a difficult moment. I did not want to upset Derek, but I knew that I could not publish his text as it stood, not even with additions and revisions. I had no idea how Bob would react, I hardly knew him at this stage, but I took the bull by the horns and said what I felt.

"To be honest, it's not a question of adding. The whole thing needs to be rewritten."

"Well, who's going to do that?" he shot back.

I took a deep breath. "I suppose I am, aren't I?"

"Good. That's what we were hoping you'd say."

I put the text aside and started from scratch.

*

Bob was the only man alive who knew what it was like to take 200 wickets in a season; furthermore, they were all for Yorkshire so he was the last man ever to take 200 wickets for a county, and he had done it in his first summer. It was one of the great achievements of English county cricket.

Yet his achievement had a second dimension, another respect in which he stood out as unusual. In the Bradford League he had been a plain medium-pacer, and only during the summer of 1950, when playing for the Yorkshire seconds, had he started to introduce the off-break into his repertoire. Then, practising those off-breaks in the winter, he had developed a blister on his spinning finger. And Bob being Bob, rather than give up for the evening, he had taken to bowling off his middle finger. He found he could bowl his off-breaks with just as much accuracy and with far greater pace.

"The wickets were on springs, I hit them, and they went all over the place. Arthur Mitchell, the coach, came over. 'What's going on here?' he said. I said, 'Just watch this, Arthur,' and I did it again. He looked at me. 'If you can bowl like that, you can bowl any bugger out.'"

So in 1951 he was that rarest of cricketers, a two-in-one bowler: fast-medium with the new ball, then quickish spin off the middle finger when the ball was old. "I don't know why nobody else does it," he says. "I'm not that special. If I could do it, others could."

But there was a third dimension to his achievement, a human dimension that made the story almost unbelievable. On 30 June he had reached 99 wickets and, playing against the South Africans at Sheffield, he became ill, his temperature high and his chest infected. A doctor on the ground told him to go home, and he was visited the next morning by a locum.

"He came at 8.30, and he was smelling of whisky, either from that morning or the night before. He was a retired doctor, and he was very keen to get me back on the field to get me my 100 wickets. He said I had pleurisy. There was no X-ray or anything. He just told me to stay in bed and gave me some cough mixture. I rested for a few days, the temperature went down, and I came back. I only missed two matches."

At the end of the summer, exhausted by his efforts, Bob decided his stamina was inadequate. He resolved to play four rounds of golf each weekend – at the Halifax Golf Club, with its steep and undulating course on Ogdon Moor. On one of my visits, I walked to its highest point of 1300 feet, the spongy turf making the climb hard work. There were curlews circling overhead, and the mill chimneys of the West Riding towns seemed distant specks below.

"It's a tough course," an elderly golfer said to me.

I told him about Bob's schedule during that winter. By a curious coincidence he had delivered papers to Bob's house and remembered him out running in the streets. "Two rounds Saturday, two rounds Sunday, that's going it a bit. That is tough. It would test your lungs, that."

The punishing schedule did not have the desired effect for Bob. "I thought I wasn't fit," he told me. "I was trying to build up my stamina and strength, but I was always feeling tired."

The explanation came at Taunton during Yorkshire's first match of 1952. Bob was sent home ill, and this time he was correctly diagnosed. He had advanced tuberculosis; the whole top half of his left lung was rotten. Streptomycin had not long been discovered as a cure; it was a disease that still had a reputation as a killer.

200 wickets. 27 years old. In his first full season. Bowling in two styles, with his off-breaks spun off the wrong finger. And with half a lung destroyed. What a story it was! Yet Bob, sitting in his chair, was so matter-of-fact about it all, describing how he followed his surgeon's instructions to the letter.

"I insisted on lying on my back or my left side. It took me a while to get used to it. Sometimes the staff, to make it easy for themselves, would try to get me up for the bedpans. But I wouldn't. It might sound a bit crazy today. Probably nobody would do it. But I wouldn't get up for anything. For five months."

In all he spent eleven months in bed – five months before the operation, six months after – and the muscles in his legs became so weak that he had to learn to walk again. Yet he never gave up hope of returning to cricket; he got his wife Connie to bring him a ball and he spent hours gripping it under the sheets, trying to preserve the hardness of skin on his spinning finger.

"You know, lass," Bill Bowes, the former Yorkshire bowler, told Connie after seeing him in the bed. "He'll never get back to the first-class game."

"Please don't tell him that," she replied. "He believes he's going to play for Yorkshire."

There was a bonus for my researches when Bob told me that his surgeon – Geoffrey Wooler, now 92 years old – was still alive, and I rang him. "I don't know why it wasn't diagnosed earlier," he said. "He must have had it at least two years, probably longer."

By chance, while I was writing the book, I interviewed Michael Barton, the Surrey captain, for an article. He had seen tuberculosis at close quarters during his childhood in Liverpool, and that summer he scored a fifty against Yorkshire at Headingley. "I do remember thinking how pasty Bob's complexion was. And I thought, 'That is the sort of pastiness that tubercular people have.' But then I thought to myself, 'It can't be so. Nobody with tuberculosis could possibly do the things he's doing.'"

"I used to go to see Bob at the sanatorium," Geoffrey Wooler recalled, "and he was always looking on the bright side, saying 'Will I be able to come back?' I would have thought that he would have been wise not to have done much for some time, but you couldn't tell him. His main object was to get back and bowl again. Some people used to give you the idea that they didn't really want to be well. But not Bob. He was never depressed, even though he had such an extensive disease."

After his recovery Bob wrote a series of articles for the *Daily Express*, and in them he talked of how important it was for him to have faith and not fear: 'faith in yourself, faith in your surgeon and, most important, faith in God.'

In April 1954 Bob was back on the staff at Headingley, and the *Yorkshire Post* talked of his having 'a cautious run-out in two-day games' in the second eleven. Yet he played from the start of the summer, heard on his 30th birthday that he had been chosen for England and spent the winter in Australia.

On the way out they played a match at Colombo, and a boy, running onto the field at the end, barged into him and cracked a rib near the scar of his operation. He had already altered his bowling to deal with his reduced physical state. Now in Australia, once he had recovered from the rib injury, he found his style unsuited to the conditions and had to alter it again, working more on changes of pace and flight. It was the third major change his bowling had undergone since he had stepped up from the Bradford League.

Some of the journalists started to write him off as a bad selection, chosen as he was ahead of Jim Laker, but he proved them wrong. What a wonderful story it was, even down to the group of TB patients, coming out of their local sanatorium to cheer him on.

"I felt I was representing everybody who had had tuberculosis," he told me several times. "I was carrying a torch for them. I did feel that. And that gave me a great determination to do well."

But I still did not know the half of his story.

I could see that his triumph over adversity raised issues of character, and I found a paragraph in Derek's original manuscript, about his childhood, that I wanted to explore:

> The boy's character and temperament were tested in those formative days. His parents had broken up; he lost a sister to diphtheria when he was 12 and soon after the outbreak of war he lost his father, stepmother and their two small children in tragic circumstances.

By this stage I had made two visits to Bob, and we had covered a great deal of his cricketing story. His friend Ron Deaton, who had been sorting all his photographs, sat in on our sessions, and I had established a routine of sending my chapters to Bob for him to go through with Ron. Then Ron would ring through their corrections.

Bob and Ron inspected every line carefully. There was a detail about a part of a tank, a 'revolver port door', which Bob, an apprentice engineer, had been employed in making during the war; it took about six attempts to get the description to Bob's satisfaction. Then there was the match at Sheffield where Bertie Buse, the Somerset medium-pacer, bowled Yorkshire out for 77. "He bowled these little seamers," Bob said, "and they were going like boomerangs. Even Leonard was struggling. I've never seen a ball swing so much in my life – and late, too. Some bowlers get the ball to swing from the arm, but that's not the trick. The trick is to get it swinging in the last yard."

Ron rang. "Page 35," he said. "Where it says 'in the last yard', could you change that to 'in the last couple of yards'?"

"Fine," I replied. "I assumed it was just a turn of phrase. I didn't think it was meant as an exact measurement."

"You've no idea," Ron said. "We spent twenty minutes on the floor with a tape measure."

I included that conversation in the introduction to the book, and I think it embarrassed Ron. He said he had no memory either of saying it or of its happening. But Bob came to my rescue. "We did have the tape measure out," he said with a twinkle in his eye.

I remember my anxiety when I sent my first chapter. I knew Bob was a perfectionist, and I spent several days wondering what he would think of it. In the end I rang Ron, and he reassured me. "Bob's main worry is whether the rest of it is going to live up to the same standard."

I asked Bob to elaborate about his childhood, and he told me on condition that I did not include the detail of it in the book. He had never told his wife and children, and he did not want to pass the stigma of it down the generations.

His mother left them when he was seven. His father was a Bradford railwayman, and a broken marriage had an element of shame about it in a proud working-class family. His sister died of diphtheria, and his father remarried and had two small children. As war approached, his father, a deep thinker who had been attracted briefly to Quakerism, became gloomy and spent every Sunday afternoon with a friend, discussing the world situation.

Bob fumbled in his memory to tell me what happened next. He liked to maintain a calm, considered way of talking, but I knew by this time that he was an emotional man beneath this exterior.

"I'd normally have left school at 15, but I went back for another year. I wanted to take further exams. Some time after war was declared, I stayed overnight at my grandmother's and I went home the next morning. And I found my father and stepmother and the two babies. They were in the bathroom. There was one of those copper boilers."

He could describe with clarity his 198th wicket at Scarborough in 1951, but this, the pivotal moment of his life, had been bottled up inside him for so long that he had ony a blurred memory of the details.

I went to Bradford Library, and I found it on the front page of the *Yorkshire Post*: 'BRADFORD FAMILY GASSED'. According to the report of the inquest, Bob had been sent to his grandmother's on the afternoon war was declared. His father had said he had to go to Liverpool and, in case he could not get back, he left Bob with four pound notes and a gold watch. Bob returned the next morning, Monday, to find the four bodies in the bath with the gas on.

Bob was on his own in life. His mother had left him, his sister had died and his father had not thought life worth living. Bob, 'in the valley of the shadow of death', turned to Christianity to get him through.

How far I had travelled from the balcony at Stratford Park Leisure Centre, listening to Ken Biddulph's happy stories. Then it was a bit of fun, capturing the fond memories of a county cricketer. Now I was being trusted with a deep and shameful secret, one that Bob had not spoken about for sixty years. As a writer I knew it was a vital ingredient in the book, part of what had moulded Bob's character and made him capable of recovering from tuberculosis. Yet I was not to include it.

I sought advice from David Foot who said that, if he were writing the book, he would start with the young Bob pushing open the door and smelling the gas. But that was the journalist in him. "The first sentence is so important," Hazel used to tell us. "If the first sentence isn't interesting, they won't read on."

That did not fit with what I felt I was doing, and it would certainly not have been what Bob wanted. In any case Bob did not want me to include it at all, just to say briefly, as Derek had done, that there was an accident.

What should I do? There were personal things that my previous subjects had told me that they asked me not to include – in one case, something most disturbing – but they had been tangential to the story. This was at the heart of Bob's life and character. How could I leave it out? Yet I had promised Bob that nothing would be included without his agreement. So how could I include it?

I started the book with his debut for Yorkshire, taking the story forward through his 200 wickets to the discovery of his tuberculosis. At the end of Chapter 5 he was being wheeled into the theatre for surgery.

At the start of Chapter 6 I imagined his fear at that moment – fear that he had bowled his last ball, fear that he faced a life as an invalid, fear of an early death – and asked the question, 'What gives one man the strength to overcome such fear where others lose their will?' Then I told the full story of his childhood, as calmly as I could, and ended: 'He was no longer a young boy, playing ball in the street. He had become a tough survivor. When they wheeled him into the operating theatre, he was determined once more to survive.'

Bob was troubled by the chapter – "I did ask you not to include this" – but he recognised that I had written it with sensitivity and he understood why I wanted to include it. Connie was not well enough to discuss it with him, but he promised me that he would take advice. First, he went to see the rector at Bolton Priory where he worshipped. "You've got to put that in," was the firm reply. Then he gave the pages to his old friend Arthur Hutchinson, a retired county court judge. Bob had lent Arthur my book with Geoffrey Howard, and he had returned it one day when I was with Bob. "Oh, I did enjoy that," he said. "The way it wove back and forth, the informality and the man himself. I just fell in love with him." He agreed with the rector; the story of Bob's childhood had to be in the book.

Bob reported their reactions and told me that he would now sit down with his two daughters, Rosemary and Liz. He would tell them what really happened in 1939 and see how they felt about what I had written.

I knew that, if Bob were adamant, I would not include it. It would be a betrayal of trust. However, I did feel that his concern for his grandchildren was misplaced. Young people today would not feel the suicide of a great-grandfather as a stigma in the way that people would have done sixty years ago.

Strangely I guessed the outcome a couple of hours before he rang. I said to Sue, "You know, I wouldn't be surprised if they already know."

"It's all right," Bob said. "You can put it in. Connie had told them. Her mother had told her about it before we married, and she'd done what you did. She'd been to the library and read the newspapers."

For sixty years he had carried that burden. Now, he said, "Reading it like this, the way you've written it, it doesn't seem so bad anymore. In fact, it's a weight off my shoulders."

Bob had had a difficult life, and there were more personal tragedies for him to handle in later years: the death from leukaemia of his only son and of his first grandson, then Connie's decline with Alzheimer's disease. Often he would have to get up in the night to change the bedsheets, but he battled on, uncomplaining. He saw no point in self-pity or regret.

He was not an easy-going man, and he did not let things drop if he believed he was right. Towards the end of his working life he took on Robert Maxwell in a court case. "I know that Appleyard," the tycoon was reported to have said. "He's a bloody-minded Yorkshireman. He'll take me all the way." Bob did, too, and he won. It was an episode he recounted with great satisfaction.

A Bloody-Minded Yorkshireman. How about that for a title? But it was not right. There was much more to Bob than that.

I took to looking through the *New Oxford Book of English Verse* for a suitable title. I thought of the poem by Arthur Hugh Clough: 'Say not the struggle nought availeth'. It had that uplifting Victorian Christianity that was at the heart of Bob's faith, but I could not find the right phrase in it. Then Sue pointed out the poem on the page opposite: 'Last Lines' by Emily Bronte. Bob was in her part of Yorkshire – at one stage he had even lived across the road from the graveyard where she was buried – and this was her last poem before dying of tuberculosis:

No coward soul is mine,
No trembler in the world's storm-troubled sphere:
I see Heaven's glories shine,
And faith shines equal, arming me from fear.

There it was. Faith triumphing over fear. We could call the book *No Coward Soul*.

"Are you happy with that?" I asked him.

"Well, I am," he said, his speech more hesitant than usual. "As a matter of fact I'm very flattered."

*

In many ways Bob and I were polar opposites. Unlike me he was happy to get into arguments and, once in them, he would never back down. His strongly-held political views were more right-wing than mine, and he put much greater value than I do on social status and financial wealth.

Yet our collaboration, helped crucially by Ron Deaton, was a great success. The key to it, I later realised, was that we were both perfectionists, willing always to go that little bit further to get things exactly as we wanted them. I loved that about Bob.

The only time we argued was on the last day before I took the book away for printing. He had joined the Yorkshire committee, by chance, in the same year that Geoffrey Boycott and his supporters were elected, and for nearly twenty years he had been locked in a feud with him and with his chief ally, Tony Vann, the man whose chairmanship of the Northern Cricket Society had so impressed me. Boycott had had a long pop at Bob in one of his books, and Bob was determined to use *No Coward Soul* to have a pop back.

I dislike books that are full of score-settling, and I refused to include most of it. I told him it would lower the tone of the book. But he started on about it again on that last afternoon, getting quite het up: "Hassell is getting off too lightly ... I want Vann named ..." He looked at me: "You're not writing this down, I notice."

I was tired, ahead of the long journey home, and all I could think to say was, "It's too late, we've filled up all the pages."

"Well, you can take out all that stuff Ray Illingworth said."

I was rather proud of the section involving Ray's contribution. I had rung him and Don Wilson, and they had both painted an unflattering picture of Bob in his playing days, how he could be sarcastic and intolerant of the failings of the youngsters. When the quotes first appeared in my text, Bob wanted them removed, but I persuaded him that it might work better if he replied to their points – and this produced a wonderful response:

> When I worked in the docks in the war, there were people there from Bristol, London, Tyneside and the Clyde, and they were pretty rough, some of them. There was a lot of micky-taking, because people had nothing better to do, and some of it was quite harsh. If you didn't stand up for yourself, you could have a miserable

time. Ray Illingworth was a nice lad, and he was a very good young cricketer. In fact, he's got one of the best cricketing brains alive in the country today, but people like him and Doug Padgett, they weren't coming out of the same world as I'd come from. I'd had to learn to be hard to survive. Perhaps I was too harsh at times. Perhaps I did take the micky too much. It's just how I'd learnt to be when I was a young man.

That exchange told me so much about the gap between the pre-war and post-war generations.

What was so impressive about Bob was that, even at the age of 79, he was still looking forward, still trying to make the world a better place. He was fascinated by history, but he wanted to understand the world around him and to find ways of improving it in the future. He had that great stubborn integrity that is both the strength and the weakness of Yorkshire folk. I grew immensely fond of him. He was a remarkable man.

After our book was published, I received a phone call from Robert Brooke, who had ended his review of Bomber's book so gloomily: 'Chalke will never find another Wells. Whatever the future holds for him, it will inevitably be something of an anticlimax.'

He said simply, "I was wrong."

*

No Coward Soul was launched in November 2003: first, at an intimate evening at an independent bookshop in Ilkley, then the following lunchtime in the indoor cricket school at Headingley. A tell-all book by Princess Diana's butler Paul Burrell was top of the national bestsellers' list, much to Bob's disgust, and he set himself the challenge of outselling it in the Ilkley bookshop.

"You'll do well if you sell that many," the manager said.

At Headingley Bob and I arrived early for an interview with a young reporter, Andy Giddings of BBC Radio Leeds. We went into an ante-room, and Andy explained that he would only need ten minutes of our time.

Bob began to talk: about how emotional it had been for him to do the book, about how England's recent win in the Rugby World Cup in Australia had brought back what it was like to beat the Australians in Australia, about how he would have loved to have been a member of the present Australian side, playing alongside McGrath and Warne. Andy was more than fifty years younger than Bob, but he listened spellbound.

It was left to me occasionally to underline the extent of Bob's achievements and to reflect on his character: "Bob has faced a number of episodes in his life that have been potentially destructive to his spirit, and he's come through them all. He's got this ability to take each challenge in his life and to keep going forward, to get the most out of his life. He's not coming from a culture of wanting compensation or benefit for things that have gone wrong in his life."

It was a subject Bob and I had discussed occasionally: the conflict between the kinder society we have created, with its medical advances and its home comforts, and the need to preserve the robustness of the human stock. On the one hand, without the discovery of streptomycin in 1943, he would have been crippled or even killed by his illness; on the other hand we were interfering with 'the survival of the fittest'.

I loved this philosophical side to Bob, and Andy was captivated too. It was fifty minutes before he turned off his recording machine.

"What are you going to do with all that?" Bob asked.

"I'm going to ring the studio and tell them to run it in its entirety."

Apparently it went out four times.

The launch was starting to fill up by this time, with Geoffrey Wooler the guest of honour. "Bob's a great fellow," he told me. "He's had a remarkable life, and he's done a lot of good in the world. I wish there were more like him playing cricket today."

In my first book Maurice Hallam had talked about playing against Yorkshire in the 1950s: "They were always arguing but, when you tried to argue against them, you came up against a brick wall. They were one clan, Yorkshire for Yorkshiremen." And that day, for Bob, the clan united: Brian Close and Fred Trueman, Ray Illingworth and Dickie Bird, and many more. The only problem arose when Bob told me to make Fred pay for the book.

"Can I take a copy of this book?" Fred asked me.

"I'm sorry, Fred," I started rather hesitantly. "I would give you one as you helped me. But Bob wants you to pay."

"Pay?" he said. "Why's that?"

Bob, spotting my difficulty, hurried across.

"I had to pay for your last book, Fred," he said.

"You did no such bloody thing."

"I did. I bought three copies in the car park at church. That thing about the Dales. I paid full price for all of them."

"You never bloody did! I've just spent ten minutes with BBC television telling them what a great bowler you were, and you're expecting me to pay for this bloody book of yours."

He left with a free book, promising Bob that he would give him a copy of his next one. Bob was crestfallen: "All my years in sales, I just wanted for once in my life to make Fred pay for something."

There was plenty of publicity, with the *Daily Telegraph* first off the block. 'Appleyard: an untold story of private grief' was their headline.

> Fred Trueman was among a throng of great names at Headingley ...
> He admitted, "A lot of this is news to me ... I simply knew him as
> a wonderful bowler."

One fellow worshipper at Bolton Priory told Bob, "Every time I turn on the television or open the newspaper, you pop up."

"I don't know what it is," Bob rang to tell me one day, "but everybody seems to be treating me differently." He gave the example of a man at Headingley who had ignored him for years and who now came up and shook him warmly by the hand.

The letters started to flow in, not just from friends but from readers, some themselves coping with serious illness and finding inspiration in Bob's story. He specially treasured one from David Sheppard, reflecting on the resilience of Bob's Christianity in the face of so much tragedy.

Bob had decided to give all his royalties to the Hutton Foundation, a charity for promoting youth cricket in Yorkshire, and he got me to put a flyer in each book. By the time we had sold out the 4,000 print run, he had raised £20,000.

It was the *Wisden Book of the Year* in their next almanack, chosen by Barry Norman the film critic. But, best of all for Bob, he rang one day to tell me he had called into the bookshop in Ilkley to find out how it was going. He had outsold Paul Burrell.

15

If it had not been for your book

Most books die down after a while, but the after-effects of Bob Appleyard's book went on and on. He was no longer the forgotten man of English cricket. He had so much he wanted to say – about English cricket, about bowling, about Yorkshire, about the way the game could help to solve the problems of Bradford – and suddenly people were listening to him. Then, when eventually the book did start to die down, his life took another turn.

I was staying overnight in a Travelodge, on my way back from a cricket society talk, and early in the morning Sue rang me. "Bob's just phoned. He wants you to ring him urgently."

"I want you to know before anybody else," he said. "I've had the most wonderful news and, as far as I'm concerned, it wouldn't have happened if it had not been for your book. Yorkshire have asked me to be the next President. I'm only the second professional cricketer ever to become President – after Len Hutton. And he was Sir Leonard by then. I'm just plain Bob Appleyard."

He did it so well, too. Even with Connie to look after, he attended all the important matches and entertained the visiting dignitaries. He clearly enjoyed his duties, often ringing to tell me how impressed he was by such people as the Indian High Commissioner and the Pakistani manager.

I was at Scarborough with him, live on BBC Radio York, when Yorkshire's latest debutant, Ajmal Shahzad from Huddersfield, came on to bowl for the first time. Already in the team was Adil Rashid of Bradford. At last the Yorkshire-born Pakistani community were breaking into the county's side, even if they were playing alongside assorted Australians and South Africans, not to mention a captain, Michael Vaughan, who was born in Lancashire.

I pointed it out to the interviewer, and he immediately turned to Bob, the club's President, for his thoughts. Shahzad and Rashid playing for Yorkshire?

"To be honest," Bob said, "I still wish we could get back to a Yorkshire team with eleven Yorkshiremen in it." He paused, and my heart sank to the floor. Then he added, "And these two lads, they're a step in the right direction."

He was not one who enjoyed speaking to large audiences. We went together to Old Trafford, to a meeting of the Cricket Memorabilia Society. The idea was that I would interview him, and I began by saying how we were fifty years on, almost to the day, from his return to Headingley after his operation. I spelled out with some emotion what he had overcome and what an inspiration his story was, what a triumph of the human spirit. Then I framed my first question, and I turned to him. His eyes were brimming with tears, and he told me to carry on the speech on my own.

Yet in the intimacy of a one-to-one interview he grew in confidence, and in the summer of 2007 he astonished Christopher Martin-Jenkins. MCC were putting together a film about the Australian tour of 1954/55, and Christopher came to interview Bob on film. "I'm going to talk about bowling," he told me. "There's so much that needs to be said."

With hindsight I think I got so absorbed with the human aspect of Bob's life story that I did not give sufficient space in the book to his thoughts on bowling. He was a deep and original thinker, and that day he rather took Christopher's breath away.

With a ball in his hand Bob showed him all his grips, including the leg-cutter that George Pope had passed on to him back in 1952; he also demonstrated the different positions from which he could release the ball. Then he spoke about concentration, how he had learnt about it from studying a yoga book while in hospital.

"I was a great believer in concentration. It's all right telling someone to concentrate, but you need to learn a method. And I did this through the yoga system. There were these two words I'd learned from this book, 'sim-la', and I'd say them when I was walking back to my mark. I just wanted to be getting into my cocoon, shutting out the crowds ... It's no use trying to concentrate at the start of a 16-yard run-up because the average person can only concentrate intensely for about three seconds. The great players, Len Hutton or Jack Nicklaus, perhaps with them it goes up to five. So if you concentrate too early, it's gone by the time you get to the important point of delivering the ball. And you need to practise this. Not in the middle, in the nets. I'm a great believer in practice."

*

Bob was by far the best salesman I ever worked with. He was persistent, and he knew all the tricks. He sold 100 copies of the hardback, specially dedicated and signed, to the local Aviva offices, for them to give to their clients. They paid over the normal purchase price but, when we sold out the print run and Bob needed some copies, he went in to Aviva and persuaded them to give him back free of charge the 37 they still had. Then, when we went into paperback, with an additional chapter covering the years since the book's publication, he insisted on all his friends and acquaintances buying copies, even when they tried to refuse. It was hard to say no to Bob.

Ken Taylor, who drew the picture of Bob on the front cover, was so taken with the book that he set in motion an application for Bob to receive an honour, and eventually – with an extra prod from me – Bob was awarded an MBE, having the day of his life at Buckingham Palace. Always, when these things happened, he wanted me to know all about it. I sat on his sofa and watched his film of the ceremony.

*

For many years Yorkshire County Club had been careless with the artefacts of its great heritage, but this had now changed. David Hall, a retired businessman with great organisational skills, drove forward a series of initiatives which culminated in the opening of a museum at Headingley. All this was right up Bob's street, and he made sure that both Ron Deaton and I were involved.

I wrote two little booklets for them. One was *A Summer of Plenty*, the story of George Hirst's season in 1906 when, at the age of 35 and with a knee that needed strapping up before bowling, he achieved the unique double of 2,000 runs and 200 wickets. It was a fascinating story, highlighting the extraordinary stamina of people in that age. Hirst completed the feat by taking a wicket with the first ball after tea in a match at Scarborough on 30 August, and 100 years later, almost to the minute, in the tea break of a Yorkshire match, we walked out onto the grass. Bob, the Yorkshire President and the only man alive who knew what it was like to take 200 wickets, held the ball that George Hirst had bowled. It was a magical moment.

The other booklet was *Five Five Five*, the story of the record-breaking opening partnership of Percy Holmes and Herbert Sutcliffe at Leyton in 1932. Sue and I went to the ground 75 years to the day later, and the game we watched had the lovely twist of ending, just as the 1932 partnership had done, with a confusion over the score displayed on the board. The story was a great one, anyway, but that was a wonderfully unforeseeable extra.

David Hall's next project, in association with the Video Production Unit of Leeds Metropolitan University, was to film in-depth, one-to-one interviews with former players. The death of Fred Trueman had made them realise that they had many great players whose testimony would be lost if they did not capture it quickly. Bob was approached, and he told them that he would only do it if I conducted the interview. The upshot of that was that I was asked to do almost all of them: nine interviews, plus filmed tributes to Len Hutton and Fred Trueman.

It involved me in a lot of driving up to Leeds and back, but I loved every minute of it. Ron Deaton gave great support as always, the film crew were most professional, and Bob, with his boyish enthusiasm for all things technical, spent happy hours in their studio, finding out how all the equipment worked.

Brian Close was the first of the cricketers to be interviewed. We went up in a lift together from the room at Headingley where we had attended a lunch to celebrate George Hirst's *annus mirabilis*. After the meal I had made a short speech, ending by quoting the great man's words on the balcony at Scarborough, on the occasion of his retirement.

> If I've had any broad views on what they call the game of life, I've learnt them on the cricket field. I've loved many games, but I've been a bit more efficient at cricket. From an unselfish point of view, it's the best game. What can you have better than a nice green field, with the wickets set up, and to go out and do the best for your side? I leave first-class cricket to those who have got to come. I hope they'll have the pleasure in it that I have had.

"Did George Hirst really say all that?" Brian asked in the lift.

"Yes, he did."

"I've got to admit, when you were reading it, lad, there was a tear in my eye."

The interview that followed was a roller-coaster of emotions. The England call-up at the age of 18, the disastrous first tour of Australia, the comebacks and the droppings, the dramatic innings at Lord's when he came down the wicket to Wes Hall, the eventual appointment as England captain, then the controversial sacking.

"The MCC brought in their own man, and that was Cowdrey. It didn't take him long to jigger it all up again. I tell you what, if I could have stayed as captain of England, knowing the players as I knew them, we could have gone years and beaten all of them – because we had artists, we had skilled bowlers and batsmen, the lot."

It was yet another setback, but the narrative drove on – "Anyway, that was that; that was over and done with" – and there followed triumphs with Yorkshire, then his extraordinary sacking, his second career at Somerset and his England recall at the age of 45. For a while we stopped the camera as he coped with the tears that welled up when he told how Brian Sellers, who had sacked him from the Yorkshire captaincy, apologised years later.

"It's been a life full of enjoyment, I suppose," he said with a touch of mellowness, "and a few sad moments. But I can laugh at them now. It's been a hell of a life."

When I played it back later, I was struck by how accurate he had been when he listed the dates of all his Tests. I also noticed with a smile how, in a delightful inversion of the norm, he had referred affectionately to all his fellow professionals by their first names, Fred and Tom and Wes, and to the amateurs with a certain dismissiveness as May and Dexter and Cowdrey.

The technicians thought the film would work best as a monologue, with my questions being cut out in the editing. This did not work at all, Brian needed too much prompting, so for subsequent films they also had a camera on me, allowing the film to cut across to me when I spoke. "Next time we meet, we'll film you asking your questions to Brian," they said.

The next session involved interviews with Vic Wilson and Ted Lester, both of whom lived in the east of the county. So any eagle-eyed viewer of the Close film will spot that he is sitting at Headingley, answering questions that I am asking from the pavilion at Scarborough.

Vic Wilson had been an outstanding close-to-the-wicket catcher so I asked him about that. He said the most important thing was to have confidence in the bowler. He was happy to stand up close when Bob Appleyard or Johnny Wardle were bowling but, if it was Brian Close, "It frightened you to death; you didn't know if it would be a long hop or a full toss."

This little passage was included in a short compilation film that was shown when the series was launched at Headingley. I could not see him, as I was further along the table, but I am told that Closey's face was like thunder when Vic came out with it.

Vic died not long afterwards, and I heard how grateful his family were that we had captured him on film. It was a simple enough project that I am surprised not more counties undertake.

Don Wilson was excellent, brimming with that joy that made him such a successful coach in the townships in South Africa, then at Lord's. He told how he had suffered from chronic asthma as a boy. His father, an ambulanceman, had taken him at the age of seven to Harley Street for a consultation, and Don had told the doctor he wanted to be a cricketer. "That's the perfect job for you," the doctor said. "Out in the fresh air."

Miraculously the problem went away, but in old age it returned. I met him on the day the museum at Headingley was officially opened, and he was struggling badly with his breathing. "If I were you, Don, I'd look at it this way," I said. "You started your life with a chronic illness, and you're ending with it. And in between, against all the odds, you've had a wonderful life."

That Christmas I received a card from him: "I often think of what you said to me. I've been a very lucky man."

*

In the summer of 2014 I attended Bob's 90th birthday party at his daughter Liz's house. His mobility was not good by then, but his indomitable spirit had not dimmed. Connie had died six years earlier, and he had taken up with a kind and intelligent widow, Julie. At the meal he announced their engagement, saying it was part of his next ten-year plan. For all the ill health of his youth, he was by then, with Frank Tyson and Tom Graveney, one of only three survivors of Geoffrey Howard's tour of Australia.

Brian Close was there, smoking a fag on a wet outdoor sofa we had been told not to sit on, and so was Bob Platt, another of the 1950s Yorkshire team, a man with a mischievous sense of humour. His central memory of Bob Appleyard was that he wanted to be bowling all day long, once telling the young Ray Illingworth to 'bugger off' when the captain had asked Ray to take over. Bob even told me once that he did not understand why there was a law stipulating that a bowler 'shall not bowl two overs consecutively'.

Bob Platt had taken a great delight in a line in Geoffrey Howard's book when the selection committee in Australia had debated whether to pick Bob or the nervous Glamorgan off-spinner Jim McConnon for the Second Test at Sydney. "Put it this way," Geoffrey told them. "If Jim learns he's playing, he'll pull a muscle. And if Bob learns he isn't, he'll come and cut your throat."

To be fair to Bob he, too, thought it funny – and not wholly inaccurate.

"I have thought of an inscription for Bob's gravestone," Bob Platt said to me in a well-elocuted stage whisper. "ROBERT APPLEYARD – DISAPPOINTED NOT TO HAVE BOWLED AT BOTH ENDS."

I loved these Yorkshire folk, their warmth, their humour and the passion with which they played and talked about their cricket. It was such fun to be accepted into their world.

*

It was Bob's last birthday. He died in his sleep the following spring, in the same year that Frank Tyson and Tom Graveney died.

Shortly before his death, he had a minor bump while out driving. He told me he had had a letter from the DVLA, requiring him to report for a medical. I assumed that they had been alerted to his condition by one of his daughters, concerned for his safety. But dear old Bob, he went to his grave convinced that the culprit was Geoffrey Boycott or one of his allies.

He never admitted that it had been right to leave out his diatribe on Boycott but, after he experienced the impact of the book, he never mentioned it again. *No Coward Soul* transformed the last years of his life.

Ours was the unlikeliest of partnerships, but without question he brought out the best in me. Sue and I thought the world of him.

16

Oral history, biography or what?

"I think this book could be a trend setter," Geoffrey Howard had said one day when all the compliments were coming in. He sensed that I was breaking new ground with the way I was writing. Bomber Wells, from a different perspective, thought the same.

These books that I was bringing out – Geoffrey Howard, Keith Andrew, Bob Appleyard – what were they? Were they biographies? Each told the story of a life so, in the simplest sense, they were. Yet it was a word I was reluctant to use, as it carried a connotation of objectivity, of standing outside the subject and making an assessment. That was not what I was doing.

One fellow cricket writer coined the term 'assisted biography', which seemed to me like a variation of 'authorised biography', with its signal to the reader that the book is likely to be sympathetic in its view of the subject. But my aim was not to take a view of the subject at all.

Perhaps my books were, in essence, autobiographies, a variation of ghost writing. But that did not seem right, either. I was weaving into the narrative too much background material and sometimes other voices.

I preferred not to put a label on the books at all. If pressed, I would say simply that I was an oral historian, collecting people's memories. Yet there was a point at which even this troubled me.

Just after I had brought out my second book, I was approached by a Guyanese Indian, Vijay Kumar, who had researched and written a book, *Cricket Lovely Cricket*, about the West Indies tour of England in 1950. Based in New York, where he was a Vice-President of Deutsche Bank, he needed help with selling the book in the UK. When we met in London, I liked his boyish enthusiasm, and I offered to store the books and send them out on his behalf.

Just before the book was published, he placed an advertisement for it in *The Cricketer*, in which he said that the book contained 'over 100 amazing anecdotes' and 'a never before seen picture of Sir Donald Bradman'. In a book about the West Indies? That seemed odd.

All was revealed when the book arrived. It was a snap of Bradman in old age sitting next to the author. And the 'over 100 amazing anecdotes' that he had carefully counted? His advert made them seem like objects, akin to autographs or old photographs, that he had acquired from the old cricketers and was now selling on in his book.

I started to receive mysterious phone calls, warning me about him, and I discovered that he was suspected of having stolen a number of items, some of significant value, from cricket collectors and dealers. This reinforced my sense that he was viewing the anecdotes, the memories of the players, as objects with financial value. I sat down and asked myself, "Is that what I am doing? Collecting people's memories and making money out of them?" Sue told me not to be so silly – I was shaping the players' stories and giving them back to them, it was a creative and a generous process, not an act of theft – but, in the shock of all this, I was riddled with self-doubt and took some reassuring.

Vijay stood trial in London in the summer of 2001. His lawyer asked me to appear as a character witness, but he did not summon me. He was sentenced to nine months' imprisonment. If he had been found not guilty, he would have been running for his life on September 11, with the building where he worked suffering impact damage from the attack on the Twin Towers.

An important part of my work has been preserving the language of my subjects. I have an almost fastidious attitude to the quotes I use; I might tidy them up a little, but I never invent them or introduce words that are not in the original. The way a person expresses him or her self reveals their character to the reader, partly at a subliminal level; if the language is mine, not theirs, I am distorting that process. Maybe that is the puritan in me. Or maybe it is the Alan Lomax, wanting to preserve the authentic voices of the past.

There is a fine line between warmth and sentimentality, a fine line between sympathy and hagiography, and I hope I have stayed on the right side of those lines. I am drawn to the humorous, and that helps. Cricket humour has a sharpness about it, a built-in truth-telling, and that is a healthy check against sentimentality. I especially appreciated a review by the author DJ Taylor: 'High on idiosyncracy and local colour, Chalke's portrait is never sentimental. Some of his glances at the forelock-tugging world of the old-style professional game can still take the breath away.'

Nostalgia is another issue. Inevitably there will be readers for whom a book about Geoffrey Howard or Bob Appleyard offers them an opportunity to revisit their past, reminding them of a time when they were young, full of the hopes of the lifetime ahead of them. In my *In the Memory* books I was conscious that I was playing with those feelings, creating in the reader the sense of a lost world. But not after that.

When I listened to Geoffrey talking about his time as England tour manager – "How much easier I would have found it if MCC had provided me with the two things I didn't have: help and money" – or Bob recalling the impersonal 'Dear Appleyard' letter with which Yorkshire dispensed with his services – "I was a bit upset. You'd think after all those years they could have written 'Dear Bob'" – it never occurred to me that what I was writing was nostalgic, full of an aching to go back to the past.

I write about the past, and I try to bring it alive and to understand it. Always my aim is to write with warmth and humanity, and perhaps for some readers that has the effect of making my picture of the past too fond for their taste. But that is a different matter from nostalgia. You can look back with fondness to the people and places of your past without believing the past to be better than the present, as the 24-year-old John Lennon expressed so beautifully in his song *In My Life*.

> *Though I know I'll never lose affection*
> *For people and things that went before*
> *I know I'll often stop and think about them*
> *In my life I'll love you more.*

If somebody told me that things were better forty years ago, then as an oral historian it was my role to record that. But most of the cricketers spoke of the changes they had witnessed in their lives with much more subtlety.

My own view is that, over the course of my life, we have made great progress in many fields but, as side-effects of that progress, there have been losses, some of them in hard-to-measure qualities such as 'a sense of community'. It should be possible to raise such issues without being accused of wanting to turn back the clock or being a nostalgia-monger.

*

Following on from that mad afternoon in 2002 I commissioned Douglas Miller to work with the Glamorgan off-spinner Don Shepherd on a book. Don was a folk hero in Wales, and the memories of his long playing career needed to be captured. Then, after we had launched that book, I persuaded Douglas to take on a second project, this time with Charles Palmer, the former Leicestershire Secretary/captain who went on to be Chairman of the Test and County Cricket Board.

Douglas sat down with Don and Charles in much the same way that I would have done, but he undertook many more interviews with others. In that respect he was more like a conventional biographer, albeit with the assistance of the subject, than I was. If I used other voices, it was primarily to add a little colour, to play with the point of view, rather than to help towards an external biographical judgement.

In Don Shepherd's book *Born to Bowl* Douglas analysed why Don had never been selected to play for England, a subject that can still be guaranteed to get Welsh cricket lovers going. He looked at a range of factors, compiled tables of statistical comparison and sought out the opinions of 17 people for the chapter. It was a prodigious piece of research, throwing an original light on the element of chance in the selection process. In one table he showed how Don's only poor season, compared with the other spin bowlers in the country, occurred immediately prior to the one point at which England had an obvious vacancy, a factor which it would probably not have occurred to me to explore. It was statistics at its best, being used to understand a real question, even if Don and, up to a point, I were so befuddled by his creation of a set of index numbers that we made him recast the table in a more accessible way. He wrote to Alec Bedser, who had been a selector for much of the time, receiving a charming letter that said nothing more than that Don had been a fine bowler, there were other fine bowlers and he was most unlucky, adding the PS: "Please do not quote me on this."

With Charles Palmer, Douglas suffered the fate that inevitably hangs over collaborations with people in their eighties and nineties, with Charles going downhill and dying before he had had a chance to contribute his memories on some parts of his life. Geoffrey Howard was forever aware of the danger – "The clock is ticking," he would remind me whenever my lecturing duties slowed our progress – but fortunately for Douglas his approach allowed him to use other voices to write up Charles's story.

Playing for Worcestershire in April 1948, Charles had scored a sparkling 85 against Bradman's touring Australians. He was a schoolmaster, playing when time allowed, and had only played one more first-class match when in early July he received a letter from Lord's, asking if he was available to tour South Africa that winter. In the wondrous ways of that time, the letter went on to explain: 'The selection committee are anxious to include a reasonable proportion of amateur cricketers.'

The innings, for Charles, was 'the pivotal point in my playing career'. He took up painting in his retirement, attending a local art class, and he used a photograph of his batting that day at Worcester, with the trees and the cathedral in the background, to paint the scene in soft watercolours. It fitted exactly on the jacket of the book, when wrapped around the front and back. None of our books has a more fitting cover.

Douglas, a committee member of the ACS, the Association of Cricket Statisticians and Historians, went on from these two books to be an influential figure in that organisation's setting up a series of books, Lives in Cricket, rather along the lines of what I had been planning to do: short books about individual cricketers. I was asked to an early planning meeting at which I suggested some names of living cricketers whose stories had not been told.

Douglas himself contributed three volumes on such men – Allan Watkins, Jack Bond and Mike Smith – but he was rare in that respect. Most of the ACS members who volunteered to write titles were at heart statisticians; they opted for long-dead subjects where they could sit in libraries rather than get out and talk to people.

*

My own next venture raised further issues about collaboration and historical truthfulness. The Wimbledon Club, across the road from the All-England tennis club, were going to be celebrating their 150th anniversary in 2004, and they commissioned me to write a new club history.

With Bob Appleyard's book to complete, I did not start till late in 2003, at which point the enormity of the task – with the 150-year time span and the sports of hockey, lawn tennis and squash as well as cricket – was daunting.

The Victorian period was rich with fascinating material: the new railway line opening up the area; the early cricket on the Common, when they employed professionals to bowl at club members on practice days; the notices in central London telling the well-to-do that Wimbledon Lake was frozen, with 44 days of skating one winter; the women hockey players using their long skirts to stop the ball and being jeered at when they cycled through the local streets; and the All-England Croquet Club deciding to hold its first tennis tournament in the summer of 1877. The winner, Spencer Gore, was a Wimbledon Club cricketer who declared, "Anyone who really plays well at cricket will never give attention to lawn tennis. The monotony of the game will choke him off."

We look back at these Victorian pioneers, thinking them rather quaint. I had fun in the book's epilogue speculating what they would have thought of us if they could have looked forward.

> Spencer Gore, if he cycled up Church Road at the start of July and saw the cars, the crowds, the great buildings, the money changing hands, what would he say? Would he feel proud that his own innovative play had helped to create a game popular the world over, or would he think us daft to make so much fuss about so trivial an activity?

We worked out a way to lay out the book in double-page spreads and, hiring some help, Sue and I bolted down the historical pages. The real problems started when we reached the post-war era, when we were shaping the pages from the memories of the people on the steering committee.

One member, who captained the cricket in the 1950s, was clear that for several years they were as good a team as any in London, citing a table of results in the *Evening Standard*. But another said they were playing a sort of social cricket that was all about school tie and port at lunch, no good for youngsters wanting to progress to a higher level in the game. And I was in the middle of the argument: "Who told you that? That's complete nonsense."

The club went into decline in the 1960s, sticking to their social priorities. When the Surrey Championship was formed in 1968, the first league in the south of England, they disapproved, being one of a minority of clubs who refused to join. A secondary Surrey Cricketers' League started three years later, and this time – with Saturday opponents now hard to find – they reluctantly entered. They imagined they would be playing clubs well below their level, but they won only one game, finishing 15th out of 16. Soon afterwards Chris Brown, son of the former England captain Freddie, turned up, and with little regard for their feelings he tore into them, bringing in a new breed of player and rapidly transforming them into the strongest club in the county. Unfortunately for me, he not only swept away the old guard he was also involved in destroying much of the club's precious historical archive.

With a certain amount of diplomacy I found my way through the tension on the Wimbledon project. But I knew, and they knew, that the pages covering the modern era did not have the quality of the historical sections.

It was the most stressful book I have written, not helped by Sue being laid low with an illness that lasted for a good two months. Strangely I look back at it now – perhaps my memory has become 'roseate-hued' – and I can only recall their enthusiasm, their warmth and the pleasure I got from pulling it all together.

I remember going up to Wimbledon by train on a cold winter's day. We were sitting upstairs in the clubhouse and, as the light faded, snow started to fall. There were floodlights, spotlighting every fluttering flake, and the cricket pitch, the grass tennis courts and the lake beyond were the most beautiful sight. Repeatedly the All-England Club has offered them breathtaking sums to move away – a new sports complex, ten million pounds – but in that moment I understood so clearly what kept them there.

By the time I left them that evening, the roads were impassable to cars, and the walk to the tube station was a treacherous one. I was not sure I was going to make it. When I got there, as when I completed the book, I felt an inner glow.

Memory is a strange thing. It is shaped by emotion, but then emotions are as much a part of the truth as facts.

17

My back pages – the 1970s

History happens in continuous time, not in decades. Yet, if we group the years together, we can discern patterns of change. Certainly there was more optimism in the air at the start of the 1970s than there was when they ended. Maybe it is all a cliché, but in 1969 man was walking on the moon; in 1979 rubbish sat uncollected and graves were left undug. The uplifting good cheer of the Beatles – 'Here comes the sun' and 'All you need is love' – had been replaced by the dark nihilism of punk. The final number one hit single of the decade was Pink Floyd's anthem for anarchism:

> *We don't need no education*
> *We don't need no thought control ...*
> *All in all, it's just another brick in the wall.*

Two years later there were riots on the streets of several British cities.

*

I took a job teaching English in North London in an ex-grammar school that was coping badly with its new comprehensive intake. Elderly staff, who had developed reputations as strict disciplinaries, found themselves floundering in front of pupils the like of whom they had never encountered.

I started in January 1971, in the middle of a school year, taking over from a charismatic man with a full head of flaming ginger hair and a flamboyant dress sense that I could not match. He had enthused my 'A' level group with a passion for WB Yeats, and the Irishman's strange, mystical ideas left me cold. I did my best, even arranging extra evening sessions at their houses, but I never shook off the feeling that his departure was a great disappointment to them.

Much worse was a group called 3-3, a lower-ability set which I had on the last two periods of Monday afternoon. The sessions with them never went smoothly, often becoming quite noisy. Stuck on my own with them, I was deeply ashamed by how badly I was coping. Then one week the head of languages, a Miss Smith, one of the old guard, stopped me in the corridor. "I think you have 3-3 after me on a Monday," she said. "You're young. Maybe you'll get through to them better than I can." Two weeks later she had a heart attack in one of their lessons and never returned.

On one occasion, during a free period, I was sitting on my own in the upstairs staff room when another of the old-timers, Mr White, burst through the door. "Quick," he said. "Come with me." With no idea why, I found myself running down the stairs, up the main drive and onto the High Street. After he had recovered his breath, he said to me, "Sorry about that, but we needed to get out. They're looking for someone to cover 3-2."

One of the keys to being a successful teacher is to know, for each age group, where their understanding and their skills have reached. I had completed a year of postgraduate training, but it was a highly theoretical course and I was ill-equipped to make these judgements. If I had been teaching mathematics, it would have been easier, but English is not straightforward. Progressive ideas were in vogue, quite different from the English teaching at my public school. Where once I had sat identifying adverbial clauses and future perfect tenses, I was now encouraging free expression.

No sooner had I arrived than I was given 120 mock 'O' level compositions to mark. They were also being marked by a confident woman, three or four years older than me, who was passionate about emotive writing. I felt so inadequate as I sat in my bedsit, wondering what it was that I was supposed to be assessing in the essays. When we compared marks, I discovered that she had failed the composition to which I had given my highest mark. It was written by a boy, a science student not given to flowery language; he had adapted the 'To be or not to be' speech in a tightly written, precisely worded essay that was full of crossings out and only just over the minimum words. The discrepancy between our marks left me feeling, not for the only time in my life, that I was a complete impostor. I had no right to be teaching English.

They were the last year of the purely grammar school entry, and their 'O' level English results were appalling, setting off something of a crisis about our teaching. Out of the 120 who sat 'O' level English Language, there was one solitary grade A. It went to the boy to whom I had given the top mark.

Towards the end of my first year, still struggling with the crowd control element of the job, the headmaster told me that an inspector from the local authority would be sitting in on a particular double period the following week. The purpose of the visit was to establish whether I would pass my probationary year. The class in question was a good one, apart from three boys who sat together at the front and took every opportunity to disrupt proceedings. I was fearful how the inspection would turn out.

I knew they liked me at heart, and I decided to raise the stakes. I took them aside after one class and explained that I was being inspected. If they mucked about, I would lose my job. It was a high-risk strategy that could have gone either way but, when I arrived at the class with the inspector, it was immediately clear which way it was going to go. The three boys were sitting bolt upright in their seats, and they never said a word not in the class discussion nor during the writing task I set them. After an hour the inspector left. "The headmaster said you might have discipline problems," she said, "but I can see that you have excellent control when you need it. Well done."

After she left, the boy in the middle of the trio stood up and stretched. I asked him what he was doing, and he said, to my astonishment, "I never had a chair." Anxious not to create a disturbance, he had spent an hour in a sitting position with no seat under him.

I made him captain of my Under-15 cricket team, and he started to confide in me about his personal problems. He left school at the earliest possible age with few qualifications, got a job in a bank and came back to see me. Alas, his respect for me melted away when he discovered that he was earning a lot more than I was.

In my second year I had a wonderful 'O' level class. We had a double period at the end of Friday afternoon, when we studied poems from the *Sheldon Book of Verse Volume 3*, among them Owen's *Dulce et Decorum Est*, Keats' *Ode to a Nightingale* and Grey's *Elegy in a Country Churchyard*. I was right in my element. They were the top set in the first year of the fully comprehensive intake and, while the four sets of the last grammar school entry had got one grade A between them, my group alone got 18 in English Language and 19 in English Literature. After that, the school believed in me. I even started to believe in myself.

My greatest success in those three-and-a-half years of schoolteaching was with an intelligent and highly sensitive lad called Will. He was a keen member of the Drama Group which I ran at the end of school each Friday, but by the 'O' level year he had become alienated from the institutional environment, was often absent and was doing no work at all. I was his form tutor and, a fortnight before the exams started, I offered him a deal. "If you want me to, Will, I'll bully you for the next two weeks, force you to work morning, noon and night. You're bright enough; you can still pass these exams, you know. But I'll only do it if you agree. If you change your mind, I'll stop."

"I'd like that," he said. So, with a theatrical sense of the comedy of it, I was on his back all day every day. As a result he passed six 'O' levels.

Recently I discovered that he has become a big wheel in the world of music, a go-to producer for major stars such as Madonna. I found, to my great amusement, an online interview with him in which he said with some pride that he had dropped out of school at 14 and had no academic qualifications.

Maybe I should have stayed with the teaching, but I did not like the person I was becoming. I was growing too rigid, and there was so much of life I had not experienced. I lined up a job working in a centre for mentally disturbed adults, and I left, full of hope for my future. My 'A' level group gave me a farewell card, containing the lines from *Julius Caesar*:

> *There is a tide in the affairs of men,*
> *Which, taken at the flood, leads on to fortune.*

Alas, funding for the job fell through, and I ran into the realities of the mid-1970s in London. Unemployment was rising, and accommodation, following an ill-conceived Rent Act, was in short supply. I had some hard years ahead of me.

*

I was a lost soul, trying to find a way forward in life. I managed a college bookshop; I studied for an MA in English Literature; I worked in adult literacy. I dabbled in left-wing politics; I took up writing short stories; I joined a group that explored 'the space between theatre and psychotherapy', performing with it at the Edinburgh Festival.

My father had died in 1969, leaving me an inheritance that in my youthful idealism I gave to Oxfam. I explained my thinking to the solicitor, a personal friend of Dad, and with his reply he sent me a copy of the *Commonplace Book* written by his own guiding star, the Christian socialist RH Tawney. He dedicated it to me, adding a quotation from Anatole France: 'La miséricorde de Dieu est infinie: elle sauvera même un riche.' The mercy of God is infinite: it will save even a rich man. It was not what I felt at the time.

Dad's money would have been enough to buy a small house, and in 1975 I had no place of my own to live, outstaying my welcome in friends' spare bedrooms.

The left-wing politics was a fairly short phase, coinciding with the first referendum on Europe. I cycled out beyond the East End to a rally, 'The Left Against Europe', in a large town hall. Towards the end of the meeting, tired of the rigid certainty of all the speeches, I got up to say that maybe the Common Market was a good thing; it promoted peace between nations and international co-operation. My words were not well received and, as I was unlocking my bicycle, I found myself pushed up against a wall by a muscular man with a strong Cockney accent. "Don't you come round 'ere with your fancy ideas," he said. "The bosses are for the Common Market so we're against it. That's all you need to know." It was not dissimilar to the boys pushing me up against the coat pegs at prep school, only this time, scared for my facial features, I meekly agreed with him, apologised and cycled away as fast as I could.

Life seemed to consist of meetings. I went to one, 'The Working Class View of the Common Market', in the upstairs room of a pub in Liverpool Road, north of The Angel. The speaker – Dave, no surname – was introduced as a long-distance lorry driver just back from the south of France. He had a rough accent, but it did not take me a moment to recognise him as a boy three years younger than me who had always spoken in our Debating Society at school. He had been rather fat with a squeaky voice, and he spoke up for the less well-to-do in society, using phrases such as 'your typical Joe Bloggs'. A lot of the boys laughed at him and, as Chairman, I tried to protect him from their cruelty. I shook his hand at the end of the meeting, our eyes met knowingly, but I did not betray his secret. "Good to meet you, comrade," he said as I left.

*

On YouTube you will find a clip of the American folk singer Tom Paxton coming up to sing his gentle *Last Thing on my Mind* in a packed club. When he reaches the stage, the audience are still yelping with joy after a rousing performance by the great Irish singer Liam Clancy. "That's tough to follow," Paxton says, "but ever since the day in a quarry in the middle of Germany that I followed Black Sabbath I have not known the meaning of fear."

Our audiences at the Edinbugh Festival were not on the scale of the quarry, often not reaching double figures, but our performances were so bad that, like Tom Paxton, I reached a place beyond fear. The venture was a disaster, and we had to appear with it in front of paying spectators every day for three weeks. In the afternoon we were our normal therapy group, albeit with onlookers, but in the other four sessions, between mid-day and midnight, we created shows. It was an intriguing idea, but it was obvious, long before we reached Edinburgh, that we lacked the talent to produce anything worth watching.

Our group leader, pursuing a fantasy that he was the next Samuel Beckett, had written a play, *Fungus and Curmudgeonly*, about two out-of-work Shakespearean actors stuck on a ledge in the London sewers. In our lunchtime show two of us had to read his script as if we were preparing for a production. We were not actors, the writing was terrible – rhyming couplets full of puns – and it had nothing to do with the space between theatre and psychotherapy. It was best summed up when one audience member stood up in mid-show: "This is complete rubbish. I can't believe I've paid 50p for it." On another occasion, when I was not a reader, I was having a sandwich in a nearby café when I heard that a fight had broken out, with one of the readers hitting our group leader over the head with a microphone. That, at least, was exploring the space between theatre and psychotherapy.

I stuck with it to the end, my curiosity trumping my fear of making a fool of myself. Deep down I was yearning for a sense of belonging, though they were never my sort of people. One of them was a personal assistant to the progressive rock musician Keith Emerson; she turned up at one of our sessions with three expensive watches, all belonging to Emerson and all in need of repair.

Several of the group became devotees of Shree Rajneesh Bhagwan, wearing orange and taking new names. The cult, which attracted many Westerners of my generation, relocated from Puna to the desert in Oregon where their idealistic community ran into local Christian opposition. It ended up as a heavily armed authoritarian sect, bugging its own members and trying to win a local election by spreading salmonella through the area.

The leader of our Edinburgh group was a highly qualified psychologist who had lectured at London University and practised at the Tavistock. I last saw him being interviewed as a sports psychologist on the BBC News, talking sense about Paul Gascoigne. In the 1970s a lot of people went a little crazy.

*

My life started to settle down when Sue and I formed a relationship. It took me a while to make the commitment, but I made a symbolic step forward when one Christmas, instead of going home to Salisbury, I spent the holiday with Sue. On Boxing Day I read *Antony and Cleopatra* to her, using different voices for all the characters, while she painted a portrait of me in oil.

I was living in Archway, she in Peckham, close to the Camberwell School of Art where she was studying. Normally I would have cycled down but on Christmas Eve, carrying a case of spare clothes and a present, I took the 137 bus. I was sitting upstairs when somewhere near Oxford Street a row broke out between the conductor and a passenger who had sat down on the seat across the gangway from me. The passenger had offered a 50p bit for his fare, and the conductor was refusing to accept it.

"I'm not handling that," he said. "It's dirty."

"It's legal tender. You have to take it."

"No, I don't. What else have you got?"

"I'm not giving you anything else. I'm giving you this."

On and on it went, till the conductor stopped the bus.

"That's it. Everybody off. This bus is going no further."

We all trooped off and waited for the next bus. Nobody thought of taking the matter further. It was just how things were.

*

On Christmas Day 1978 Sue went into labour with our first child. She was 27 weeks pregnant. Our daughter Ruth, when she appeared in the early hours of the next morning, weighed only two pounds.

For six weeks Ruth lay in an incubator, battling for life, but she did not make it. We sat with her for as much time as we could, but we were helpless. On the last evening, when all hope was lost, they let us hold her, and we did so till she died around breakfast time.

It was the twentieth anniversary of Buddy Holly's death. He was my first musical love, and early in our relationship I told Sue how happy I was to find somebody who could join in when I sang his songs in the car. That night, as Ruth lay dying, the radio in the baby unit was playing his records repeatedly.

> *I tell my blues they mustn't show*
> *But soon these tears are bound to flow*
> *'Cos it's raining, raining in my heart.*

It was the worst of winters, with deep snow on the ground. One day, leaving the special unit with its incubators full of wires and gadgets, I took our washing to the launderette. Suddenly, in mid-wash, a group of young boys came in and, from a carrier bag, started pulling out pocket calculators, throwing them about the room so that bits of battery and casing were everywhere. The other customers cowered but, whether it was my 'have a go' personality or the association with the wires in the hospital, I decided to confront them, chasing them out of the launderette and up the hill, every footstep a nightmare in the snow and ice. Eventually I grabbed one and called for help from a passer-by, a man of my own age. I wanted to give them a severe talking-to, but his reaction was to round on me as the assailant. "Let that boy go. What the hell do you think you're doing?" The boys slipped away as, despite my protests, the chap continued to call me a thug and a bully. It seemed in that moment that the world around me had lost all sense of order.

The industrial action of the 'Winter of Discontent' was in full swing, with the hospital porters and ancillary staff on strike, leaving nurses to collect the laundry and wheel around the patients. At one point, when Ruth was fighting for her survival, we were asked to wait in an ante-room where a little television set was broadcasting the news.

My left-wing ideals had their roots in Christian principles, helping others less fortunate than myself. I still have a strong streak of that, not comfortable with a world that over-rewards the successful and those born with advantage, but that sort of 'I want more' trade unionism, as it had reached by 1979, did not speak to me. On the television a striker was standing by a brazier outside a hospital. "If it takes a few deaths for us to get a proper wage," he said, "it will be a price worth paying."

It was a low end to a low decade. I did not get over it till Martha was born three years later.

18

A real all-rounder

Late in 2003 the two cricket magazines, *The Cricketer* and *Wisden Cricket Monthly*, joined forces to become *The Wisden Cricketer* under the editorship of John Stern, who had been Stephen Fay's deputy on *Wisden Cricket Monthly*. I got on well with John; he was a thoughtful editor, open to ideas, and he ran a happy team. He set in motion some excellent series, an early one of which was 'The real all-rounders', about cricketers who had achieved success in a second field. There was Aubrey Smith the Hollywood actor, Johnny Douglas the Olympic boxing champion, David Sheppard the bishop and, of course, CB Fry who excelled at almost everything. To add to the fun of it, there was even one about Donald Weekes, a West Indian batsman who had played Othello in Moscow, swum the channel, coached the US Olympic fencing team and been voted by a group of journalists 'the greatest all-round athlete in the world', only for people to rumble eventually that he was nothing more than a fantasist.

John asked me for a contribution, and I had no hesitation in plumping for Ken Taylor, who had illustrated my first two books. Here was a man who in the mid-1950s was simultaneously playing cricket for Yorkshire (and later England), football in the old First Division for Huddersfield Town and studying art full-time at the prestigious Slade in London. Meanwhile his brother Jeff, five years older than him, played in the First Division for Fulham and, after completing a Geography degree at London University, trained as an opera singer at the Royal Academy of Music. They had grown up in Huddersfield, with a father who struggled to find regular work in the 1930s, and the two boys had shared a bed till Ken was 11. It was an extraordinary story, unimaginable in the 21st century.

With the Journeymen touring Norfolk in late May, I took the opportunity to meet up with Ken, and he gave me plenty for a two-page feature. He told me about his elementary school headmaster who, with no key-stage tests or national curriculum, was determined to find and develop a talent in every boy. One term, with 120 children, they had 100% attendance.

Ken's multiple talents were not always appreciated. Brian Sellers, the Yorkshire chairman, said he would never play for the county again if he did not shave off the artist's beard he returned with one summer, and Bill Shankly, his Huddersfield manager, told him that cricket was "a lassie's game". But, a quiet man, Ken was happy to have so many options. "If I didn't get any runs," he said, "I would think, 'I'll be back playing football soon,' and that made it easier for me."

The idea of working together on a book, combining his story with his art work, appealed to me, and Ken was keen. As a result of the two books he had illustrated for me, Harper Collins had employed him to produce 20-odd drawings for a book called *Botham's Century* and, though this was a best-selling title by a major publishing house, he had been paid only a small fraction of what he had earned from my books. Not only that but, rather than make a feature of the drawings being by a Test cricketer, he was acknowledged with just four words, 'Illustrations by Ken Taylor', in a small font on page 4, between the ISBN and the printer's details. Another book with me, showcasing his art work, was a much more appealing proposition.

I had just finished the Wimbledon book, which had brought home to me the advantages of laying out the material in self-contained doube-page spreads. In Ken's case there would be the added attraction of being able to bounce the words and pictures off each other – so that his memories of Fred Trueman and Denis Law could sit opposite his portraits of them. It had to be printed in colour, of course, and that created fresh challenges, but by this time we were using Bath Press, the ancient printing firm, and they had a most helpful pre-press man, Alan Stedman, for whom nothing was too much trouble. On one occasion he spent ages restoring the red glow of an electric fire in the image of a life study Ken had painted while at The Slade.

Ken was not like Bob Appleyard. There was no point in my interviewing him systematically about a season; he did not think like that. He had an artistic mind, drifting about, and the trick was to spend plenty of time with him and to wait for the gems to emerge.

"Fred Trueman wasn't a bad footballer," he said over tea one day. "In a rugged sort of way. Occasionally the Yorkshire team would play a football match, and Fred liked to play centre-forward. But then so did Closey. And neither of them had any idea of passing the ball. We needed three footballs: one for Fred, one for Closey and one for the other twenty of us."

"That's going in the book," I said, reaching for a piece of paper.

Another day, in a casual remark, he threw a revealing light on the mental strain of being a professional batsman. "I often used to dream about going out to bat with a golf club. I'd take guard, and I'd look down and think, 'Christ, what am I going to do with this?'"

Ken was an easy person to be with. He had left the world of sport behind, and he looked back at it with a wry humour. He was quick to emphasise how much luck there was in it all, and his memories were endearingly full of disasters. He had hit 160 against the Australians and scored five goals against West Ham. But I was much more likely to hear about the bad shots and the goal-line disasters.

> I was trying to cut an off-spinner. I don't know what made me do it. You should never cut an off-spinner in your whole life ... Both Ron Staniforth and I had got back onto the line, ready to head it away, and Jack staggered back and knocked us both into the back of the net. I can still see that ball coming down. All three of us were lying on the ground, watching it.

He had known at close quarters some of the great sporting names of his era – Denis Law and Fred Trueman, Bill Shankly and Brian Close, Ray Wilson and Geoff Boycott – and he spoke about them all in an uncomplicated, down-to-earth way. There was a bit of the amateur about Ken, not in the sense of social class, far from it, but from the way he pursued his various interests. He enjoyed the games he played, but he never saw them as his life's work.

So many people – from Michael Parkinson to Jim Swanton, from Ray Wilson to John Arlott – thought he was a sporting under-achiever, but he never seemed bothered by that thought. "I might have done better," he said, "if I hadn't done so many things. But I've been a very lucky man. I've had to work hard, but I've always enjoyed what I've done. So it's never felt like work."

I visited Ray Wilson, left-back in England's World Cup winning side. He had started at Huddersfield Town on the same day as Ken, and it was fascinating to see how a combination of luck and character had caused their paths to diverge.

Ken was a young prodigy, in the first team at 18, but Ray was about to be released when at a training session he was asked to have a go in the left-back position. To Ken, that proved how much luck there was in sport.

Ray had come from a hard night-time job, repairing wagons for the railway at Shirebrook Pit near Mansfield, and he was determined to be a successful footballer. Ken had his cricket and his art, and he was happy to enjoy the mix rather than to strive hard to reach the top. To Ray, that proved the importance of character and motivation.

Ray sat in the kitchen of his remote house on the moors north of Huddersfield. He was a reclusive man, but he came to life as he told his stories. There was one in particular that chimed with my own experience of Ken:

Ken was a dreamer. I remember a year when we were sitting near to the danger zone in Division Two. And one Friday we all had to go into the board room for a talk. We were all sat around the table, and we had this talk about the game the next day. I can't remember who we were playing. It might have been Leyton Orient. 'It's imperative that we win this game ... A great club like Huddersfield ... If we can't beat Leyton Orient ... If we go down to the third division and Leyton stay up ...' On and on it went, and I looked across at Ken. It was obvious his mind was wandering. 'You've got to do this to Leyton Orient and that to Leyton Orient.' I think Ken was looking out of the window at one point. Then eventually, when it ended and we all got up and left the room, I was walking along and Ken caught up with me. 'Who do we play tomorrow?' he said.

I went to stay with Ken's brother Jeff in Scholes in 'Last of the Summer Wine' country. He had retired as Professor of Music at the Glasgow Academy, but top opera singers were still visiting him for coaching before taking on major roles. He was a different personality from Ken, much more forthright, and he gave me plenty for the book. In the early 1970s he had given a radio talk on the Third Programme about the connections between football and singing. It began with Maria Callas singing 'Qui La Voce' from Bellini's *I Puritani*, followed by commentary on a Bobby Charlton goal in the 1966 World Cup. Then he went on to describe the physicality of both activities and the need for the self-discipline that would allow both Callas and Charlton to express themselves fully.

Jeff gave me a tape of the talk. I thought it would work well if I printed it on the left-hand side of a spread and had Ken's views on art and sport on the right. I rang Ken with the idea, and he promised to give the subject some thought and come back to me.

He rang three days later. "I'm sorry," he said gloomily. "I can't think of anything at all to say." I might have abandoned the idea, but I thought I would have a shot at getting him talking, see if I could squeeze anything of any use out of him. Within minutes, and so typically of Ken, he was saying the most wonderful things.

"You're at your best," he said of his art, "when you get beyond thinking, when your concentration is so great that the line just flows. You feel as if you're in another dimension ... It's the same with sport. You have to be completely wrapped up in what you're doing at that moment. There were times when I batted when I could feel that something else had taken over and I could play shots without thinking ... In football I was a defender, but it was still all about timing: reading the game, knowing where the other players were, timing your tackle and playing the ball away. You lose yourself in the concentration, and unconsciously you find yourself making the right decision."

He talked of his school pupils in Norfolk. "You can tell the ones with a bit extra, because of their concentration. The ones who are fiddling about, dropping their pencils, talking, they may have talent, but they won't get to that point where their work flows."

He went on to apply his thinking to the players of his day. Denis Law, George Best, Garry Sobers, they all had in abundance the ability to lose themselves. Brian Close did not, however; he could be distracted. And Geoff Boycott, he had the concentration but "he didn't let himself go into that other dimension; he was conscious all the time."

I thought it was the best page of text in the book. It said so much about Ken, and it made you think about everything in your own life. And it was extra special for me because I knew how nearly it never happened.

The book was launched in the spring of 2006, at Ottakar's Bookshop in the centre of Huddersfield. Ken had just come out of hospital with a replacement ankle, and he hobbled into the shop on crutches with a great pod on his foot. Two of Ken's friends from primary school turned up, chuffed to find themselves in a photograph in the book, and Ray Wilson was there, complaining about the pressure he was under to attend 'Forty Years On' events ahead of that year's World Cup. "They ring up, saying all the others are going; you don't feel you can say no."

My Journeymen friend John, cousin of Johnny Wardle, came with his elderly mother. "Look at them all," she said as the queue formed for Ken to sign books. "They're like little boys with their Christmas presents."

John wrote a review in the left-wing paper *Tribune*: 'This is Chalke's latest book to paint the post-war world through the eyes of its quiet sporting heroes … His work echoes that of CAMRA, when real ale was in danger. In Ken Taylor we have another recruit for Chalke's campaign for real people.'

Ken and I spoke at several cricket societies, and he exhibited his art in the Long Room at Headingley. Sue and I also drove to north Norfolk and back in a day, for an evening at the bookshop in Holt. The Norwich-based author DJ Taylor had written a fascinating, little book called *On The Corinthian Spirit*, about the way the word 'amateur' had declined during the twentieth century: from being 'someone who did what he did for the sheer love of doing it' to 'someone who was second-rate and incompetent'. 'Meet The Two Taylors', the evening was called, with me chairing the discussion.

What a challenge it was! On my right I had David Taylor, who spoke at high speed, his mind spinning with intellectual ideas that belonged in the world of books and language. On my left was Ken, cheerfully telling down-to-earth stories about the people and events of his own life. They were both talking about sport, but somehow their worlds seemed to have nothing in common. We were meeting the two Taylors, but they were not meeting each other.

The growth of the universities has had such an impact on our culture. I have always been grateful to Hazel for the way she knocked the academic pretensions out of us at the evening class: "You can chuck that out. Nobody's going to wade through all that. That's how they teach you to write in universities."

Hazel would have approved of the letter I received from a sports sociologist in Belfast. 'As an evocation of sporting memory,' he wrote, 'your work says far more than most of the jargon-laden texts that I'm obliged to read.'

I thought David Taylor's book was a little gem, elegantly written and not jargon-laden, but I struggled as chairman not to show my preference for listening to Ken.

*

I would love to have worked with Ken again. At one stage we were going to put together a book on Norfolk churches, with his artwork, but it never happened. And now he is starting to struggle with his memory, with all that heading of the old leather footballs taking its toll.

In 2014 an old friend from his youth, Anne Denham, a Liberal Democrat councillor in Huddersfield, organised an exhibition of Ken's art at the town's Tolson Museum. Ken worked hard for it, producing a series of some twenty large paintings of the long-gone mill buildings of the old Huddersfield. Displayed around the staircase and on the upper gallery, they were magnificent.

One of them, a long landscape of smoking chimneys, was exhibited in the art gallery in the town centre, and it was stunning, by far the most striking picture in the room. Ken's landscapes are not comforting chocolate-box images. There is a real confidence of brush stroke and a gritty realism. That was what won him a place at The Slade, where William Coldstream, the Professor of Art, was a member of the Euston Road school of painters, wanting to turn art away from the abstract that was so fashionable in the 1930s to a depiction of real-life urban scenes.

For Ken's book I interviewed Harry Riley, a fellow Slade student who has gone on to have great success as a portrait artist, commissioned by – among others – three popes, two American presidents and Nelson Mandela. "I've always respected Ken's art hugely," he said. "He's got a fine eye, and he'd got everything technically. I know William Coldstream admired him greatly as an artist. He had the ability to say a lot of things. But his obsession was with the sport."

I am sure this was true but, in comparing their differing fortunes, it was also true that Ken had none of Harry's commercial acumen. He was much too happy to bob along in his own little world.

Ken asked me to be the speaker at the Tolson Museum when the exhibition was opened, and the evening went well. But, for me, the really special evening of the trip was the previous night when Ken, his wife Avril and I stayed with Anne Denham and her husband in their house on the outskirts of Almondbury, with its open view over rolling hills. They invited to supper another couple, the man a film-maker whose career had lost its momentum when he went to Australia for a while in the 1960s. All six of them had been friends in the youth clubs of the 1950s, where they played jazz music and were full of the new ideas of the post-war world. Over a delicious lasagne we got to talking politics and, though I was younger than all of them, I felt at home in their company.

At one point I tried to articulate my own thoughts about the world in which they had grown up, about the vibrant working-class communities that were centred around chapels, choral societies, sporting clubs, trade unions and more. Social mobility has sucked so much of the strength from those communities and, with the industrial base destroyed, those that are left – though they might have more money, more home comforts – have lost most of that old collective pride.

It is a dangerous argument. If you phrase it wrongly, it sounds like you are against social mobility, wanting the cream of the working class to be kept down at the bottom of society like it used to be, but somehow that night, in that company, it came out right. Avril was so intrigued by it that she asked me to repeat it all.

Among the friends in their youth club was Brian Jackson, author of *Education and the Working Class*, one of the pioneers of the Open University. At The Slade with Ken was David Storey, the rugby league player who wrote *This Sporting Life*, the best novel ever written about sport. Such a burst of energy and creativity emerged out of the world of their youth. And there in the middle of it all was Ken, with so much talent yet so unassuming. If you met him and you did not know, you would never guess the half of it.

Because of its visual quality and because of the wry, self-effacing honesty of his contributions, I often think my book with Ken was my best.

19

Memories are made of what?

I have always been captivated by the reminiscences of the elderly. They bring alive whole worlds of people and places and conversations, and there is always this extra poignancy that you know that soon they will be lost.

My father was no raconteur at all. I would ask him about his time as a stretcher-bearer in the trenches of the First World War, and he made it all seem so dull. By contrast, my mother brought everything in her past alive. She had played the leading role in a school play, knowing every line of every member of the cast, and in one scene she had to kick off her shoe so that it flew across the stage. There was nothing special about the story, but she made it so vivid that I never tired of hearing it. I could sense the young girl in her, full of excitement, before life's disappointments quietened her down.

Being sent to boarding school at thirteen was a great shock, the most traumatic time of my life, and I coped to some extent by developing a sense of humour, particularly when it came to observing the masters. I would bump into one of them somewhere in the school grounds, he would say something slightly bizarre, and by the time I got back to the house I would have found a way of entertaining the others with it. My friend Mike did the same, though he had a richer imagination than me. We told the stories over and over, to the point that on one occasion I found him telling one of mine as if it were his. "Hold on," I said. "That happened to me, not you." But he was adamant, and I could tell that he believed it. Somehow, in his imaginative memory, my experience had become his.

We had a scheme called Personal Service which I organised. We would cycle to the nearby town and visit old people who needed help: gardening or decorating or just someone to talk to. I remember a lady called Mrs Drew who lived by a smallholding, where chickens wandered about the yard. After we had done some practical jobs for her, she would sit us around a little table in a cramped room and tell us wonderfully amusing stories from her childhood in the 1890s. We loved visiting her.

Others were not so cheerful. There was a Mrs Fripp; I discovered later that her grandson played guitar with the progressive rock group King Crimson. Every visit she would describe to us in gruesome detail her brain tumour. Then there was Miss Pinhorn, Ivy Mabel Violet Pinhorn, who was a Miss

Havisham-like figure, with a wispy beard, living on her own in a house that was not only a mess but smelled terribly. Our job was to paint her hallway, and we took a can of air freshener with us each time. "This paint smells lovely," she would say.

We were teenage boys, half wanting to help her, half wanting to have fun. On one occasion, rifling through her personal belongings, we found a large batch of love letters, sent from the Isle of Wight before the First World War.

"When you've finished the painting," she said, "I'm going to bake a cake and we'll have a tea party." When the day came, as I feared would happen, the others all made excuses, and I cycled there alone. Miss Pinhorn and I sat down formally at the cluttered, unclean dining table and, sensing her disappointment, I tucked into two extra-large slices of her rich sponge cake. Then back at school I vomited violently and spent two days in the sick bay.

In my short stint as an English teacher in the early 1970s, I set up a class project in which the pupils would visit old people to learn about their area's history. I collected some names from social services and called on them all. One woman was outstanding, telling me how the area, in the north of London, had been a separate village when she had been a child. She had recall of so much detail, and I sat there entranced from four o'clock till after six. Unfortunately, when the pupils arrived a few days later, she sent them packing with short shrift: "I've already told all this to your teacher."

I worked for a while in adult literacy, where one of our techniques was to help the students to write down their life stories. That involved teasing out memories, which I loved doing. Some were immigrants, who enjoyed reliving the cultures of their early years.

I love the reminiscences of the famous, too. Late in the 1970s there was a series of radio programmes in which the actor John Gielgud talked about his life. He had the lot: a good memory with plenty of visual detail, a sharp eye for the oddities of his fellow thespians and a wicked sense of humour in telling the stories. One I have never forgotten was of him as a young man playing Osvald in Ibsen's *Ghosts*, in the scene where it starts to dawn on him that he has inherited syphilis. His mother, Mrs Alving, was being played by Mrs Patrick Campbell, a grand old dame who, despite having put on weight and lost her beauty, still had to be the centre of attention. Just as Gielgud was delivering the crucial line, she said in a loud aside, "Oh, I am so hungry."

There was a compelling series of programmes on Channel 4, in which Mike Brearley sat with John Arlott across a table. There was much coughing and spluttering, much reaching for another glass of red wine, as Arlott, through a great fog, reflected on his life. There were so many subjects covered – the gentleness of Jack Hobbs, the cruel sacking of Alf Ramsey, a fight in a railway carriage, his time as a mental hospital nurse, the supreme loneliness of the opening batsman – and always there was this melancholic humanity running through it all. The effect was mesmerising.

More recently, there have been several series on Radio 4 in which Peter Hennessy has interviewed retired politicians. At the other end of the spectrum from Jeremy Paxman's impatient cross-examinations, he has treated his subjects with respect and, in a relaxed atmosphere, allowed the listener to get close to them. I loved one story Shirley Williams told, from her youth, about a meeting of East Anglian ladies at which Clement Attlee droned on about China for an eternity. By chance she had been given an emotional poem about the East London poor that Attlee had written in 1912, and she got up and read it. It showed the beating heart of the man beneath the matter-of-fact exterior, and the hall was in rapture. Afterwards, the chairman introduced her to Attlee – "and all he did was look at me and say, '1911, actually.'"

I also loved a book in which Thomas Grant, a barrister, sat down with Jeremy Hutchinson, the eminent QC and one-time husband of Peggy Ashcroft. Hutchinson was in his late nineties, but he offered lucid insights into some of the great cases in which he had been involved, among them *Lady Chatterley's Lover*, Christine Keeler, the art faker Tom Keating and the spy George Blake. It was not only compelling to read but of considerable historical value.

When I think about all this, it seems almost inevitable that I should have finished up doing what I do. In fact, I started out on the road, most briefly, in my last term at school when I contributed to the school magazine an interview-based profile of an elderly member of the domestic staff, Sam Wolstenhulme. I have just found it at the bottom of a drawer, and I am struck how little my writing style has changed. The piece has a nice mix of respectful sympathy and humour, all the better for being about a man whom many of the boys would have ignored, even looked down on.

*

Ken Biddulph paid me a great compliment when he said, "You always get me remembering so much." I did not think a lot about it at the time, but others have said it since so I have come to realise that there must be something in it.

There are no great tricks. You need to be a good listener, not to keep butting in. You need to be patient, not to create a sense of hurry. You need to show respect and sympathy, not to be judgemental. And, above all, you need to be interested – genuinely interested.

It does not always work. I once drove 125 miles for an interview for one of my magazine articles, and my host never turned off the television. He told me enough for me to write an article, but in that atmosphere, half-watching a basketball match on Sky, I could not get him in the mood to open up.

Cricket in the family

(above) Scoring, with my brother Andrew operating the board, at Fenner's, Cambridge.

(left) Martha, at the non-striker's end, doing what I never did: batting on a Test match ground, Edgbaston. One of only two girls on Finals Day of the Primary School National Softball Competition, 1994.

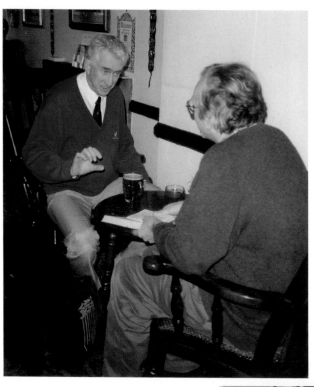

This page
(above) Ken Biddulph reminisces over a pint, *(right)* Geoffrey Howard over a cup of coffee.

Opposite page
(top) With Bomber Wells at the Cheltenham Cricket Festival, *(bottom, left)* Cotswold forester Charlie Light, *(bottom, right)* Bomber with the Journeymen at the Brasenose College ground, Oxford.

With Bob Appleyard, watching cricket at Park Avenue, Bradford.

Ken Taylor at work in his studio and *(below)* his landscape of old Huddersfield.

(top) Anthony Gibson *(left)* receives the MCC/Cricket Society Book of the Year award from John Barclay, winner the previous year. *(bottom left)* Mark Wagh writes his diary of the season in the dressing room and *(right)* David Foot at home.

(top) Tom Cartwright's last bowl, during Bob Barber's 70th birthday match.
(bottom) 'Seven minutes of fame': being interviewed by Helen Castor for
Radio 4's *Making History* at the Ageas Bowl, Southampton.

LIFE BEYOND THE AIRING CUPBOARD

John Barclay
foreword by Mike Atherton

Team Mates

Edited by John Barclay and Stephen Chalke

Charles Palmer's painting of his own innings against the 1948 Australians at Worcester, Renira Barclay's portrait of her husband John's prep-school ritual in the airing cupboard and Susanna Kendall's drawing for the charity book *Team Mates*.

Worse was a 450-mile round trip to the north to interview a man about his famous father. He had previously had a bad experience with a journalist, and initially that made him reluctant to open up. But, even when I put him at his ease and he tried for me, he could not remember much of value. After three hours I left with little more sense of his father than when I arrrived.

However much you try to make yourself a neutral figure, there is always a personal chemistry and, when that clicks, you are away. A person where that happened straightaway was Alan Townsend, who came down from County Durham to play for Warwickshire after the war. The purpose of my visit was to talk about Tom Cartwright, but Alan warmed so much to my company that he went on to talk about all sorts. In particular, he relived an extraordinary day in his childhood, one that he admitted still gave him nightmares seventy years on.

It was the summer of 1934, he was twelve years old, and at close of play on the Saturday of the Headingley Test Bradman was on 271 not out, with all the world wondering if the Don would pass Hammond's Test record of 336. Alan's father asked him if he would like to go with him on the Monday, and he said yes with little understanding of what this would involve. Setting out before six o'clock on a bike with no gears, he cycled 65 miles from Middlesbrough to Leeds, arriving at the ground too late to get a seat. They stood for hours on a hot, sultry day and, shortly after they set off for home, the weather broke.

Sitting with me, he seemed to be reliving every minute of the horror.

> I never want to go through that journey again. I'm sure it did me mentally. I'd been standing all day in the heat. And somewhere – I can't remember where we'd got to – this thunderstorm came and it absolutely belted down. It was so dark and lonely on the road; we never saw a soul. Just miles and miles of blackness. And Dad kept saying to me, "Keep going, lad, keep going." I'm sure I was asleep. I was that wet and miserable, really soaking, fed up and tired with the heat ... "We're not far off Thirsk," he said. "If we get into Thirsk by midnight, we'll catch the fish and chip shop open. And I'll buy you some fish and chips and a bottle of pop." I suppose it was a spur to keep me going ... There was a big clock in the square and, sure enough, just before midnight, my dad and I got there and we bought some fish and chips ... The hardest part of it was the loneliness. There were no cars in those days, not after night time. We just cycled along, with our capes over the handlebars. It was well after two o'clock when we finally got home ... In those days, as a kid, you accepted things as they were, but now I look back and it frightens me to think about it.

Entirely unplanned, a short chat about Tom Cartwright had yielded a double-page spread in the *Wisden Cricketer*, one of the best pieces I wrote for the magazine.

*

Trust is a crucial part of the relationship. It works best if the person talks freely and trusts me to judge what should and should not go in the book. In that respect it is like psychotherapy. If you do not trust the therapist, if you hold back, then it does not work.

I have been told a lot of things that I have not put into print. At one extreme there was Bomber Wells telling me about the team-mate who only sat down on the loo once a week. "And when he did, by Christ, the smell! We all used to clear the pavilion." At the other end, one subject told me that he suspected that his father's death had been murder. He did not want to include this and, as it happened relatively late in his life and threw no great light on anything, I agreed not to do so. Part of the trust I establish is based on the assurance that I will not put into print anything they ask me not to.

The line marking what is acceptable to put in the public domain shifts with each generation, and I try to respect that. Usually my judgement is good, but I have occasionally been surprised. A former bowler told me of a time when he got Ted Dexter out. First ball the great England batsman, a superb player of pace, played and missed a leg-break; then next ball he was bowled through the gate by a googly. "They talk about another Wally Hammond," the umpire, a broad northerner, exclaimed. "Bloody hellfire!"

It was a whimsical little tale that was just about worth including in the article, but the bowler struck it out. "That's dressing-room talk," he said. "I don't want that in print."

*

Memory is not always a reliable window into the past.

I read an article in the *New Scientist* that compared a memory with a piece of string. Every time you pick it up, you put it down in a different shape so that, over time and with repeated picking up, it changes. In extreme cases, where strong emotions come into play, people can even come to believe in past experiences that never happened to them at all.

A friend sent me an extract from a legal judgment on a 2013 commercial case by Sir George Leggatt. In it he elaborated this 'string' theory, referring to 'a faulty model of memory as a mental record which is fixed at the time of experience of an event and then fades (more or less slowly) over time. In fact, psychological research has demonstrated that memories are fluid and malleable, being constantly rewritten whenever they are retrieved.' A subsequent paragraph focused on the especial unreliability 'when it comes to recalling past beliefs. Our memories of past beliefs are revised to make them more consistent with our present beliefs.'

Cricket has an army of statisticians who will be quick to point out where a memory is at odds with the printed facts: "He was stumped, not bowled" or "He never played against Tyson." They used to drive Bomber Wells bonkers, especially when he was in a wheelchair and could not walk away from them. He would be halfway through a lovely story, and somebody would fish out a book and be contradicting him before he had finished it.

He knew the tales he told were not accurate; that was not the point of them. That was why I structured his book in the way I did, with him sitting at the boundary's edge, telling his stories to a gathering, as he often did. That way I did not have to do more than say, 'These are his stories. Enjoy them.'

Bomber belonged in an older tradition of oral story-telling, the sort of story-telling that created the Bible, and that tradition does not sit well with our age of information. Five loaves and two fishes feeding a crowd of five thousand? There would be statisticians and investigative journalists crawling all over the story.

Bomber told a story that his first coach at Gloucestershire, Charlie Parker, had told him about bowling to Ranjitsinhji. "Ranji kept glancing him to leg. That was his shot, wasn't it? So Charlie went up to the captain – an amateur, Champain, I think – and he said, 'Excuse me, sir, do you think I could move second slip onto the leg-side to stop him doing that?' And Champain looked at him: 'Good God, man, are you trying to spoil the game?'"

I tried to look it up. I only found one game when Parker bowled to Ranji, and Ranji did not make many runs. What is more, Champain, though he was playing, was not the captain. But that was missing the point of the story. It was not about filling in exact words spoken by exact people on exact dates. Bomber was no fool; he knew that. It was about shining a light on what the world of cricket was like in those days – and, of course, making you laugh. "It's easy to make people sad," he used to say. "It's harder to make them laugh."

Bomber was a one-off, though. In my other books I place the memories in the speech of the old cricketers, so the reader can assess them how they will. At the same time I try to ensure that what is being said is consistent with known facts so that the reader can have a reasonable expectation that it is broadly true – though, when conversation is recalled, nobody will assume that the words of the conversation will be exact, just the gist of them.

Dickie Bird's autobiography remains the best-selling cricket book of all time, but it would not have done nearly as well if I had edited and published it. It is a great read, especially for that outer rim of people who quite like cricket but do not follow it closely; it is full of good stories, full of fun, with

Dickie's loveable personality running right through it. The problem for the hardcore cricket lover, though, is that you can look up the games and find that a lot of the stories cannot have happened.

One option is to let the subject tell his story as he remembers it, then point out in the following text that it is not quite right. I have seen that done in books. My own preference is to go back to the subject and say, "We've got a problem. Can you think about this again? Are you sure it was at Yeovil?"

Apart from the straightforward misremembering of details, there are two sources of distortion that I look out for. One is when people have reshaped past events to justify their own actions or to cope with something that would otherwise sit unpleasantly in their mind. That is tricky territory. I think I have a good nose for self-justification and score-settling, I try to create a relationship in which people do not feel the need to do that, but sometimes it is all so long ago that the person is no longer aware that the memory has been reshaped.

The other distortion occurs with people who have done a lot of after-dinner speaking. Looking to entertain, they have turned events into funny stories, often rolling two or three separate occasions into one, usually adding amusing embellishments. Some will retain an awareness of the original or, at least, know they are fictionalising – but there are others for whom the oft-told story, like the piece of string, has become the memory. My friend Mike at school was like that. He had a good imagination and he lived the stories fully while, in contrast, I had a stultifying streak of Methodism, with an omnipresent God demanding that I tell the unvarnished truth. Maybe that is why he became a successful theatre director, and I went into education.

The Glamorgan cricketer Peter Walker asked me to publish an autobiography he had written. His next-door neighbour had pulled out so I inherited the project at a late stage, which is never ideal. The designer I was using at the time did not help by passing as fit for purpose the scanned images Peter supplied. It was only when we went into a reprint and I had them all rescanned that I discovered that the long blur at the top of a photo of Peter and his father at the quayside in Durban was neither the horizon nor a passing ship but a strip of sellotape. It made me deeply ashamed of my work.

Peter had a fund of wonderful stories, especially from his life away from cricket. Growing up in South Africa, he had run away to sea at the age of sixteen, and his tales of his maritime adventures – nearly murdered while passing through the Suez Canal, penniless on the streets of New York, improving his catching skills by throwing potatoes back and forth with a Dutch fellow crewman – were as lively as anything I had published.

After cricket he went into television, first as a frontman for BBC's Sunday League coverage, then with his own Cardiff-based company, and again the stories tumbled out: a disastrous sequence of events when his company was covering a Test series in the Caribbean and, best of all, the story of a documentary in post-apartheid South Africa where his team drove down a dusty track in search of an interview with the far-right Afrikaner Party leader Eugene Terreblanche. Peter had a terrific turn of phrase, and he relished the tale as he told it:

> There were some dozen men and a few women leaning against the open-air bar. As I approached they oozed suspicion and hostility of such intensity one could almost touch it. Dusting off my rudimentary schoolboy Afrikaans, I explained that we were a television crew from Wales, not England – always a good opening gambit, this, when confronted by any group who were mentally still fighting the Boer War in 1900 – and that we were hoping to interview Commandant Terreblanche. They lightened up at my attempt to speak their language and visibly thawed, particularly when I invited them all to have a drink while they phoned ahead to see if Terreblanche would see us.
>
> As their confidence in us grew, I thought to myself, "A few quick interviews with this bunch should be interesting! I can just imagine what they think about the prospect of living under black rule." I explained what we'd like to do and that, although Emyr would ask his questions in English, if they so wished, I was happy to record their replies in Afrikaans and, when we did the editing, we'd sub-title these in Welsh. Some decided they had good enough English to respond but, when a typically bull-necked, thickset man stood in front of our camera, he launched off in a tirade in Afrikaans against 'uitlanders' (foreigners) and in particular the overseas media, who were misrepresenting his country and in the process destroying his way of life.
>
> Emyr was standing alongside cameraman Dean so our interviewee was looking virtually straight at the camera lens. Sound recordist Eddie, too, had no idea of what our interviewee was saying. I did. His final words were chilling: "Die erste kaffir dat sy kop or my grond sit, sal ek hom dood skiet!" (The first black who puts his head over my land, I'll shoot him dead!) Midway through this sentence he had reached into his jacket pocket, pulled out a revolver and, to emphasise what he meant, pointed it directly at the lens!

Both Emyr and Dean must have thought they were about to be shot but, to their credit, stood their ground and Dean kept the camera rolling. Slowly, ever so slowly the gun was returned to its holster, unfired.

I was excited to be publishing something that was written in such a lively style. The cricket pages were not as colourful, but the mix, reflected in the title *It's Not Just Cricket*, was good. The only problem developed when I found myself clashing with him on some of the factual details. He had the order of the islands wrong in his superbly comic tale of their attempt to film the Test series in the Caribbean, and he refused to accept it, even at one point insisting that both *Wisden* and *The Times* had got it wrong. "Don't forget, I was there," he kept telling me.

The text was agreed eventually. I suspect it would have been an easier ride if we had worked together from the beginning.

*

At this stage I had worked on books with five individuals: Bomber Wells, Geoffrey Howard, Keith Andrew, Bob Appleyard and Ken Taylor. Each had his strengths as a collaborator, and my task was always to find the right way to write to those strengths.

There were five key attributes I looked for in each subject: memory, articulateness, an interesting life, emotional honesty and a distinctive point of view. A sense of humour, too, but that was a bonus.

Bomber certainly had a distinctive point of view – "Doesn't he have a lot of opinions?" Geoffrey said when he gave me back the book – and he had a rich turn of phrase and vocabulary, reflecting a good ear and an intelligence unspoilt by too much education.

Geoffrey opened his heart as much as any of them, his long and varied life gave him an awareness of so much history, and he was highly articulate, though in a different way from Bomber, forming beautifully constructed sentences when he spoke.

Keith had warmth and strong opinions and could come up with some delightful ways of putting things; Bob had the most interesting life story, he was more open emotionally than I expected him to be, his memory was sharp, and he spoke well. Ken was engagingly honest, had a rich story, some refreshing idioms of speech and, of course, what he lacked in memory he more than compensated for with his art work.

The person who came closest to having all these attributes – an exceptional memory, an engaging story, a surprisingly good turn of phrase almost poetic at times, a willingness to express his feelings, a wry humour and, above all, plenty of challenging things to say – was my next subject. Tom Cartwright.

20

The way it was

By the end of 2006, my tenth year of writing and publishing, we had produced 16 books, four in 2006 alone, with my offering on Tom Cartwright scheduled for early in 2007. *Runs in the Memory* and *No Coward Soul* were the stand-out successes, each selling more than 4,000 copies, but all the others had made a reasonable profit.

I wrote a monthly column, now called *The Way It Was*, for *The Wisden Cricketer*, and I contributed two sets of five articles to *The Times* on famous Ashes victories. I was also developing a new line, as an obituarist, after John Stern had given me a real shock by asking me to take on the *Wisden Cricketer*'s tributes to David Sheppard and Fred Trueman. Into my late fifties, I was still playing plenty of cricket – twice, to my astonishment, topping the Journeymen bowling averages – and I was giving talks here, there and everywhere.

It was my most creative time, and I cut back my lecturing, retaining only my work with the Open University, to focus more on it all. None of it paid as well as the lecturing, of course, and my tax returns made pitiful reading, but we had paid off our mortgage, Martha had graduated and left home, and I was carried forward by a strong sense that I was 'going places'.

The subjects for my monthly column were left to me to choose, and I liked it that way. Sometimes I could find a way to put a piece together from material I had already gathered. One that I have always liked focused on the Somerset-Yorkshire match of May 1954, when for the first time the newly recruited Ken Biddulph walked through the gates as a Somerset cricketer ("Don't you ever refuse a boy an autograph"), when Harold Gimblett, crippled by stress, left in mid-match, never to return, and when Bob Appleyard came back after two years out with TB, taking 12 wickets. 'A beginning, an end and an extraordinary return. Three lives meeting in one match.'

More often, I travelled the country in search of fresh stories, just as I had done for my first books. Geoffrey Howard had given me some letters that George Duckworth, his baggage man/scorer in Australia, had sent him from the next tour, and one of said how, needing to summon another spinner, they had opted for Hampshire's Peter Sainsbury, only to change their mind overnight and send for Gloucestershire's John Mortimore. Peter had coached Andrew and me as boys, and I drove to Southampton to show him the letter. "To think I got that close," he said. "Between going to bed and getting up. I'd like a copy of that letter for my family. You've made my life!"

A trip to Torquay to see the reclusive Stan Cray, hoping that he would tell me about the Essex team of the 1940s, ended up with a piece about a wartime match in Bombay which took him a hair-raising 12-day journey to reach from his posting on the Imphal plain in Assam: "We were 6,000 feet up, and every time we came to a sharp corner our Indian driver just put his foot down. When I looked down the mountain side, I could see all these vehicles that had gone over the edge."

He was a lifelong bachelor, living in an almost hermetically sealed flat, the joy of his life a top-quality stereo system and a large collection of jazz and classical records. He sat me in an armchair with an antimacassar on the headrest and matching cloths on the arms, and whenever I got up he rushed to tidy and straighten them. It gave me such a feeling that I was intruding but also – more romantically – that I had chanced on a gem of history that would otherwise have been lost. When he died, only four people attended his funeral.

I interviewed the last two men alive who had played county cricket in the 1920s. Frank Shipston, a Nottinghamshire professional, was living with his son, himself now a pensioner, hoping soon to go to sleep one night and not wake up, while Michael Spurway, a Somerset amateur, was bedridden at home, with a daughter and carers to support him. "Come at twelve o'clock," he said. "That's gin-and-tonic time." I noticed when I arrived that he had nearly completed that day's *Times* crossword.

I interviewed Geoff Edrich about his time as a Japanese prisoner-of-war, about the way it formed his character as a cricketer: "A lot of the boys died of a broken heart. They couldn't see the end. There was one march, when we moved camp, maybe 20 miles, when some of us were ready to pack in. And if you dropped out, that was it – you got a bayonet through you from the guards. But 'Keep going,' my friend Dick Steward said. You had to have one or two decent chaps with you to get through. That's probably what made me feel that to have success at cricket, you've got to have team spirit."

He had not talked about it for many years, he said, and now his memory was starting to fade. The bravest of men, he told me that he had cancer of the throat and had not eaten a solid for eight years. I only had 750 words, but I wrote up his story more fully in a later book of essays, *A Long Half Hour*.

I interviewed Lord Wigram, who in 1934 had played – and top-scored – for the North of Scotland against the touring Australians. His father had been Private Secretary to King George V and, away from the cricket, he threw light on all manner of subjects: how the King had liked Ramsay MacDonald, how his father had persuaded the King to be seen not just at horse racing but at the Cup Final, Lord's and Wimbledon and how his father-in-law had invented snooker while stationed in India.

I met Jim Laker's widow and Hedley Verity's son, both of whom shared fascinating insights with me. I talked with Alan Castell and Bill Bridge, two spin bowlers who, after glittering starts, lost their actions completely. I asked Julien Cahn's son about his wealthy father's private team, an extraordinary story that inspired Cahn's granddaughter Miranda to write a full-length biography of him.

I took the opportunity to renew my acquaintance with Peter Wight, who had coached Martha. He had moved to Ross-on-Wye to be near his daughter, and I got him to tell me the story of his life, how as a 20-year-old wanting to study engineering he had caught a boat out of British Guiana in early 1951. Dressed only in light clothes, he was a frail, shivering figure when he got to his destination in Lancashire. The landlady, where he was taken for lodgings, was full up, but "We'll have him," she said. "He looks pathetic."

I visited his Somerset team-mate Graham Atkinson who spoke glowingly of his batting: "There was always a lovely ring to his bat. He seemed to middle the ball so well. If he'd gone out with an old chair leg, there'd still have been a nice ring to it." Peter was very happy with what I wrote – until one evening he rang me in distress. His brother Arnold in Canada had seen the article, thought it was an obituary and fallen into a depression. Peter had reassured him on the phone, but the depression had not lifted.

I got myself invited in September 2005 to the 70th birthday party of the former England cricketer Bob Barber. It took the form of a cricket match at Broadhalfpenny Down, the ground in Hampshire where the game enjoyed its first years of glory in the 1770s. The West Indian Lance Gibbs flew in from Miami, Yorkshire's Jimmy Binks from California and Bob's university friend Aizaz Fakir from Karachi. There were four England captains, three chairmen of selectors and a host of stalwarts from the cricket of my youth, some watching, many playing. Even Bomber in his wheelchair was there – "Do come and add a little class to our day," Bob had written to him.

"I've never played here," Tom Cartwright told me, "but I did visit here once. I went out on my own into the middle, and I listened to all the ancient voices. And I knew which end I would have bowled. Uphill, into the wind, like Lumpy Stevens used to do." Where others played in track suits, Tom was immaculate as ever in his whites – and uphill into the wind he bowled for one last time.

There was strictly no press coverage, but Bob was happy for me to wander about, chatting to people, and to write it up for *The Wisden Cricketer*. It was such a special occasion, such a uniquely magical day, that I felt the enormity of the task with which I had been entrusted. I wanted to capture the romance of it, but I also wanted to inject into it some gentle humour, such as Tom Cartwright wondering how many of them had had their flu jabs, Alec Bedser the world's greatest moaner saying of a sprightly innings by the 59-year-old Roger Knight, "He's a bit young to be playing this sort of stuff" and Bob's old friend Owain Howell in seventh heaven: "Isn't it wonderful? I've been bowled by Mike Brearley."

Had I struck the right note, or would they think it a little too irreverent in places? When I sent it for approval, I was as nervous as I had been that evening when I waited to read my homework to Hazel. Fortunately they loved it and, when Bob brought out a book ten years later, it was reproduced as a postscript.

I was every bit as nervous when John Stern persuaded me to write the magazine's obituary of David Sheppard. I was in a state of shock when he asked me to do it. Surely someone grander than me was more appropriate, I told him. But he sounded desperate – I think he had had several refusals – and I let him prevail upon me.

I spent a long day in research, reading David's two autobiographies, but at the end of the second day, when I planned to complete the piece, I had written only one sentence. 'My, this is a tough task,' I wrote that night in my diary, 'and it is churning me up having to do it. The canvas is so large, his life's work so immense, that it is difficult to focus on the cricket appropriately.'

As so often happens, I slept on it, let it take shape in my subconscious, and by lunchtime next day it was in John Stern's inbox. Was it any good? I was not sure, but John seemed to like it and next month he printed a reader's letter commending it, saying that I had fused the cricketer and the Christian in 'a complete obituary'. Most of the newspapers, it seemed, had dealt with the two strands in separate tributes.

The following year John landed me with an even greater bombshell: would I write the main obituary of Fred Trueman? Again others had turned down the task – Frank Keating and John Woodcock were mentioned – and again I found myself gasping at the enormity of the challenge.

Yet, in a strange way, the format of the obituary suited my writing. It calls for a certain warmth, and it also requires you to go to the heart of the person, to see their life in the full. It is not enough just to string together a few stories and achievements.

I developed a good link with *The Times*. When *No Coward Soul* was published, they printed three lengthy extracts. On one of the days, when I was on a train to Wimbledon, a woman across the table from me started to read the extract, and I watched her face with interest. She was barely halfway through it when her husband, without a word, pulled the paper out of her hands. In time he, too, reached the page, and for a while he seemed absorbed. Then, with his eye a long way from the bottom, he turned over.

For the summer of 2005, twenty years on from the last time England won a home series against Australia, I proposed a series of five articles in which I would reconstruct famous victories in the company of a participant, and they liked the idea. Then, before the winter of 2006/07, they agreed to my doing the same for five victories in Australia. The last of these involved the Melbourne Test that started on Boxing Day 1986, for which I interviewed Gladstone Small at his house south of Birmingham. He was in sparkling form, with some lovely turns of phrase, and I left in high spirits. But horror, when I got in the car and checked the tape, it was silent. I drove to the nearest layby, took a sheet of paper and scribbled every little phrase or story I could remember. Fortunately it proved enough for a 1,000-word article; only I would know how much better it might have been.

I tried to interest *The Times* in another idea, one that would have drawn on my skills as an interviewer and researcher but beyond the field of cricket. I wanted to take a year in the late 1950s and to pull an article out of *The Times* for each week of that year: a news item or a comment column. The articles would span a full range of topics – from agriculture to pharmaceuticals, from commercial television to urban development – and I would interview somebody involved, asking them to comment on the thinking at the time and how things subsequently panned out. *The Times* would run the pieces through the year, then put the full set in a book. Alas, they showed no interest at all. I was just a bloke who wrote articles on cricket's past; I was not even a proper journalist.

Over the years I have dreamed up a fair few books that never happened. That is the one I most regret, and it is too late now. For me the 1950s was the pivotal decade in the post-war reconstruction, and there will not be enough people left now who were involved in making those decisions.

*

Away from all this writing I got drawn into a bizarre dispute.

When Sussex won the county championship for the first time in 2003, Matthew Engel, editor of *Wisden*, commissioned Robin Marlar to write an article for the almanack on all the times that Sussex had nearly won the title. One of these was in 1953, David Sheppard's year as captain, when Robin had come down from Cambridge and joined the team in mid-season. 'I was personally convinced we were going to win in 1953,' wrote Robin, 'until Rupert Webb missed a vital catch behind the stumps at Hastings against Yorkshire. There may be an element of bias here since I was bowling at the time, and had turned an off-break away from the left-hander.'

Rupert's wife Barbara rang me. She was an actress, who had appeared on the West End stage with Spike Milligan, whom she loved dearly, and also in a film with Elvis Presley who had proposed marriage to her but whom she did not love. She told me that Rupert was in quite a state about Robin's article, and she was worried. She had seen him like this a couple of times before, and it had not ended well. Was there anything I could do to calm him down?

She passed the phone to Rupert, who was indeed in a state. As he saw it, he had been named for all time in the bible of cricket as the man who had cost them the 1953 championship, and he had no memory at all of any such catch. He had checked with the county's archivist who had consulted the scorebook where there was no mark to indicate a drop.

He went on to tell me that he had calculated Robin's bowling figures in the second half of the summer, and they compared unfavourably with those of Alan Oakman, who broke a finger in the Hastings match and had been the off-spinner before Robin's arrival. As far as he was concerned, this was a better explanation of why they had not won the title. It was very unpleasant, and I could not see what I could possibly do to defuse the situation.

I never said it to Rupert, but the report in *The Times* did refer to Vic Wilson having 'an escape at the wicket when 65'. At that point the score was 172 for six, with Yorkshire in their second innings 11 runs ahead with maybe an hour and a half to play. Perhaps Sussex would have won, and perhaps as a consequence they would not have lost momentum in the games that followed, but it was not clear cut.

I knew how much Rupert, a devout church-goer, looked up to David Sheppard so I rang David. He and Robin had been at Cambridge together, but they were not kindred spirits. Robin disliked the way David mixed his cricket captaincy with his missionary work as an evangelical Christian.

At the end of his one summer as Sussex captain, David had written to each of the team, thanking them for their efforts, a rare gesture in those days, and, after hearing of Rupert's distress about the *Wisden* article, he undertook to write once more to him.

A few days later Rupert rang to say that he had had the most wonderful letter from David. He was going to frame it and hang it on the wall; he was now at peace with the world.

I glowed with the sense of a good deed done.

I also rang Matthew Engel, who said that it was all his fault. Robin's original article had lacked a little colour, and he had asked him to spice it up.

A few weeks later it was all over the newspapers. 'Cricketers still argue over 51-year-old dropped catch,' was the headline above a long article in the *Telegraph*. My intervention had achieved nothing.

Eight years later Sussex asked me to write about Rupert for a booklet celebrating his 90th birthday. I drove to his flat in Rottingdean, and we had a sparkling five hours in which he took me with his great story-teller's gift through his life: from the evening in 1921 when his father, after a spell of unemployment, found work – "He and Mother went out for the night and got pissed, and nine months later I came along" – to his reincarnation in old age as a model and actor, appearing as the father of the final bride in *Four Weddings and a Funeral*.

He still wanted to talk about Robin Marlar, but I was determined not to re-enter that territory, writing a 2,000-word piece without a single mention of Robin. 'Ted Dexter was the last of Rupert's captains at Sussex,' I ended, 'after Hugh Bartlett, Jim Langridge, David Sheppard and Hubert Doggart. There was one other, I think. I seem to have forgotten his name.'

*

By the start of 2007 I had written some 80 articles, for the cricket magazines and for *The Times*. I was beginning to wonder whether there were many more interesting characters or whether the well was running dry. Then in quick succession I discovered two of the best: Alan Rayment and Frank Parr.

Alan was writing his autobiography and had been recommended to speak to me. "What is the normal length of a book?" he asked.

"It varies – but a hundred thousand words, maybe."

"I've written seventy thousand so far."

"Yes? And have you nearly finished?"

"Oh, no. I've only got to the age of seventeen."

He was living in an attic flat near the front at Milford-on-Sea in Hampshire. I arrived there at 10.30, and we were still going strong at six o'clock. He was full of laughter, a free spirit like Bomber Wells but also somebody whose life had taken many twists and turns as he sought a deeper, more spiritual meaning. He had been a professional cricketer, a ballroom dancing teacher, an estate agent, a community worker and a psychotherapist. He had had several intense relationships, including two marriages. He had lived in Malibu and Honolulu; he had been an active member of the Church of England, then in his fifties had suddenly found himself believing in reincarnation. Even in eight hours together I felt we were only skimming the surface of it all.

Mark Ramprakash had just succeeded Darren Gough as the *Strictly Come Dancing* champion on television, and we talked for a while about the dance studio he and his wife Betty ran in a hotel next to the ground at Northlands Road. He persuaded a few of his team-mates to beginners' classes. "Peter Sainsbury was the only one who stuck with it. He got his Bronze, but he wouldn't do the Silver. He thought the tango was a bit too sexy."

Inevitably he started to observe his fellow cricketers through the eyes of a dancing instructor. "It's a trained response. If Marilyn Monroe were to come past me, the first thing I'd take in was how she walked. And movement is beautiful in cricket."

He was on his feet, demonstrating as he spoke. "Derek Shackleton, when he ran up and bowled, was wonderfully upright and elegant like Fred Astaire, whereas Fred Trueman was down and muscular like Gene Kelly. Roy Marshall was well co-ordinated and relaxed, but there was also a Caucasian stiffness in him."

"Do you think any of the present England team could follow in the footsteps of Gough and Ramprakash?"

"Ian Bell could be a good dancer ... Dear old Harmy, I don't think he would ... Hoggard would have the potential to be as good as Darren Gough; they're both more loose-limbed than Harmy ... But not Flinty, though. He's too big, too much of a yeoman build. Rather like Peter Schmeichel ... Pietersen could be a very good Latin American dancer, but he wouldn't have the total discipline for all-round ballroom dancing. It would take him too long to learn the foxtrot and the waltz. He'd get bored."

"What about Shane Warne?" "He'd fit the razzamatazz of the American version, but I don't see him doing it on British television."

He paused for breath. "I'm just thinking on my feet, you know. Monty, he's got it. There's no doubt about that. But he would have to stand up straight."

"What about David Gower?" "Oh, yes. He had the beautiful co-ordination, the grace, the timing, the nonchalance, the sophistication, and he wouldn't be embarrassed. He would be the tops."

"Botham?" "No. Not Botham. He'd be hopeless. I don't think he'd even begin. I don't think he'd want to."

Alan's first wife Betty was still involved in the world of dance teaching, and she was horrified when it all appeared in *The Wisden Cricketer*. "What do you think you were saying? You haven't even seen them on the dance floor. You're not supposed to talk about people like this." But Alan just laughed.

Tom Cartwright thought it was brilliant. Still coaching the Welsh Under-16s, he was sick to death of all the initiatives coming out of Lord's, all the directives about how people should bowl. Alan's take on the cricketers was a breath of fresh air. "He's looking at them as individuals, isn't he? He's starting from their natural movements. That's what we've completely lost from English cricket. He's not trying to make them fit into some perfect biomechanical template."

From Alan I moved on to Frank Parr, who had kept wicket for Lancashire. I noticed in an obituary of the jazz trumpeter Mick Mulligan that Frank had played in his band, and I thought he sounded an intriguing character.

His address was Abbey Road in North London. I knew he had been Acker Bilk's manager at one stage so I had an expectation that he would greet me at the door of one of the detached houses at the bottom end of the road, near the recording studio and the legendary zebra crossing.

George Melly had been the singer with Mick Mulligan's band and, on the train journey up, I read his account of those years, *Owning Up*. It was a quite different window into the world of 1950s England, full of boarding houses and sexual encounters, and Frank was described affectionately as quite the scruffiest and most anti-social member of a band not noted for personal hygiene or conventional manners.

> The professional cricketer has a social role. He is expected to behave within certain defined limits. He can be 'a rough diamond', even 'a bit of a character', but he must know his place. If he smells of sweat, it must be fresh sweat. He must dress neatly and acceptably. His drinking habits must be under control. He must know when to say 'sir'. Frank, we were soon to discover, had none of these qualifications.

I walked past the recording studio, on and on to the top of the road where Frank's address turned out to be on the sixth floor of a block of council flats.

"It's a bit untidy in here," he apologised.

"Don't worry," I said. "I've read the book."

Something on the floor stopped us opening the door into the main room straightaway, there was muddle everywhere, and the chair he invited me to sit on was covered with all sorts, including *The Times Jumbo Crossword*, a battered dictionary and a library book with the title *Filthy Words – A History of Swearing and Obscene Words*.

At one stage he had me crawling under his bed for a photograph which, when I did find it, left me coated in dust. His diet seemed to consist of whisky and cigarettes and, after I had been there for a while, he suggested going down to the pub. I was all set to agree till I realised I had been with him for over four hours and I would be pushed to catch my train out of Paddington.

175

I had thoroughly enjoyed the afternoon. If Geoffrey Howard had opened up for me the origins of the garden city movement and Charlie Light had fascinated me with the technique of nurturing ash trees, Frank had introduced me to his world of revivalist jazz so engagingly that I bought two CDs of Mick Mulligan's band that I still play regularly.

> *I wanna pay a visit to the devil down below*
> *Hung and killed my woman, wanna reap just what I sow*
> *So judge, judge, good time judge*
> *Won't you send me to the 'lectric chair*

In July 1952 Frank, a grammar-school boy from Wallasey, broke into the Lancashire team as their wicket-keeper, making a great impression at The Oval in only his second game. "This boy is the most promising I've seen in years," the old England keeper Herbert Strudwick said while *The Times* wrote that he had 'strongly suggested himself as a successor to Evans.'

The following May the selectors looked at him in an early MCC game at Lord's. Then, he told me, they wrote to ask if he was available, if selected, to tour the Caribbean that winter.

Alas it did not work out. "All jazzmen are kicking against something," he told me. "It comes out when they blow." And his kicking was not to the liking of Cyril Washbrook who took over the captaincy of Lancashire in 1954, a stern disciplinarian who liked his cricketers deferential and well turned out.

I asked Frank if other cricketers had ever shown any interest in his music, and he said that Ken Taylor and Bryan Stott had come to see him play at the 100 Club in London. I knew Ken had "fiddled about with the clarinet" in the youth clubs of Huddersfield, so I got him to talk about the way jazz was perceived at that time: "It was looked on as the poor man's music. Playing for a county cricket club, especially one like Lancashire, was all about being smart and respectable. If you were involved in anything like jazz, in their eyes you'd be a drop-out. They'd be thinking drugs and all sorts."

Bryan Stott agreed, laughing with delight at the memory of Frank Parr.

"I don't think Cyril Washbrook liked him," I said.

"No, oh no, he wouldn't. Oh dear, no. Frank Parr!"

Frank seemed to be one of those characters, like Bomber or Roly Jenkins, whose mere mention was guaranteed to bring a smile to the face. Bob Barber had a story about him turning up at a reception at the House of Lords wearing – the horror of it – a *blue* shirt.

"Did you ever play your trombone in the dressing room?" I asked Frank.

"Just once," he said. "At Oxford. Bob Berry knocked out the beat with a stump. Much to Washy's disgust."

"What did he say?"

Fifty-four years had passed, but he could still repeat the words verbatim: "What do you want to play that fucking nigger music for?"

Washbrook hung like a dark shadow over Frank's life. His predecessor as Lancashire captain, the amateur Nigel Howard, was an easy-going type and got on well with Frank, often giving him lifts in his car. But Washbrook, breaking the mould as the county's first professional captain, was a grammar-school boy, with none of the relaxed confidence of a public school education; he rose to leadership by acquiring the more formal traits of the English upper classes. "He was the second biggest snob in English cricket," Doug Insole, another jazz lover, told me once. "After Jim Swanton."

"Cyril was too stiff," was Geoffrey Howard's kinder verdict. "He didn't understand young people. He was one of those men, you can't ever imagine him being a boy."

For many of the post-war players – even for Washbrook's near-contemporaries Alan Wharton, a Labour-voting schoolmaster and magistrate, and Geoff Edrich, who had come through hell as a Japanese prisoner-of-war and knew the value of team spirit – his approach was unpopular. "We should have won the championship two or three times in the '50s," Geoff Edrich told me. "We had a good enough side, but we never had the leadership."

It was a sad story. Washbrook, a fine cricketer, was doing what he felt was right for Lancashire cricket, upholding the values of the pre-war world which had moulded him, but the fault lines of his years in charge did not fully disappear till the quiet Methodist Jack Bond took on the captaincy in 1968.

My article for the *Wisden Cricketer* was about Frank and his sad demise, and I had to decide what to do about Washbrook's words on jazz music. The social historian in me felt that they needed to be recorded, but another part of me – not wanting to tarnish Washbrook for all time with a phrase that he will not have been alone in using in the 1950s – held me back.

'Washbrook's vitriolic words, on the origins and nature of jazz music,' I wrote, 'are perhaps best left unprinted.'

I am still agonising over the rights and wrongs of it. It was a quote that was at the heart of Frank's story, and it threw a sharp light on an unpleasant aspect of the world of his youth, a light that we should not pretend did not exist. But would I now be putting the quote into print if Cyril Washbrook had living descendants?

The new captain dropped Frank from the side after a handful of games. Frank was in his prime, and in the second eleven his keeping improved further – "I don't think I ever kept better in my life" – so much so that Worcestershire's new captain Peter Richardson tried to recruit him. Terms were agreed but, at the last minute, Worcestershire wrote to say they had opted instead for Yorkshire's Roy Booth. "I soon found out why. A girl in the office at Old Trafford showed me this letter. 'I hear that you are thinking of taking on Frank Parr as a wicket-keeper. I should inform you that he can be a grave social risk.' Signed: Cyril Washbrook."

'We never knew the reason for his quarrel with the captain of Lancashire,' George Melly wrote, 'but after a month or two in his company we realised it must have been inevitable.'

For a while Mulligan's band was a popular act, then one night they saw the future. In a cinema on the outskirts of South London, in front of an audience of unusually young girls, they played the first half to little applause. After the interval Tommy Steele appeared, the girls shrieked, and Frank sank into an alcohol-fuelled depression: "He'll have us all on the bread line."

Alan Rayment had also talked about the birth of rock'n'roll. On a rainy day in Nottingham in August 1956, some of the Hampshire team went to the cinema to see *Rock Around The Clock*. "They stopped the film because people were dancing in the aisles. I rang Betty straightaway: 'We've got to do this.'"

That autumn they converted an old building in the town centre, and *The Alan and Betty Rayment School of Dancing* became *The Grosvenor – Southampton's Gayest Ballroom*, with an 11-piece band on Saturday nights. "Thursday was always the dead night, the night before people were paid, so we advertised a rock'n'roll class. The first night we had 185 people, queuing all down the road."

Alan left cricket and dancing behind him, pursuing his religious faith into a training as a community worker. Meanwhile Frank's cricket was confined to keeping wicket for the Ravers Club on the Paddington Recreation Ground. "Looking back, I've no reason to grumble," he said. "I would have gone to Worcester, I'd probably have married a local girl and spent my time in oblivion. So it all turned out for the best in the end. I've been very lucky in my life, and I don't regret a moment of it."

I think that was only 90% true, an old man determined not to give in to bitterness. He loved cricket more than anything, it was the passion of his life, he watched it on television all the time in his flat, and he clearly felt the injustice of his lost career. "At the time I thought it was the end of the world," he said. "It's probably why I took up serious drinking."

And serious drinking he did take up, telling me of a time he was staggering around behind the pavilion at Lord's.

"Are you Parr of Lancashire?" a member with a cut-glass accent asked him.

"Yes."

"Good God."

Alan knew Frank from National Service days in the RAF; he thought Frank had been unlucky to run up against Washbrook. "He'd have been fine if he'd been with us at Hampshire, with Colin Ingleby-Mackenzie as his captain."

Alan completed the first volume of his autobiography six years after our first meeting. Punchy had been his cricket nickname, and he called it *Punchy Through The Covers – The Early Years 1928-1949*. It ran to nearly 400 pages, bringing alive his family, his childhood in Finchley, his holidays on the Isle of Wight, his National Service and his first steps into cricket, a magnificent slice of social history which I page-set and took through the printers for him.

Disappointingly there was a five-year hiatus before he started work on volume two, his cricketing and dancing years, so my next task is to spur him on. He is 91 now, but he has lost none of his mental sharpness. In a recent telephone conversation, to my delight, he was comparing and contrasting Colin Ingleby-Mackenzie and Boris Johnson, both of them 'Captains of Pop' at Eton.

I wish I had done something more with Frank. I liked him greatly, there was something about his story that touched me deep down, but he was not much of a raconteur. I kept in touch with occasional phone calls – I can still hear the musical way he gave his name when he picked up the receiver, the major third interval that fell from the E of 'Frank' to the C of 'Parr' – and I had a second long session with him. I had it in mind to write a little monograph but he died, of cancer of the throat, before I had cleared the decks for it.

I spoke at his funeral. A jazz band accompanied his coffin down the hill to Golders Green Crematorium, and we had a two-hour service, full of laughter and music. From the world of cricket, amid the large congregation, there were only two or three Ravers and me, and my speech was wrong; I struck far too formal a note for the jazzmen. I had expected some people from Lancashire to be there; I had given the details of the service to a committee member at Old Trafford, but the club did not even send a wreath. It upset his stepdaughter Fiona, though it would not have bothered Frank.

I wrote his obituary for *The Independent*, deciding this time to put into print Cyril Washbrook's infamous words. The obituaries editor was not so sure, however. The paper did not use asterisks, it printed obscene words in full or not at all, and after some deliberation he told me, "You can have the nigger but not the fucking." In the interests of historical accuracy, I left it out, as did the *Guardian* when Fiona, who was determined not to let the matter drop, tried to include it in some lines she wrote for their 'Lives Remembered'.

Frank had come to terms with the slings and arrows of his life, but Fiona still felt the pain of what had happened to him, the sense that he had suffered a great wrong. Perhaps getting the quote into print was her way of dealing with that.

21

Tom

At the time of Bob Barber's birthday match at Broadhalfpenny Down I was collaborating with Tom Cartwright on a book. We had been working on it on and off for two years – bursts of activity, followed by fallow spells while I was completing other projects – and I loved the idea of witnessing what was almost certain to be Tom's last cricket match.

The new ball was taken by two England cricketers: Fred Rumsey, whose arm was very low, and Ian Thomson who, at the age of 76, was decidedly slower than medium. David Allen was only prepared to umpire: "I'm afraid my bowling mechanics have completely gone," he told me. But Tom still ran in with purpose and with a high arm. "He wouldn't know how to bowl a bad ball," the watching Donald Carr said.

Perhaps it was not surprising. Tom had spent the last 25 years, driving the length and breadth of Wales, coaching cricketers of all ages. He was bowling every day in the nets.

In the evening we gathered in a marquee where, after the meal, the principal speaker was Dennis Silk, the former headmaster of Radley College and MCC President. He told some witty stories, expressed appropriate thanks, then startled me by singling out for special praise one of the many gathered there. Not Ted Dexter or Mike Smith, not Lance Gibbs or Mike Brearley – but Tom. Tom, the lifelong Labour voter who had stuck to his principles and gone his own way into the Welsh hills and valleys. At the end of his heartfelt paean, there was a great, swelling round of applause from every part of the marquee.

I did not make a note of Dennis's words, but I rang him some time later. "I've always had this thing about Tom," he said. "He's tremendously respected by his fellow cricketers. He's kept up such high personal standards without making a meal of it. And he's put so much back into the game, patiently and generously. He's one of the great unsung heroes of English cricket."

*

Two months earlier Sue and I had been with Tom at Callington Cricket Club in Cornwall where his Wales Under-16 side were playing. It was July 7, the day the bombs went off in London, and, knowing that Martha was planning to be on the underground at the time, we had a moment of great alarm.

Then we settled to a special afternoon, with Tom meeting Lorna and Liz, the two daughters of the schoolmaster, Eddie Branson, who had introduced him to cricket sixty years earlier in Coventry. Over a teatime tray of sandwiches and cakes, Tom waxed lyrical. "Your father was brilliant. He taught me the basics but much more than that; he taught me the love of the game. There was a passion he transmitted ... I never speak to young kids without hearing his voice in my head ... I wouldn't be here talking with you today if it hadn't have been for him. My whole destiny has come from what he did."

"Dad went to Trent Bridge that day you made your debut," Lorna said. "You got 82, didn't you? It was one of those very special days in his life."

"The whole family lived and died on your efforts," Liz added. "And the injustices. We all suffered the injustices. It seemed to centre around the selectors and Dad not agreeing with them. We didn't really know if he was being partial."

"We used to get the *Coventry Evening Telegraph* every night and look at the back page. 'What did Tom do?' You seemed to be scoring 20, 25, 30, no spectacular scores. And that went on for several years. Then you switched over to bowling. And suddenly your career took off."

By then I knew the full story of Tom's career: the fairy-tale debut as a 17-year-old batsman, the extraordinary day seven summers later when he found he could bowl an out-swinger, the years as the best medium-pace bowler in England, the chequered Test career, the move to Somerset. He became a coach, teaching Ian Botham to bowl, and now he was hidden away in Wales, quietly passing on his passion and his technical skill.

"Often I've ended up in places," he said, "and I'm not sure how I've got there. It's almost as if you're born with a little chip and someone's guiding you."

I also spent a day with Tom in Coventry, meeting his three sisters and visiting the oak tree where his parents had courted after Christian Endeavour classes at the local Methodist chapel. They had eight years of courtship, followed by 69 years of marriage; they barely spent a night apart. Everybody in Tom's family seemed to have that steadfastness.

They were proud working folk, strong believers in the Labour Party, and their pride came with a strict discipline.

"You were brought up to call people Mr and Mrs, to say please and thank you," Tom's sister Sheila said. "I was 25 when I got married and, right up till then, I was still having to get home by nine o'clock."

"We'd be sitting in the cinema," her husband John said, "and, halfway through the film, Sheila would say, 'We've got to go.' We're only now seeing the ends of them all on television."

"I used to worry like mad. Dad was very strict, but you loved him and you could have fun with him."

"Black was black, and white was white. He was straight down the middle. You knew where you were with him. Tom is just the same."

"He taught us to know the difference between right and wrong," Tom added. "Between truth and lies. And to treat other people in the way you'd like other people to treat you."

Back in the spring of 1997, when I had been writing my first book, I had been captivated by Tom. He had an extraordinarily good memory. He had a deep understanding of cricket. He was fascinated by the human character, and he could describe incidents with a wry humour. He had a romantic streak, and he also had strong opinions. And he wasn't going to compromise those opinions to advance himself or to fit in with any ruling orthodoxy. He was a man who exuded integrity, at times to the point of tormenting himself.

I visited Mike Brearley, a great friend and admirer of Tom, and we sat in his kitchen with cups of tea. Mike was busy as a psychoanalyst, but he made time for me and he spoke about Tom with feeling and with precision. He compared him with Mary Garth's father in George Eliot's *Middlemarch*, a novel set in a fictitious town not far from Coventry. "It's ages since I've read it, but I remember that Caleb Garth was a man of total integrity and honesty. He would never do anything that had a smattering of dishonesty according to his standards."

It is my favourite novel, and I took it out when I got home.

"What care I about their objecting?" said Caleb, with a sturdiness which he was apt to show when he had an opinion. "There's no sort of work that could ever be done well, if you minded what fools say. You must have it inside you that your plan is right, and that plan you must follow."

"But Tom didn't get on a high moral ground. He'd say his piece, and you knew where he stood. He wasn't moralistic. He'd be humorous about human failure, in a warm way that most people could take. As I'm talking, I can see him speaking and chuckling."

*

More than three years passed between my starting work with Tom and sitting down to write the book. In part, this was because I had too many other projects on the go, even allowing Peter Walker to push ahead of Tom in the queue. If Tom had not been so kind and patient, if he had been more like Bob Appleyard, this would not have happened – and, as things turned out, it was immensely sad that it did.

The delay was also because I never felt I had got to the end of what Tom had to offer. With the others I had worked with, I would reach a point at which the same stories and opinions kept recurring, when I sensed I had collected everything I needed, but with Tom there was always more. It chimed with what Brian Langford said to me about the end-of-day conversations when they played together at Somerset: "Tom was always the last to leave, but he wouldn't drink. He'd talk cricket all evening. His pint lasted all night. And the young ones all listened to him. He knew so much about cricket, more than anyone I've met. You spend day in, day out with people, and after a bit you get fed up with hearing the same things. But Tom wasn't always saying the same things. With him there was always something different."

Apart from the trips to Cornwall and Coventry, we met ten or twelve times for four-hour sessions, including a bite of lunch, at *Y Mochyn Du*, the pub on the corner near the Glamorgan ground. I also visited his house a couple of times, out in Neath, and talked with his wife Joan. And, more than any other book, because I became so involved, I spoke to about twenty cricketers he had played with or coached.

In his time as Somerset's player/coach, he had argued for a budget of £6,000, to employ six young cricketers for the summer. Viv Richards, already completing his residential qualification, was one, and for the other five Tom selected local lads: Ian Botham, Peter Roebuck, Vic Marks, Philip Slocombe and John Hook. He had a vision that, if Somerset could build a team from the talent spread around the county, rather than recruit old stagers from elsewhere as they had been doing, the people would flock to watch them. And, though he had gone by the time it happened, leaving after a row with the chairman ("in a smelly toilet in Weston"), he was proved right.

"Any county could do it, you know," Tom said. "You only have to have somebody in charge who knows what he's doing."

From this group of 'Tom's boys' I interviewed Vic Marks, Peter Roebuck and Ian Botham. Three more different interviews, it would be hard to imagine.

First Vic, at home in Exeter, speaking gently and warmly about Tom: "He wasn't the archetypal old pro. He wasn't severe, down on you; he didn't treat you in a patronising way. He was excited by all us young guys. Not only did he know our names, which a lot of coaches wouldn't have done, he had ideas that were designed for each of us individually. In that era of bog-standard truisms, he was very different."

Then Peter, on the phone during a brief stay in England, talking at a phenomenal speed, almost like a machine gun, yet every sentence a pearl of reminiscence or insight. He spoke of the twin influences of Brian Close, the captain, and Tom Cartwright, the coach, on the young Botham: "He was lucky to have those two influences. I don't say they put things into him, but they brought things out of him. Ian was always a very keen learner. He'd go and practise on his own, you know. He had this larger-than-life thing, this hail-fellow-well-met, but there's a solitude inside him that most great sportsmen have. An ability to listen. He was a great admirer of Brian Close. They had furious rows all the time, but he'd listen. And he listened to Tom about the technicalities of bowling – because Tom was an absolute master. Botham took a lot from him."

Finally Ian, whose mobile phone number I was given: "It's not a good time. I'm at the Ryder Cup. Ring me next week ... I'm on a charity walk. Can you leave it for now? ... Give me a ring me when I'm in Australia ... I've just come off a 12-hour commentary session. I'll tell you what. Ring me an hour before the start of the game on Sunday ... I can't possibly speak now; the game starts in an hour."

He did speak to me in the end. There was water lapping in the background, and I imagined he was in the bath: "There were times when I got a bit down. But Tom kept pegging away at me. 'You're an all-rounder, you can be a very good one – so get on with it.' He had a lot of time, a lot of patience and he gave me a great deal of encouragement. As a youngster, if you've got somebody like that pushing away at you, it's a real buzz. I owe him a lot."

Botham had come back from a year on the ground staff at Lord's where they had thought his bowling a joke, not even letting him bowl in the nets. But seeing his desire to bowl, Tom set to work: "I can honestly say that Ian was one of the most receptive people I've ever worked with. He learned to swing the ball both ways in a very short time, literally in weeks, and to have control in doing it. He had so much ability to grasp what was going on around him and to work ... It really is down to the individual: the learning, the ability to teach yourself. You have to do so much for yourself – and Ian did. People may think that life came easy to him as a cricketer, but he worked damn hard. He really did. I have as much admiration for him in the way he buckled down as for anybody I've ever been with."

*

Tom was forever fighting battles. He told me one day that he had received a directive on how many balls youngsters should be able to bowl in the nets, and he spent three hours on the phone to Lord's, being passed from extension to extension, trying to find out who had issued it.

On another occasion one of his youngsters, a most promising if rather overweight batsman, was sent to Lilleshall for a week's course. His father drove him up from Pontypridd and, when he arrived back home, the boy was on the phone. He was at Pontypridd railway station; could he come and pick him up? "They did the Pinch test, to check his bodyweight index, then the Bleep test, timing him as he ran between cones, and they failed him. He hadn't even opened his cricket bag, and they sent him home. You can imagine how the lad must have felt. I was furious."

'I thought this was supposed to be a class act, not a crass act,' Tom wrote to the ECB.

"I don't think the letter went down very well. You think of some of the great cricketers of the past, people like Colin Milburn, they wouldn't even get close now."

Tom never gave up. In a different way he was like Bob Appleyard, a perfectionist striving for what he believed in. I admired him greatly for that.

"Not many people want to take up issues, you know. They don't. They really don't. Sometimes I wish I could walk away, but I can't."

Tom had so much to say about bowling in the modern game. He thought the coaches worked too much to biomechanical templates, that there was an excessive focus on speed to the detriment of control and that the coaching system, promoting people with good marks in examinations ahead of people with experience, was all wrong.

"You've got people bowling for England who have served no apprenticeship in the game at all, and they're being guided by coaches who have never even been successful in county cricket. They're nice lads, good coaches in the right setting, but they're like the St John's Ambulance. You're pleased to have them at the village fete, but they aren't expected to perform heart by-pass operations, are they?"

Every book has its problem passage. Keith Andrew was forever picking at the text about a catch he was supposed to have dropped at Brisbane. Bob Appleyard was never satisfied with my description of the revolver port door he was manufacturing during the war. And Tom kept returning to this paragraph about the England bowling coaches. He must have raised the subject with me four times.

"I'm not sure I want to say that."

"But you haven't given any names."

"I don't think it's really fair."

"I think it's fine. These coaches are earning a lot of money. They should be prepared to take criticism."

"Oh, it's not the coaches I'm worried about. It's the St John's Ambulance."

*

The part of the book that everybody was waiting to read covered his role in the D'Oliveira Affair, when he was selected in the original party, then – after all the furore of Basil's non-selection – dropped out, citing a shoulder injury. Basil was picked to replace him, and the South African government, calling it the team of the Anti-Apartheid movement not the MCC, cancelled the tour.

Knowing his radical views, many people had always suspected that he had pulled out for political reasons. It would have been great for the book if he had come out and said that to me; in truth, I was hoping he would. During several sessions in *Y Mochyn Du* I probed him hard about it. But Tom not only had an exceptional memory, he also had an honesty that went right to the core of his character. He was not going to claim more credit than he was due.

He and Joan had spent a winter in South Africa shortly after they had married, when he had coached in Johannesburg. He had also been on the 1964/65 tour of the country, when he had formed a close bond with Mike Brearley. On both trips he had not liked what he had seen but, despite that, he had told the selectors that he was available for the 1968/69 tour. He was even prepared to justify Basil's non-selection, saying that, before his century in the Oval Test, the selectors would have had a tour party in mind; one innings did not have to change their thinking.

Perhaps he was a little too prepared to think well of the people involved. He never liked the argument becoming personal. Of the selectors he said, "There was so much confusion, so much interference, and they were trying in the middle of it all to do what was for the best."

He withdrew, he told me, for a mixture of three reasons. First, he had a bad shoulder, and the consultant told him his career would be shortened if he did not rest it. Secondly, he was deeply committed to his family, and his two children hated it when he went away. And finally, he read in the paper that the MPs in the South African parliament all cheered when they heard that D'Oliveira had not been picked. "When I read that, I went cold. And I started to wonder whether I wanted to be part of it."

And that was what he wanted me to write. We went over and over it, and he was wholly happy with the chapter.

He had just one memory that suggested that there were some at Lord's who were conspiring to keep D'Oliveira out of the tour. It involved a phone call from the England captain Colin Cowdrey, which Tom received as he arrived home from the meeting at which he had told them of his withdrawal.

"Colin said, 'Will you agree to go, at least to start the tour? When you get out there, if things go wrong, there are people out there who are coaching, like Don Wilson, who we could bring in.' Basil certainly wasn't mentioned.

Nobody had suggested to me that, if I dropped out, Basil would be the one who took my place. I wasn't privy to anything like that. It was Don Wilson's name I remember being mentioned. But I just said no, and Colin said, 'OK, fine.'"

Tom moved to Somerset for the summer of 1970, when the South Africans were due to tour, and he told the Secretary that he was reluctant to play against them. If selected, he would honour his contract, he said, "but my contribution to the game will be very minimal."

He was proud to tell me that.

*

Originally I had planned to put a fighting sentence from Tom at the bottom of each page, in a box, but I soon realised that his thoughts were more joined up than that. So I saved up some subjects till near the end of the book, and I put them in one chapter, 'A Six-Ball Over', in which Tom could let rip. The fifth ball, one of my favourites, dealt with the top-down administration of the game:

> It was the people's game when I played. Then it started to shift from that to becoming financially driven. Now marketing and sponsorship have totally taken over. The game was run by people in sports jackets, and now it's become suits, hasn't it? It may sound glib, but it tells a huge story.
>
> The more people become organised, the more it detracts from why they are there. I remember Peter Cranmer, one of my first second-team captains at Edgbaston, saying, 'You can be over-organised if you're not careful.' You lose the free natural progression; you've strangled it at an earlier point.
>
> Most of the people in these jobs – because of their lack of ability, or confidence in their ability – try to have cushions. They have people between whatever they're dealing with and themselves. The responsibility is deflected; they bring in people to absorb the pressure, whereas people before stood on their ability.
>
> They create work to keep themselves going, to pay their salaries and their pensions. They're not interested in passing on their knowledge and skills – because their interest is not there in the first place. They could be organising transport, couldn't they?
>
> So much of their innovation is born of job justification.
>
> The people who used to be in charge of cricket were ex-cricketers. The other people were brought in and used for what they were good at. Now they've stayed and they've multiplied, and the ex-players, with a conscience about how the game should be, have gone.

I'm staggered by my own thoughts now. I'd rather see the thing go back to being controlled by the MCC of yesteryear, that type of person, rather than the hard-bitten professional who's come out of the City. I look at John Barclay at Arundel, an Old Etonian, and he's trying to spread joy. His bounce is telling you that. It's joy. And I find myself wishing that people like him were running the game.

Tom was so articulate, especially when like this he gave expression to his feelings. He was always thinking, wrestling with the changes he had witnessed in his life, wondering if they were for the better or not.

There was much more of a rhythm of life then. A rhythm of going to work and coming home at the same time each day, a rhythm of learning a trade and progressing with it, a rhythm even in people's leisure pursuits, and it gave people good manners and a consideration for others. People had settled lives. They did things which were within their reach – going out into the country, doing the garden, spending a day at cricket. Now people are striving for things they can't attain, the structures break down and the natural rhythm is lost.

I was enchanted when he talked like that. It made me think of the Ten to Spot on my childhood journeys to school. There was even a rhythm in the way he said it. As a writer, he was a joy to work with.

*

Tom had only been to an elementary school, but he enjoyed the company of the young university-educated cricketers – Vic Marks, Peter Roebuck and, of course, Mike Brearley – and in the same way he enjoyed working with me.

Mike dedicated a chapter to Tom in a section called 'Heroes' in his recent book, *On Cricket*, and Vic called him "one of my two favourite people in cricket – him and Arthur Milton."

Eventually, in late January 2007, I completed the book. I set my home printer to run off a copy of the text to send to Tom and, while it was doing so, the telephone rang.

"Stephen? It's Arthur here." I knew two other Arthurs, but he did not need to say Milton. There was only one Arthur with a Bristol accent like that. "I've had a couple of health scares, and I've been thinking ... I've decided I'd like to do a book after all ... I've asked Mike Vockins to do it with me ... We wondered if you would publish it."

"Of course I will, Arthur. Really, I'd love to have written it myself."

"I know."

"But I'll happily publish it."

*

188

Tom rang back after he had finished reading the final manuscript, and he had very few changes to make. "I've come to the conclusion this chap wasn't a bad player," he said with a chuckle. "In fact, if I'd known about some of these statistics at the time, I'd have put in for a pay rise."

There was an 11-year-old boy across the road, Sanjit, who often came round to talk cricket with Tom, mostly about what a good batsman Rahul Dravid was. He too had been reading the statistical appendix. "I caught him looking at me out of the corner of his eye, as if he was thinking, 'Have you really done all this?'"

At three o'clock one Friday afternoon in late February I collected the printed book, and I drove to a motorway service station outside Cardiff where Tom was waiting for me. He was sitting in the driver's seat of his Rover, with a completely blank look on his face, no expression at all. He was far away, not worrying about the world around him, and he looked a different man. Then he saw me, and his face became animated again. He signed some books and took some boxes away for himself.

By this stage I had got to know his wife Joan well. Her sense of humour, seeing the funny side of human pretensions, reminded me of women in my own Nonconformist childhood, people like my Auntie Katherine who saw through all the 'fuss and bother' and the 'swank'. I had woven into the book's narrative a little of Joan's story, how as the daughter of a tin-plate worker in South Wales she had fallen in love with the green fields and white clothes of cricket. She and Tom had had the closest of marriages; Tom often told me how they would sit up into the small hours talking about cricket.

When I rang Tom the next day, Joan answered. "He won't tell you himself, Stephen, but he really is delighted with the book."

We were organising a launch in Coventry, and such was the affection Tom inspired that guests were coming from many parts, including Bob Barber from Switzerland and, best of all for Tom, Sir Alec Bedser at the age of 88 making the trip up from Surrey.

Then things started to go wrong. Tom took to bed with a sickness, and Joan fractured a hip falling downstairs. Joan went into hospital in Swansea, and Tom became agitated about the standard of care she was receiving. "I never thought I'd hear myself say it, but I don't think some of these nurses deserve the pay rises they've been given." And, when Joan was kept waiting two days for her operation, "I was ready to go out and shoot Tony Blair and the lot of them."

I rang him one morning while Joan was in hospital. I wanted some more signed copies of the book so I arranged to call in on him about eleven o'clock. I had cracked a rib, tripping while carrying a box of books, and I was in a hyperactive state, planning several visits around shops in South Wales. After Tom had signed the books, he suggested going out for a spot of lunch, and I nearly said no. Then I thought, "Slow down, Stephen. Joan's in hospital. Tom's on his own. He wants to go for lunch. Go for lunch."

"That would be very nice, Tom," I said, and we drove up to the local Harvester where, as always, Tom insisted on paying.

The book was finished, and the conversation became more relaxed. I was no longer needing to listen to every word for possible inclusion in the text. Soon we would be telling each other about the reactions to the book, and he would be getting phone calls and letters from people with whom he had lost touch. It would be a special time in his life.

A friend of Joan, a former headmistress, had already called at the house to tell Tom how good the book was – "It's not easy to write that well," she had said – and he was eager to pass on the compliment.

"Oh no," I said. "If it's a good book, it's because of what you've got to say in it."

I told him that Pat Murphy of the *Birmingham Post* was keen to interview him, and Tom said how he liked Pat's enthusiastic voice on the radio. "I've never spoken to him. But I think he was eating at the next table to us once. The children bought us a weekend in a hotel for our 40th wedding anniversary."

We talked for a while about the commentators. He said how good Trevor Bailey had always been at reading the state of a match. "The one who gets it wrong a lot is the Australian." I wondered who he meant, and he surprised me when he came up with the name: "Richie Benaud." I wish I had asked him to elaborate, but we were just chatting.

We drove off in separate cars, I to pick up the M4, he to visit Joan in hospital. At the roundabout where we parted he stuck his arm out of the window and waved.

22

What cricket can be in people's lives

The next time I saw Tom he was lying in a hospital bed.

On the day after our lunch at the Harvester he had persuaded the hospital to discharge Joan, preferring to carry her up and down stairs at home than to leave her surrounded by patients with dementia. We were due to go to Headingley three days later for a cricket society meeting, ahead of the book's launch the following week, and he was not sure he could make it. I could tell that he did not want to let me down, but I told him not to worry; I would manage without him.

At lunchtime on the day before the trip north he rang to say he would be coming; the children, Jeremy and Jane, were going to help out. We both had busy afternoons ahead of us – I had the car in for a service, he had shopping to get done – and we agreed to talk first thing in the morning.

At 6.15 I was unwinding in front of the television quiz show *Eggheads*. 'Who scored the winning runs to win the Ashes in 1953? Was it Len Hutton, Denis Compton or Ray Illingworth?' was the question, and Judith Keppel was just plumping for Len Hutton when the telephone rang. It was Jeremy on his way to Swansea Hospital: "Tom has had a fall, no details yet." Then five minutes later it was Joan: "He's critical."

He had had a massive heart attack while shopping in Marks & Spencer. He had been without oxygen for some minutes before paramedics had revived him and, as a result, he was in a very feeble condition. He might live for years, but he was not expected to regain many of his faculties.

I went up to Leeds on my own. It was the hardest speech I have ever given. I told them how, in 26 years as a first-class cricketer, Tom had only been to the ground once, when he was twelfth man for England, and he had been looking forward to the visit. Bob Appleyard came along to support me, and I got through it, at one point lightening the mood by reading some of Tom's memories of Brian Close's driving.

Each Wednesday I drove down the M4 to Neath, to have tea with Joan, then to sit with Tom in hospital, and on each visit I could see little improvements. He had been a strong and fit man, only 71 years old, and he astonished the specialists by the way he battled. At first he was lying with little life or speech, and the family took to reading passages of the book to him. Then he started speaking: a few words, then nineteen to the dozen, mostly about cricket though little of it made sense.

It was never clear that he knew who we were, but on my third visit I managed to stop him talking for a moment. "You've had a knock, Tom," I told him slowly, gripping his arm. "You've got to keep trying. If you do, you may be able to get your brain working again."

"It would be good if it could," he answered, then he lapsed back into confused talk about 'extra balls' and 'got to practise'.

Normally, when I was driving in the car, I would listen to music on the radio, but I found after sitting with Tom that I wanted to drive home in silence. It was a harrowing experience, testing my sense of what life is, just as those children in the mental hospital had done forty years earlier.

By my fifth visit Joan was starting to regain a little of her spirit, laughing that Tom had responded to one of Jeremy's pep talks by shouting "Fuck off", then a little later "Bollocks". That had cheered them all up. In my diary that night I wrote, 'He listens carefully to what I've got to say, and his replies always make sense at first. And I feel I am starting to understand him. He talks of going into the nets to relearn how to play, and he says that he is happy enough at present. And, when I say goodbye and thank him, he thanks me back. All his qualities shine through in his struggle.'

Bob Appleyard was a rock for me. He understood what I was going through, more than anybody except Sue, and he rang regularly.

I was feeling flickers of hope for Tom, but then I wondered if it would be worse for him if he came to understand his situation. There was talk that he could not stay for ever in the hospital. I knew absolutely that he would not have wanted to put his family through this.

My sixth visit, at the end of April, was my last. His temperature had become unstable, he slept throughout the hour I was with him, and I left in low spirits. I was driving on to Yorkshire and, when I stopped for a meal, I found a message from Sue on my mobile phone. 'Please ring.'

"David Foot has called," she said. "He's heard that Arthur Milton has collapsed and died."

The following Monday morning Jeremy rang to say that Tom had died.

*

Tom's book went into a strange limbo. It was in the shops and out for review, but that no longer seemed appropriate. Several obituaries drew heavily on it, some without even acknowledging its existence, and I was left with an awkward ambivalence: knowing that Tom had wanted his views to be heard, yet not wanting to be pushing the book in such circumstances. Even the title, *Tom Cartwright: The Flame Still Burns*, was now inappropriate.

Pat Murphy quoted from it seven weeks running in the *Birmingham Post*: 'It should be compulsory reading for everybody who worries about cricket's direction in this country.' When he rang, I told him that Tom had recognised him in the hotel, and he seemed really touched.

Frank Keating, as ever, understood what I was trying to achieve: 'Always the delight of Chalke is that while he invariably casts for depth in his subjects, he never once throws back a single tiddler's nuance, realising that each one landed adds substantially to the whole gleaming weight of the catch.'

I sent a copy to Peter Roebuck in Australia. He was out of love with England, having being put through a court case that centred on his regime of caning young overseas cricketers. For all his great gifts, sporting and intellectual, there was a strangeness at the heart of him, yet Tom retained a fatherly affection towards him. 'Peter really doesn't get the recognition he deserves,' he said in the book. 'I feel the world hasn't treated him as well as it should have done.'

Peter wrote back: 'I enjoyed the book so very much. It was rich and informative and conveyed both a sense of character and period. It was also pleasant to read something favourable about myself in England – has not happened for a long time!' Then he asked me to pass a message to Tom and Joan: 'Tell them that the world has treated me fine and that my life is rich and varied – and that I am highly regarded in many places and by many young people.' Alas, as his death four years later made clear, it was not the whole truth.

There was something poignant about my being the conduit for such an emotional communication. My only previous contact with him had been one phone call, yet he signed his letter: 'Your friend Pete'.

I was never able to pass on his message to Tom.

*

For the seven weeks in March and April that Tom lay in Neath and Port Talbot Hospital, the sun had beaten down as if it were midsummer. Then on the day of the funeral, at a church in a secluded spot at the bottom of a wooded hill, the rain came, the rain that fell all summer.

Joan had asked me to give the tribute and, after we had sung 'Jerusalem', I went up to the lectern. The church was packed, with family and friends, old team-mates and youngsters Tom had coached. I started by saying the things that needed to be said: about Tom as a family man, about his service to the game, about some of the people who had been important in his life. Then I read three passages from the book.

When I am writing a book, I can sit for days hearing almost nothing but that person's voice in my head. It is an intimate experience and, as I spoke the words to the congregation, I could hear Tom saying it all to me.

If I go onto a ground in the morning, an hour before a game, it's the loveliest of times. Especially at a club ground, in a nice place. There may be a mower still ticking and the groundsman marking the ends, but there's a silence as well. You can stand and think and listen. You've got the birds singing, the craftsman working, the mower ticking, the smell of everything. That's something that makes cricket different from all other games. I used to love to go out to open the batting at the start of a match and to see the white lines and the 22 yards of beautiful strip. No ball marks, no foot marks. All the preparation. It's something very special.

Sledging is infantile playground behaviour, isn't it? I can't believe it goes on. The wicket-keepers are expected to orchestrate all this noise, and the players are telling you all the time who they're going to target. It's pathetic. It's a huge tragedy that it's been allowed to happen like this. Not enough people speak out against it.

Step outside cricket and think. Is that the sort of ethic we want to encourage in the world, the way we want adults to deal with each other? They say it's a test of mental strength, but it's got nothing to do with that. It's a complete abuse of what sport is about, and we just accept it.

I say to my kids, 'The umpires are responsible for the laws of the game; the players are responsible for its spirit.' Unless people understand that, the real feel for the goodness of the game will go.

Religion brought a semblance of order to the community, and it's gone. And sport did a similar thing. There was a discipline and an order. These things fashioned people's lives.

What was precious in our game is being destroyed, thrown away.

My third passage was from the end of the book, set on that special day at Broadhalfpenny Down:

It was a magical day. A living evidence of what is really good about playing cricket. When you looked at the different backgrounds of all the people there and the way they'd come together in cricket and played on equal terms, it really brought home what cricket can be in people's lives.

Cricket has given me such enormous pleasure. I suppose that's why I've done what I have with my life, why I still do it. Cricket has been such a wonderful life for me, and I try to provide for other people something that might come close to what I've enjoyed.

Headmasters should insist on its being played in their schools. Parents should take their kids along to play.

Cricket is not like any other sport. It has a purity, and that purity is being taken away. It's so important that people who love cricket stand up and fight for it.

When I stepped down, the whole congregation burst into loud applause: not for me but for Tom, for the words I had spoken on his behalf and for everything he had stood for.

"Thank you so much, Stephen," Joan said at the reception, trying to find some cheerfulness through her tears. "I think he must have been a pretty good bloke, this Tom Cartwright, mustn't he?"

*

Five years later, at the Herbert Museum in Coventry, we assembled for the unveiling of a specially commissioned portrait of Tom. Tom would not have wanted it – he would have sooner the money was given to youth cricket or a homeless charity – but, nevertheless, we gathered: a whole team of Warwickshire cricketers, led by Mike Smith and Bob Barber, nearly all of Tom's family, both from South Wales and from Coventry, and various local dignitaries. The mayor spoke, then Mike Smith, and I brought up the rear, reading those same three extracts. By then, with the grief having abated, I felt proud to be Tom's posthumous voice.

The portrait was a good likeness, though Joan was not that keen on it. "He's made it look as if I haven't washed his sweater," she said.

I talked with Clive Leach, who had made money at Yorkshire/Tyne-Tees Television and become the chairman of Durham County Cricket Club. An Anglo-Indian from Coventry, he had started at Edgbaston at the same time as Tom. Tom had talked with a chuckle about him in my first book, how in those early years he had tried his hand at so many things including recording a cover version of 'The Yellow Rose of Texas'. "He was like a little bumblebee, buzzing about. He was always going to be chasing something."

I had often wondered if he really had recorded 'The Yellow Rose of Texas', it seemed a fanciful touch, but Tom, as I came to realise, rarely got a detail like that wrong. Yes, Clive told me, he had won a talent competition at Butlin's and spent a winter in the Republic of Ireland, singing with the Jack Ruane Band.

"I must get out Tom's book again," he said after I had read the extracts. "There was a real poetry in those passages you read."

*

Bob Barber did not manage a cricket match for his 80th birthday, though he still looked fit as a fiddle. Instead, we gathered for a meal on *HMS Victory* in Portsmouth. He rang to ask if I would speak, and I did not feel I could say no. Then he sent me the guest list, full of so many of the great and good of English cricket, and I began to wonder if I had made a mistake. It was bad enough speaking about county cricket in the 1950s, flanked by Hubert Doggart and Colin Cowdrey. This time, as it turned out, I would be flanked by Ted Dexter and Bob, with a dozen or more England cricketers around the room. What could I possibly say that they would want to hear?

We split into groups for a tour of the ship, and to my delight I found myself with Ken and Avril Taylor. That helped to keep me calm. Unfortunately I had had a busier day than I expected, and my speech was still in something of a muddle, with headings on several scraps of paper which I was adding to during the meal.

A formula emerged. I wove much of my speech around the people who had been at Broadhalfpenny Down and were no longer with us, mixing a few uplifting remarks with some funny stories. It did not go on too long, and I finished with those words of Tom about the enormous pleasure cricket gave him, how it brought people of all backgrounds together and how important it was to cherish the game and pass it on.

They are wonderful sentiments, beautifully expressed, and Bob's guests on the *Victory* applauded them as loudly as the congregation at Tom's funeral.

*

I kept in touch with Joan, visiting her from time to time till she died in 2017, ten years after Tom.

Two months later Jeremy and his partner Alison had a short break in Bath, and they took me for lunch in the Abbey Courtyard. We had a most pleasant two hours talking. Then, as we were about to go, he said he wanted to give me something as a thank you, and he produced a long, thin object wrapped in a couple of black bin bags. It was an umbrella, I could tell, with a spiky end. I am not a great one for umbrellas so I opened it very slowly, trying to compose the right words to show a proper appreciation.

When I pulled it out, I could not get out any words. There was a lump in my throat, and I was almost crying. It was not an umbrella; it was a stump from Tom's first Test match, given to him by his captain Ted Dexter. I am not a collector of cricketing memorabilia, but I shall never part with that.

23

Welcome to the real world of publishing

The summer of 2007 was the wettest since records began in the mid-18th century. The rain began on the day of Tom's funeral in early May, and it never went away for long. The jet stream drifted south where it stayed for months, bringing widespread flooding to the north in June and to parts of the south in late July.

I played two games of cricket on the weekend before Tom's funeral, and I only played two more in the rest of the summer – one in the drizzle in the only match that survived of the Journeymen's five-day tour of the West Country, one on a damp pitch in Surrey in the middle of September.

For the most part I did not want to play. I had had the stuffing knocked out of me by Tom's death. I did not fully realise it at the time, but it brought to an abrupt end my ten-year exploration of the cricket of my childhood. Tom was the man I consulted most often through those years – for the sharpness of his memory, for his insights into his fellow cricketers, for the clarity and freshness of his thinking and for the way he wrestled with the wider social issues. He felt, as I felt, that we were losing important qualities in our way of life, but he was not a reactionary; he did not want to turn the clock back to the world where honest, proud working men like him had to know their place and accept a pittance for their labour.

Arthur Milton's death hit me, too. I had just agreed to publish his book, and he had hardly started work on it. Mike Vockins wanted to press on with it, by interviewing others to tell the parts of the story that Arthur had not yet shared, and it was published four years later – but not by Fairfield Books. The sadness of the task, on top of Tom's death, was too much for me.

Within days of their two funerals, another death was announced, this time of Bath Press, the long-established firm who were printing our books. They had been keeping their prices low, to make sure their machines were always busy, and the French company that had bought them could not resist an offer for the site from a firm hoping to build a supermarket on it.

They were the fourth printers we had used, as local firms closed down or were taken over, and they were the best. We had established a good working relationship with Alan Stedman, the pre-press man, and Jenna Wilcox, our account manager. On one occasion, when I took the design of John Barclay's jacket to a firm of young designers, Alan expressed horror. "Why on earth didn't you give it to me?" he said. "These garish colours, they are like a holiday brochure. Not at all in your style." Within the hour he had it looking a whole lot better. Then, when I apologised one day to Jenna for taking up her time ahead of printing, she put me right. "You're the best customer I've got," she said. "All the big firms send through their work unchecked, then they want it reprinted when it comes out wrong."

Alan had learned his trade long before the days of computers. "I printed a book once," he told me, "with the four colours of charcoal grey, deep green, terracotta and beige. Who nowadays is going to do a job like that?"

I did not always understand the detail of what he was telling me, about midtones and solids and dot gain. But I was certain he knew what he was talking about, just as I had been when Charlie Light had talked about nurturing ash.

"People have lost the ability to read what even black-and-white pictures will look like on different types of paper. They use these cheaper papers, to save money or to make the book look bulky, and they just press the buttons on a computer. Everything's done automatically. Nobody feels the need to learn it for themselves. They don't understand dot gain so all they get is a mass-produced blob. Every picture is the same. No definition, no lift. Nobody any longer knows how to address a picture according to the particular surface of the paper. There are very few things I look at now and think, 'That's a good job.'"

"I go by local woods now," Charlie said, "and, dammit, it upsets me."

"The artistic skills of printing have all gone. It is very sad."

*

We toured several printing firms and finished up at Midway Colour Print in a village outside Trowbridge. They were not the cheapest option, certainly not as cheap as Bath Press had been, but they had an older man, Bob Preston, who talked the same language as Alan Stedman. Alan knew him; he said he was a good craftsman of the old school, and that clinched it.

They only printed the pages, sending them off for binding and jacketing elsewhere, which was not ideal, but they had a pre-press specialist, Rob Taylor, who, though a lot younger than Alan, shared his understanding of the relationship of the computer screen to the printing press, and working with him became the big plus of the firm. Up to this point I had been writing my books in Word, then giving them to a man in a nearby village to lay out in InDesign. The programme looked fearfully complicated, but Rob told me firmly that I could easily learn it – and, with his occasional help, I did so, saving myself a great deal of money in the process.

My next publication was the most ambitious I ever undertook. Frank Keating had recommended me to Simon Lister, a news producer with BBC television. Simon kept wicket for Kew in the Thames Valley League and had come up with the intriguing idea of a book in which he would seek to improve his glovework by talking to the greats of the game while simultaneously telling the story of the evolution of keeping. He had had a session with the Australian Rod Marsh, and his writing sparkled. Would I publish it?

I should have said yes, it was a great idea, but I was not sure it would sell well enough – an unknown author, cricket's least fashionable skill – and I turned it down. He was keen to write for Fairfield Books so, rather than take his book to other publishers, he talked to me about other possible books. By this time he was writing a regular *Eyewitness* feature for *The Wisden Cricketer*, one of which involved him ringing Clive Lloyd, the former West Indian captain. The interview went well, and he asked me, "What about a book with Clive Lloyd? Would you publish that?" "Yes," I said, without much thought, and the next thing I knew I was in the deep end, taking on a book with a potential to sell far more copies than any of my previous books.

A reader in Essex used to ring me. He had made money in a minicab business and regularly offered me two pieces of advice: "Work from the smallest premises you can and stick to what you're good at." On this occasion I did not follow his advice.

Clive, for the first time in his life, had employed an agent, a North Londoner called John, whom I met regularly for meetings. He was not my type at all, talking all the time about money, but strangely I found I liked him. He was refreshingly straightforward. The problem with him was that there was rather more talk than action. In an hour-long meeting I might say six times, "To get back to Clive's book." I have just found, with some incredulity, an entry in my diary in which at one meeting he set himself a target of selling 5,000 copies of the book at corporate events. As far as I am aware, there were none sold in this way.

One evening the four of us – Clive, John, Simon and I – met in the basement café of the Institute of Directors in Central London. John launched into a long story of how the BBC had asked to interview Clive for a programme about West Indian cricket. "Well, put your hand in your pocket," he told them. "What are you offering?" The answer was fifteen hundred pounds. "You've got to be joking. This is Clive Lloyd you're talking about. I know he's a nice man, but people have been taking advantage of him and I'm here to stop that. He will need ten thousand." On and on the story went till finally they agreed a figure of four thousand. "I know it wasn't ten thousand, but I had made my point."

Some weeks later I had a call from Clive. "How much did John say I was going to be paid for that television interview?"

"Four thousand, Clive."

"Well, why has he sent me a cheque for fifteen hundred?"

Simon, with a demanding job and a young family, put in long hours to get the book finished on time, even flying to Guyana and Trinidad to further his research, and he wrote it all up in a lively style. I was delighted to be publishing a book by a younger author and on such a major subject.

Much of Clive's greatness as a captain, the respect in which he was held by his team, came from an emotional maturity born out of his early experiences. Simon captured that beautifully, even getting Clive to talk movingly about the slavery that his ancestors had endured. After the book was published, when I visited their house, Clive's wife Waveney told me how impressed she was by the extent to which Clive, a naturally reticent character, had opened up to Simon. She thought it helped that Simon was so much younger than Clive.

At the last minute we had a crisis when an old friend of Clive in Georgetown read the text and told Clive that some of the language he was using was not sufficiently formal, not in keeping with his status in the world. The three most problematic words, often used by Clive when talking about his team-mates, were 'fellows', 'guys' and 'boys'. I forget what was wrong with 'fellows', but 'guys' was slang from the world of jazz and 'boys' had connotations of slavery. The suggestion was that I, as editor, would go through the text and replace the three words with 'men', 'players' and 'team'.

It was a tricky moment. We were close to going to print, and it offended against my sense of purity, my belief in the importance of recording Clive's voice as he spoke. Eventually we agreed a compromise: leave the 'fellows', cut down the 'guys' and strictly no 'boys'!

The finances of the book did not add up. I had paid out far more in advances than I could afford, I was having to increase the discount to my distributor to get the book into the main chains, and the take-up from my mailing list – the customers who would pay full price direct to me – was relatively insignificant. Before publication I constructed a spreadsheet, based on the cost of printing and selling 5,000, and it left me with a loss. So, at the last moment, buoyed by John's fighting talk and by the printer offering to store 5,000 of them, I increased the print run to 10,000.

Getting the print run right is the hardest part of publishing. Because of set-up costs, you are better off if you print too many and have a few left over than if you under-print and either lose sales or have to set up a second printing. That is the rational way to look at it, but we are human beings and somehow I always feel better if I print 2,000 and sell them all than if I print

2,500 and have 300 left over, even if the latter has made me more money. The other irrational factor, which I have never overcome, is the surge of optimism I feel whenever I am in the last days of getting a book ready for the printers. Time and again at this stage my heart has overruled my head and I have increased the print run, never more so than with Clive's book.

It was to be launched on a Monday lunchtime at Old Trafford, but on Wednesday of the previous week there was no sign of the copies. They were still being bound and jacketed by a firm in Wolverhampton. I drove up there to see what was happening, only to find that the jacketing was going to be done by hand by a group of elderly women sitting around a table. Worse, when I tried to sort the problem out with the supervisor, I could not make head or tail of his thick Black Country accent.

Finally it was arranged for a van load to be sent up to Manchester on Friday afternoon, only for the van to break down. "We'll have another go on Monday," they said cheerfully. I forced them to agree to a delivery on Saturday morning, arranging for a friend to meet the lorry outside a community centre between ten and twelve. He stood in the rain for the full two hours, only for somebody then to tell him that a lorry had driven up at 9.30 and gone away. I finished up ringing the managing director of the haulage company at home, and by sheer persistence I got the books delivered.

There followed three weeks of intense promotion. I organised two long days of press interviews for Clive in London, I accompanied him on some bookshop signings in Lancashire where I saw at first hand how he still turned heads in the street, and I set up a special lunch at Old Trafford, an evening at his old club Haslingden and several more appearances at bookshops, one of which created a display all across their front window. Then, in the midst of all this, the West Indies Cricket Board put pressure on Clive to be a last-minute stand-in as manager of their tour of South Africa, and he was gone, leaving me to cancel all the remaining events and to take a lot of flak. The bookshop with the display was almost incandescent with rage, refusing to be appeased by my abject apologies.

Simon had written a very good book – it was Mike Selvey's Book of the Year in the *Guardian* – and I liked Clive a lot. We shifted about 5,200 copies in all, my most successful title, and Simon went on to write an award-winning book, *Fire In Babylon*, about the golden years of West Indies cricket. For me, however, the bottom line was that I made a whacking great loss, wiping out the combined profit on Keith Andrew, Charles Palmer and Peter Walker.

It was welcome to the real world of publishing, where the profitable titles have to carry the losses of all the others. It was quite a shock.

*

For three years after Tom's death I did not write a book. I continued to submit monthly columns to *The Wisden Cricketer* and, remembering Stephen Fay's words when he took me on – "When you've done a hundred, you can put them in a book" – I did just that in a volume called *The Way It Was – Glimpses of English Cricket's Past*.

For several years, following my Geoffrey Howard book, the people at Surrey tried to persuade Micky Stewart, their former captain, to work with me on a book. He had liked Geoffrey's book greatly and was interested, but it never seemed to happen. In early 2008 I had a long session with him, talking through the great Surrey side of the 1950s for my magazine column, and the subject of the book came up again. When I sent him the article for his approval, I attached a letter, setting out what a book would involve. He rang to say that he was going to think it through over the weekend. "I'll give you my answer on Monday," he said. But he did not ring and, when the months passed, I decided to forget it. The most important requirement for a subject for one of my books is that they want to do it.

John Barclay had greatly enjoyed writing his first book, and he came back to me with a set of 15 or 18 unpublished articles, each focusing on an episode in his life. Would they make a second book? No, I thought, the format was not quite right but, if they were to be more consciously linked up and supplemented, that could work well.

I looked on the map to find a suitable meeting place, halfway between Bath and his home near Horsham, and I came up with the Grosvenor Hotel in Stockbridge. Little did I know that this was owned by, and housed the records of, the Houghton Association, the MCC of trout fishing – and that John, a keen angler, had caught his first fish in Stockbridge. Our project was blessed.

At each meeting we would talk around the next section of the book, then John would go away and write it up. This he did with a great care for the words he was choosing, and I loved his style. It had a depth below the plain English, and he had the rare gift of comic timing in his prose. He was always at his happiest when recalling a disaster on the playing field, like the achingly funny story of his catastrophic Sussex debut at Swansea when, after the game's conclusion, he managed to tip a whole tray full of drinks into his captain Tony Greig's kit bag: 'As I watched items of Greig's equipment bobbing about in the smelly and unattractive mixture of beer and milk, I came to the conclusion that I must have played my first and last championship match.' And, to this day, whenever I try to read aloud to Sue the story of his goalkeeping in a prep school football match that they lost 12-0, I finish on the floor, gasping for breath, with tears rolling out of my eyes. I am not exaggerating.

There was another side to the writing, with John revealing that he had been on antidepressants since his teens, his one attempt to come off them ending in something of a breakdown. He called the book *Life Beyond The Airing Cupboard*, recalling how on the days of prep school cricket matches he would shut himself away with his mid-morning milk, talking quietly to his bat.

> In the pages which follow, the airing cupboard is left well behind and becomes but a distant memory. And yet, as I developed and played the game in a grown-up world, there was always the little boy inside me, alone with the burden of expectation as he faced fresh challenges. Echoes of that childhood can be heard below the surface of the pieces that follow, and perhaps those echoes add something to the tales.

What beautiful writing, so clear and so emotionally honest. John has lived a most successful life, but he has never been uncomfortable with his streak of eccentricity.

In my early years at public school, every minute of every day was organised, all except an hour and a half on Sunday afternoon. My brother Peter, still at the school in my first two terms, would take me for a walk onto the heath, to see how I was getting on.

"You know what they are saying about you, don't you?" he said one week.

"No," I said a little nervously.

"They think you're eccentric."

I had no idea what the word meant but, when he explained it to me, I thought to myself, "That's all right. I don't mind that."

Working with John was always a joy, and his book was a great success, going into three reprints. Paul Coupar, who warmed my heart by comparing me with Alan Lomax, wrote a spot-on review in *The Wisden Cricketer*: 'These moving reflections on cricket and life glow with a winning generosity of spirit, soaring above petty rivalries to approach, at times, the level of spiritual meditation.'

He even saw the strength of the decision John and I had made when we sat down together: 'The book comprises 30 episodes, each carefully evoked. This eliminates dreary stretches of routine reportage – a format other publishers could fruitfully investigate.'

"He's really got it, hasn't he?" John said when he read the review.

We launched the book in November 2008 in the Writing Room at Lord's. Two days before that, Sue and I sat down for a crisis meeting. The gist of it was that we had taken on the publication of far too many books. Sitting on the carpet with a low table in front of us, Sue made me write down all the definites and all the possibles. There were more than a dozen titles on the piece of paper.

First up, for publishing the following spring, were three books: an update of Pat Murphy's *The Centurions*, one of my all-time favourite cricket books, about the batsmen who had hit 100 hundreds; the Nottinghamshire batsman Mark Wagh's diary of a season that I had rescued when another publisher had disgracefully jettisoned it; and *Bradley Brook – An American Walks Down an English Stream*, a book the journalist Dudley Doust had been writing when he died and which his friends Scyld Berry and Mike Brearley wanted to see into print.

There were others: the diaries of the umpire Nigel Plews; a social history of Essex County Cricket Club; the story of the cricketing summer of 1959; the memoir of a retired coroner, a friend of Bob Appleyard; a book by David Foot about his life in journalism; Robin Martin-Jenkins's account of the rise of Sussex from its revolution in the mid-1990s. And yet more that have now faded from my memory. The list was frighteningly long.

One by one Sue and I went through them, reducing the list to four or five, at the end of which she made me promise that I would not take on anything else – "absolutely nothing at all" – until these had all been published.

We were still sitting on the floor at the end of this when the phone rang. "Stephen, it's Micky here. I'd like to get started on that book."

Sue was pulling a dreadful face when I put down the phone.

"Well, I couldn't say no to Micky, could I?"

Two days later we were at the launch of John Barclay's book at Lord's, where I got talking to Marcus Williams of *The Times*. A book of writings by the *Yorkshire Post*'s cricket correspondent JM Kilburn had just been published, to which I had contributed a short piece at the back. I wrote how I liked to quote from newspaper reports of games, to counterpoint the memories of my subjects and to add atmosphere – and, for this purpose, my favourite two writers were Kilburn and Alan Gibson of *The Times*.

"The book I would really love to publish," I said, "is a collection of Alan Gibson's writing."

"That's funny," Marcus replied. "We had his son on the phone last week, asking us if we would publish exactly that."

My heart sank. I had been pipped to the post.

"And what did you say?"

"We said we couldn't take it on, but we'd look for a publisher for him."

A week later Anthony Gibson was sitting in our kitchen, talking through with me how we were going to lay out the book. Another title for our list.

24

My back pages – the 1980s

We were a divided nation in the 1980s. The deregulation of the City of London, the privatisation of public companies and the new computer-led technologies created a sense of easy money for some, with house prices rising rapidly. For others there was widespread unemployment, with communities hollowed out by the loss of traditional industries.

It all happened so very fast. Government stopped trying to control the forces of the market place, laying the foundations for a new age, one that was radically different in ideology from the Welfare State consensus that had held sway for the previous forty years. Individualism was celebrated and rewarded, with people from all backgrounds encouraged to use their initiative and make money. The Conservatives were no longer so much the party of the old school tie, while Labour slowly began to disentangle itself from its militant wing.

*

Cricket was back in fashion, with the perfect working-class hero for these times in Ian Botham. Having played little in the 1970s, I helped to set up a team of friends, the Lost Graces, that played in the parks of North London. A host of such teams were formed around this time, playing on pitches that had lain half-idle during much of the 1970s.

We took it all immensely seriously. One of our team even produced an annual called *Swisden*, with witty articles and statistics galore. One year he got me to write all the match reports in literary pastiches. One, in the style of Housman, described a ground in Hackney, where the outfield was a mess with holes dug for rugby posts left unfilled.

> *Loveliest of grounds, Spring Hill today*
> *Is clothed with grass as high as hay.*
> *In place of winter's rugby poles*
> *They've jammed down traffic cones in holes.*
>
> *Now of my three score years and ten*
> *Forty will not come again,*
> *And take from seventy years two score*
> *It only leaves me thirty more.*

And, since to gaze at upturned cones,
Thirty Junes is no great bones,
I'll slip and slide in mud and slime
To see Spring Hill in summertime.

The *Swisden* editor, a genius of surreal humour, produced a spoof 'souvenir brochure' for a tour of East Anglia. In it I was described as having been 'born and nurtured in a home which breathed the very essence of cricket, the laundry at The Oval', of bringing 'a Wittgensteinian approach to captaincy and a cricketing skill to logical positivism' and of gaining fame at Oxford 'for singing Dylan's *Desolation Row* 26 times during a marathon innings of 36 in six hours'.

It was great fun for a while, with park cricket producing more than its share of the unexpected and the comic. But I yearned for it to have a greater formality, for the rituals of the game to be taken more seriously. In one match I went out to bat at about 100 for two, looking to make runs against a poor team who were one short in the field, only to find that they had just recruited a passer-by, a lean and distinctly fit-looking West Indian. He was immediately brought on to bowl, sent my middle stump cartwheeling with a lightning-fast yorker, then said "That'll do for me" and wandered off.

Before the end of the decade a group of us set up the Journeymen, establishing some agreed rules of behaviour and creating a fixture list at grounds beyond the M25.

*

My friend Mel, who had been grubbing a living of sorts as a piano tuner and home tutor, enrolled for a 13-week course, an introduction to computing, run by the government's Training Opportunities Scheme. He got a job with a firm who were charging companies £25 an hour for his services, and on his first call-out he took nearly two hours to work out how to insert the floppy disc. Yet nobody complained, it was a new world, and soon enough he had moved to a company who were paying him an annual salary of £80,000. "If others are making all this money, why shouldn't I have a bit of it?" he said.

He had grown up in the East End, a working-class lad, and he had less difficulty than me in shaking off the egalitarian baggage of the 1970s.

My brother Peter, still running the family timber business, had several letters from people starting up businesses. One, which he threw in the bin, came from a chap planning to spend his redundancy money producing croquet sets. Two or three years later he was featured in the *Daily Telegraph*; he was selling 100,000 sets a year.

My only step into such entrepreneurial activity came when, at the height of the Coe-Ovett rivalry, I designed a board game called 'The Mile' which

I planned to produce and sell into shops. I worked out how to simulate the tactics of middle-distance running, with a track that rewarded the athletes on the inside and playing cards that penalised the pace-setter. Then, when Sue had created the board, I invited round a friend and his two teenage boys. Unfortunately, part way round the last lap, we all ran out of playing cards, and life moved on.

My work in adult literacy led to my taking on a numeracy class, a group of middle-aged men working in manual jobs. Each week we generated the maths out of their daily problems, and it became a delightful session, one of the highlights of my time in education. One man, a little younger than the others, was a dustman with Westminster City Council. He was thinking about buying a starter home in Milton Keynes, coming into work each day on his motor bike. It was a perfect subject for one of our evenings, and painstakingly we itemised all his bills, concluding that, if he were lucky, he would have a pound or two a week left for food and other expenses. "You can't do it, Bill," we all said, but he went ahead. Out in Milton Keynes he stopped coming to our group, but I saw him a year later, emptying bins. Since we had last met, he had been on two foreign holidays.

Having put my head above the parapet as someone not frightened by numbers, I was soon in demand all over North London, teaching maths in adult education centres and further education colleges. At Tottenham College I was allocated the sub-'A' level work that the full-time staff did not want to teach: a return-to-study course for the unemployed and a BTEC diploma in Science where we took a bunch of youngsters, gave them 30 hours a week of tuition and some supervised work placements, and turned them into desirable employees.

An epiphany came for me one day when I was discussing one lad's work with their Physics lecturer, a former boilerman who had gone to university in his forties. As always I was trying to see the positive in the student, and the man rounded on me. "I don't know what sort of education you've had, but I've got higher standards than this."

I stood there, thinking, "I was supposed to sit for a Cambridge scholarship in Maths. I was asked to apply for a lectureship in Drama at Bristol. What has become of me?"

I enrolled for a Maths degree with the Open University, and in 1989 I took a full-time job, with responsibilities, in Bristol.

*

In our last year in London the teachers went on strike from Tuesday to Thursday every week. We arranged our lives so that each Tuesday, while Sue worked, I would look after Martha. I took her to all the sites of London – St

Paul's and Westminster Abbey, the various museums and art galleries, some of them places I had never been myself – and she had an excellent attention span, making the most of the days. It was a better education than she would have got at school, but I was fed up that London was not working better. It would be a wrench, leaving so many friends, but it was time to go.

*

Through the 1980s we lived in a self-managed housing association, a co-operative where, in exchange for rented accommodation, we were required to give four hours of our time each week, doing practical or administrative tasks. I rarely put in less than twenty hours, sitting on various committees and becoming something of an expert on the funding of public housing.

In Maslow's Hierarchy of Needs housing comes in the most essential category – food, water, warmth and rest – and many of our new members, often single parents with young children, were at a desperately low point in their lives. On one occasion, against my advice but clutching at the only solution on offer, a woman accepted a flat too small for her and her child. Three months later she was accusing me of hard-heartedness for putting her in it.

Mostly we converted large houses into two or three flats, and this created inter-tenant problems that I was not good at dealing with. One such dispute involved a woman with a young child in an upstairs flat where, below her, was a single woman who objected on some sort of mystical grounds to the cutting of the grass on the shared lawn. To add to this, the downstairs tenant had acquired a boyfriend who was constructing a large, unstable sculpture in the back yard. Feelings on both sides had hardened, and my efforts at mediation were pathetic.

I was not sorry when we left. Sue wanted to transfer into another housing co-operative, but I was determined to become a home owner. With little capital we bought a shabby house in an unfashionable district of Bristol, spending a lot of money – money we barely had – doing it up.

After two years we decided to move on, but the housing market had crashed and we were stuck. Eventually, by dropping our price substantially below what we had paid for the house, we found a buyer and moved to Bath.

At this point I did a calculation: the loss on the house, the money spent on renovating it, the interest our savings would have accrued, the new incentive scheme for tenants leaving housing association accommodation. It turned out that we would have been better off if, instead of working flat out at the college, I had spent the three-and-a-half years lying in bed in London.

Such was the financial roller-coaster of those times.

25

Writing can be a lonely life

In October 2008, when *The Way It Was* and John Barclay's *Life Beyond The Airing Cuboard* were printed, it brought our set of publications to 21, prompting me to host a 'Coming of Age' lunch for Fairfield Books.

There were thirteen of us for lunch at The Bear in Hungerford: Sue and me, my brother Andrew, John Barclay and his wife Renira, Douglas Miller, Mark Wagh, Peter Walker, John Stern, David Foot, Ivan Ponting, who had co-written with David a book on post-war Somerset cricketers, and my most trusted adviser and proof-reader David Smith and his wife Silvia.

The highlight of the day was the conversation around the table. At my end Mark Wagh, still playing for Nottinghamshire, and Peter Walker, who had retired 36 years earlier, were comparing their different eras, captivating those around them with a fascinating exploration of how close-to-the-wicket catching had evolved. I was so taken with the conversation between Mark and Peter that I hatched the idea of a series in *The Wisden Cricketer*, called 'Then And Now', in which players of different generations would sit down in this way. John Stern was keen so I set up the first such encounter, pairing Bob Appleyard with a current Yorkshire and England bowler. Bob loved the idea, and the Chief Executive of Yorkshire instructed the bowler to speak to me. I left him two messages on his mobile phone, but he did not respond – so, without the thick skin of a journalist, I let the idea die. If the young Bob had been invited to talk with Wilfred Rhodes, he would have leapt at the opportunity, but times have changed.

The following year I set up a second lunch, this time at the Ibex Inn in Chaddesworth, just off the M4 in Berkshire. This time there were sixteen of us. Mark Wagh, John Stern, David Foot and David and Silvia Smith could not make it, but they were replaced by Peter Walker's wife Sue, Anthony Gibson, Don Shepherd, the former *Times* cricket correspondent John Woodcock, Ken and Avril Taylor, making the trek from Norfolk, and, best of all, coming down by train from Yorkshire, Bob Appleyard with his friend Ron Deaton.

My great regret was that Frank Parr could not come. He so much wanted to meet up with Ken Taylor and with John Woodcock, whose time on the *Manchester Guardian* had coincided with Frank's time in the Lancashire team, but, alas, he had booked a place on a jazz weekend in Norfolk. It would have done him so much good to be a special guest in that company, and my sadness – and his – only increased when he told me afterwards that the jazz weekend had been a disappointment.

Bob and Ron were late, held up by a death on the line near Peterborough, and, when they finally appeared, there was quite a buzz in the room. Bob, this forgotten man of English cricket, had such an aura about him. John Barclay, who had just become MCC's President, sat next to Bob for a while, seeming like a star-struck schoolboy as he asked him about Len Hutton and Denis Compton. "He's not Bob Appleyard to me," John said. "He's *the* Bob Appleyard, one of the legends of the game."

Bob, who was always impressed by status, was delighted to meet John, and he was even more thrilled to be reunited with John Woodcock, whom, I suspect, he had not met since they toured Australia together 55 years earlier.

Unlike the previous year, when the table was long and thin, we sat in a square, and after the meal we talked as one, with stories bubbling up from all round the table. I brought with me some cricket balls, and I got Bob Appleyard and Don Shepherd to display their bowling grips. Bob, in his heyday, had bowled his off-breaks with the ball between his middle and ring fingers, adding to the force he could impart on the ball. He had enormous hands and even at the age of 85 he could get the ball right down into the gap, with not a chink of daylight between the fingers. Don had hands barely half the size.

Peter Walker was at his wittiest, Ken Taylor chipped in with typically modest humour, John Barclay radiated joie de vivre, and those of us who had not played cricket at a high level listened in wondrous joy. It was intimate, and it was very, very moving. John Woodcock, who himself was 83, shook my hand warmly as he left: "I don't know anybody else who could have arranged such a special day."

So much of my life as a writer and publisher has been spent at home, typing onto a computer screen or packing parcels. So these days, all too rare, stand out in the memory.

*

John Barclay and I set up a hilarious evening at the Cricket Society in London. The idea was to tell the story of a match, keeping the audience in suspense about the outcome in much the way I did in my first books. We opted for a game against Kent at Hastings in which Derek Underwood, nearing the end of his career, scored his only century. John persuaded Derek to take part so we had one player from each team, with me setting the scene and moving the action forward. If their memory lacked detail during a passage of play, I would set up a diversion – "Who was the best batsman you bowled to, Derek?" – just as I did in my first books.

At first Derek, a naturally quiet man, was bemused by the format. Then he realised that, if he did not assert himself, John would talk all evening. John was full of nervous energy, dancing back and forth around the low stage – and, when I finally got Derek into the action, his first words were, "I don't remember your feet moving this much, John, when I used to bowl at you."

The game moved to its denouement. The last Sussex batsman – the reserve wicket-keeper David Smith making a rare appearance for the county – faced Kent's Australian fast-medium swing bowler Terry Alderman with one run needed for victory.

John had added a quirky touch, involving an old man in a long coat who, spotting John the Sussex captain looking nervous as the end neared, had offered him advice: "Years ago I used to coach high-jumping. Do you know what I used to tell my young jumpers?" John described beautifully the scene, of this stranger trapping him with some long, seemingly irrelevant advice. "I used to tell them to throw their hearts over the bar and that their bodies would automatically follow. It used to work wonders with athletes who were anxious or nervous. Tell that to the team."

As the last ball was bowled, John held the tension beautifully. "The ball was there to drive, and David Smith? He threw his heart over the bar ..." – there was a long pause – "and he was caught at slip."

*

Micky Stewart surprised me when we joined forces on a tour of the cricket societies. As England manager he had never come over as a bundle of fun, but that, as I had already discovered, was deceptive. He had a theatrical gene, a grandfather who had appeared in Fred Karno's troupe with Charlie Chaplin, and it would come out when least you expected it.

He had fielded in the leg trap to Jim Laker's off-breaks, often telling me how much closer to the bat they would stand than the fielders at other counties, so I invited him to show the audience what distance he was talking about.

"Here I am," I said, waving up and down an imaginary bat. "I'm taking guard against Jim Laker. Where will you be?"

"I won't be anywhere," came this voice from behind me. "I wouldn't need to be. He'd bowl you first ball."

On another occasion we were in Derbyshire where our audience included Harold Rhodes, at one time the fastest bowler in England. He was a long way back in the large room, not quite a cricket pitch away, and he stood up to ask a question. "Nice to see you, Harold," Micky replied and, before he answered the question, he ducked his head as if swaying out of the way of one of Harold's bouncers. The timing of it was perfect.

*

211

On 8 January 2013 I drove to Sheffield and back to deliver a six-minute reading. Yorkshire County Cricket Club had been formed on 8 January 1863 at a meeting at Sheffield's Adelphi Hotel, which stood on the site of our venue, the Crucible Theatre. So we were gathering on the very spot on the very evening 150 years later, and there was a great turnout of players, staff and committee. Unfortunately many of the old players, including Bob Appleyard, chose to stay away, unhappy with Geoffrey Boycott's appointment as President of the club and thereby the evening's master of ceremonies.

The feud between Boycott and many of his contemporaries is a sad business which has never died down. I remember a man ringing to order a book from us and, like so many customers, he got talking. He told me how he had once been required to administer an anaesthetic to Brian Close, asking him if he had any allergies. "Just the one," came the reply. "Geoffrey Boycott."

Brian was not one to let such matters get in the way of his loyalty to Yorkshire cricket, and he, almost alone of his generation of Yorkshire players, attended the evening at the Crucible. The audience was on all four sides of the performing area and when, in the second half, Geoffrey was in the spotlight, telling the story of how Brian had encouraged him to open the innings early in his career, Brian's disembodied voice came out of the darkness: "That's not what I said, Geoffrey. I said you had to choose between opening and being bloody twelfth man."

I love these anniversaries when past and present are joined together in this way, and my own contribution, the first of the evening, focused on George Hirst and Bob Appleyard, the two men who had taken 200 wickets in a season for the county. Geoffrey introduced me warmly, paying tribute to my work for the county, and, after I had done my six minutes, I was ushered to a seat near the back where I found myself sitting next to his wife Rachael and their daughter. Only days before this, Theresa May, then the Home Secretary, had given an interview to the *Daily Telegraph* in which she had revealed that her teenage pin-up had been Geoffrey – so, to strike up conversation, I asked Rachael if she had seen the piece. The exact words of her reply, which I have never forgotten, were, "What do all these women see in Geoffrey?"

*

Between 2007 and 2013 I spoke at four funerals and a wedding.

For the funerals of Tom Cartwright and Keith Andrew I used the same format, celebrating them as people, then reading some of their words. Both times their quoted words were greeted with applause. Such clapping was something that was 'not the done thing' in church till Charles Spencer spoke so powerfully at the funeral of Princess Di.

My speech at Frank Parr's funeral was much too formal for the jazzmen, but the real disaster was my speech for Bomber Wells in Gloucester Cathedral. Bomber's great gift was his humour so I built my eulogy around that. But nobody in the large congregation laughed; nobody even smiled or looked happy. It was all wrong, I realised, and, as I stood there, I tried to find short cuts through the text I had written. I had struck the wrong tone. Bomber's irreverent humour did not belong in a cathedral.

It was only after the service that I discovered that nobody had heard any of it. My voice, amplified by a microphone, had bounced up into the vaulted roof, and the words had jumped around till they were just an ugly cacophony. "I tried putting in the hearing loop," Tom Graveney told me. "I even tried shaking it and hitting it."

For some days afterwards I felt terrible. Then I thought of Bomber. I imagined him looking down on me from above: this chap at the lectern taking it all so seriously, sweating away as he talked nineteen to the dozen at the top of his voice. And not a soul could hear a word of what he was saying. Bomber would have found it hilarious.

The wedding speech was for Martha, at the reception on Worthy Farm in Pilton where she is a finance worker for the Glastonbury Festival, a full-time, all-the-year-round job till she became a mother and went part-time.

In the week before the wedding I put aside a day to read my diary for the years when she was small. Children see things differently from adults, and Martha was certainly no exception. I built the main body of my speech around some two dozen of the quirkier things she said.

A time when we played I-Spy in the car
"I Spy with my little eye," she said, "something beginning with f..."
After an age of guessing – a field, a farmer, a fox, a forest – we gave up. It turned out to be Far Away.

A conversation over dinner
"You know that man at Westminster Abbey," Martha says. "What was his name? The one who said nobody should pay when they go to hospital." "Clement Attlee." "Yes. Well, when I grow up, I'm going to say you shouldn't pay to have your car mended, Sue."

Shortly after we had had our video player stolen
"We don't see many policemen," Martha says.
"Not everybody can be policemen," I explain. "If they were, there wouldn't be any bus drivers or teachers or people who make televisions."
Straightaway she retorts, "And there wouldn't be any burglars."

June 1987 (soon after the General Election)
"Did Mrs Thatcher win?" Yes, I reply. "So she's going to run it for another year." "Five years." "You should have done it," Martha says.
Three days later
"If you had won the vote to look after England," Martha asks me during her bath, "would you have had time to look after me as well?"

I suppose the day of her birth was the happiest of my life, but this came close. It was a do-it-yourself venue, with no swanky wedding organisers, and we ended the evening on top of a hill, gathered around a large bonfire. Martha spoke beautifully, about the importance of family and friends, and I was inwardly happy that I had not let her down.

Every quote from my diary was met with a great roar of laughter, with several of Martha's friends telling me later that, when they became parents, they were going to write diaries. At one point during the speech I looked across at Michael Eavis, and he was almost falling off his chair. For some years after that, whenever he met me, he would say, "Oh, it's you," rather as if I were the lead singer of one of his headline acts.

Martha's co-workers tried to persuade Michael to do a book with me about his life. Anthony Gibson, who had known Michael from National Farmers' Union days, thought it an excellent idea. "For a man who's made so much money, he's got remarkably few enemies," he told me. It would have been a best-seller, far, far beyond the sales figures for Clive Lloyd and Bob Appleyard, neither of whom have had a railway locomotive named after them or appeared in *Time* magazine's list of 100 most influential people in the world.

Somewhat to my relief, Michael thought I was not rock'n'roll enough, and he was absolutely right. I can sing along to 'Waterloo Sunset' and 'Mr Tambourine Man', but I could not start to distinguish Coldplay from Elbow. Sue goes to Glastonbury each year, but I have not been to a pop festival since the Isle of Wight in 1970. My main memory of that experience is of sitting at two o'clock in the morning in a cold, windswept field, listening to Joan Baez singing 'The Night They Drove Old Dixie Down'. The stage seemed about half a mile away.

*

There are some thirty cricket societies around England, meeting through the winter months. Some are struggling, but others are in rude health, attracting large audiences. When I first spoke at Stourbridge, there were barely 30 there; now they pack the pavilion with 80 to 100. Leicester, meeting at the County Ground at Grace Road, get 150 to 200, as many as they get some days in summer for the cricket.

A special favourite is the Dorset Cricket Society, who meet every Thursday afternoon. Sometimes they have an outside speaker; sometimes they find somebody from their own ranks. Because it is weekly, it becomes a built-in part of the routine of their lives, rather like the Methodist Women's Fellowship my mother attended each week.

They meet at a sports centre near Bournemouth Airport. When I first went there in 2005, they were in a little office upstairs with sixteen chairs. There were seventeen of us there, a record attendance; when I got up to speak, somebody took my chair. Now they are in the main hall downstairs, attracting an audience of fifty or more. I have just been booked to speak in the 2019/20 season; it will be the eighth time they have heard me.

In Bath the West of England branch of the Cricket Society folded up some years ago. The numbers attending the evening meetings had dwindled to about twenty, and the committee grew old and retired together, leaving such a gap that nobody wanted to step forward. In spring 2016 a group of us, including Anthony Gibson and me, re-established it, switching the sessions to the afternoon. At the first talk we were delighted to attract just over 40; now, after a succession of excellent speakers, we think nothing of getting 150 to 200, many of whom come from far away: from Torquay to London, from Weymouth to Witney. With the venue close to the bus and train stations, we have even had audience members making their way from Suffolk and Cheshire.

Our normal format is for me, as chairman, to interview the speaker in the first hour, then after a break to have questions from the audience. Most of the speakers are more relaxed this way, happy to talk about their lives rather than to stand up on their own and make a speech.

As chairman I try to make the afternoon as uplifting as possible. The audience is elderly, and there is a danger in the second half that the questions can become negative, focusing too much on what is wrong with the current game. On one occasion there was a long question, more of a speech than a question, about slow over rates, which the speaker – David Leatherdale, the PCA's Chief Executive – answered intelligently. When the next questioner took up the same subject, I stopped him in mid-sentence: "No, we've said enough about that. Let's have a more cheerful question." I called a man on the other side of the room, and his 'more cheerful question' was: "Why do so many cricketers commit suicide?"

We had Derek Randall, who was great fun, as was Farokh Engineer. Mike Procter inspired us with the story of his charity work in South Africa. They are greats of the game, and it was special to have them with us. But others, when we had less idea what to expect, could take the breath away. John Holder, the umpire, was stunningly good. His way with words, when he brought alive the experience of flying from Barbados into England for the first time, wearing a light jacket and looking down on the grey rooves and the leafless trees, was superb. He also spoke with admirable passion about the need to uphold the highest standards of behaviour among cricketers at all levels.

John Barclay was brilliant, but he was not new to me – so, for me, the most enjoyable speaker so far has been Fred Rumsey. At the age of 80, he spoke for two and a half hours, generating much laughter and holding the rapt gathering in the palm of his hands. He had not addressed an audience for some years, so for him the session was a glorious surprise, discovering that he was not a cast-off has-been. There were still people out there whom he could entertain.

Out of that discovery was born another Fairfield Books title.

*

Then there are the Book of the Year ceremonies that briefly put a few writers in the spotlight – or, should I say, through the mangle – each year.

After my first book was published, a reader rang to say he thought I might have a chance of winning the Cricket Society Book of the Year prize. I had no idea what he was talking about. I knew nothing of the Cricket Society, only the Cricket Lovers group in Bristol, and certainly nothing of any book prize.

In time I was told I had been shortlisted. There was no ceremony, and it was only in a roundabout way that I learned that the prize had gone to a book about Broadhalfpenny Down, written by a colourful character who would go on to be elected to the European Parliament in the colours of UKIP, spending some of his term of office in prison for the wrongful claiming of benefits.

My second book was also shortlisted without winning. So my first prize came when the Wombwell Cricket Lovers' Society rang to say that I was their Cricket Writer of the Year for *One More Run*, my book with Bomber Wells. Would I come to Barnsley to collect the prize, then be that evening's speaker?

The Wombwell, set up in 1951 by the legendary Jack Sokell, was for many years the premier cricket society in the country, well known to all the old players. Fifty years on, when I went to collect my prize, Jack – a formidable character in his day – was still chairing it and, alas, time had taken its toll on him. The first item on the night's agenda was to choose the next set of prize winners and, with the forty or fifty members sitting around at tables with pints of beer, Jack was struggling to hold their attention.

He reached Cricket Writer of the Year and called for nominations. By this stage many of the people in the room were talking to each other so, with Jack hard of hearing, everything had to be repeated two or three times. "Has Rob Mills ever won it?" one member asked, referring to the then cricket correspondent of the *Yorkshire Post*, to which a man on the other side of the room said, "I bloody hope not." Somebody offered the name of Malcolm Lorimer, the Old Trafford librarian who had compiled a booklet of tributes to Brian Statham. I was surprised that qualified him for a writer's award, but Jack accepted him. When there were no further nominations he called for a show of hands, Rob Mills or Malcolm Lorimer, and Malcolm won by three votes to two.

If I had described the scene to Bomber, he would have laughed and laughed, but I thought better of it. He was so pleased that our book had won a prize.

My fourth book, with Geoffrey Howard, was shortlisted for the Cricket Society award, and now there was a lunchtime event at the Royal Overseas League in London, with the authors all gathered and the winner's name pulled out of a sealed envelope.

Three months earlier, I had been in the Long Room at The Oval after Alf Gover's memorial service, where the chairman of the judging panel, David Rayvern Allen, was talking to a little group about the books under consideration. Seeing me nearby, he said, "Perhaps it's Stephen's turn to win this year." Was that how it worked?

We did win, and I half-knew that from the moment one of the judges greeted me: "Are you Stephen Chalke? I can't say too much at the moment, but I did so enjoy your book." Two years later, when I was next short-listed with Bob Appleyard's book, I said hello to him and he shot past me with barely a word. At the time it felt rude, but in fairness he did spare me a tense hour of wondering whether or not I had won.

Frank Keating acquired a strange role where he was one of the judges but, out in Herefordshire, did not attend their discussions. It reminded me of a television documentary about a national poetry competition. Because the judges' meetings were being filmed, the reclusive Philip Larkin refused to attend, leading his fellow judges to spend much of their meeting asking, "What does Philip think?"

Frank had columns in the *Guardian*, *The Spectator* and *The Oldie*, and it was not uncommon for him to choose a different Book of the Year in each of them. He had a bee in his bonnet about the William Hill Sports Book of the Year, believing that its judges preferred books about the dark or seamy side of sport rather than celebrating its joys. Annually he would write an article in the *Guardian* attacking their choices, several times asking why I was not on the shortlist.

On one occasion Frank rang in advance to tell me what had won the Cricket Society Book of the Year, complaining that it was quite the wrong choice – "but what can I say?" One of my authors had a book on the shortlist, and all evening I had to pretend that I was in as much suspense as he was. When the chairman of judges was asked about Frank's role, he told the meeting that they had rung him with their decision and he had fully agreed with it.

It is 'posh bingo', as they say of the Booker Prize. It was never much fun being put through it each time, but as a publisher it gives the books a bit of publicity so it is undoubtedly a Good Thing.

There started to be other Cricket Book of the Year awards. In 2003 the *Wisden* almanack asked its reviewer to single out a book, and we won twice, with the Bob Appleyard and Tom Cartwright books. The same year the National Sporting Club introduced the British Sports Books Awards. It was much more corporate in style, looking to sell tables to companies, with awards such as 'Best Promotional Campaign for a Sports Book' and 'Best Sports Book Retailer', the latter being won in its first year by WH Smith.

At first the Cricket Writers' Club was responsible for the National Sporting Club's cricket book award, and Fairfield Books won twice with *Sixty Summers*, David Foot and Ivan Ponting's book about post-war Somerset cricket, and my *The Way It Was*. Then they peeled off and created their own award, which I have won with *Summer's Crown*. So now, as well as Wombwell's Cricket Writer of the Year, there are four Cricket Book of the Year awards. Often there are four different winners.

In 2009 the Cricket Society joined forces with MCC for their Book of the Year, moving the awards evening to the Long Room at Lord's. There is a keynote speaker and, unlike the National Sporting Club's evening, the books are all available for purchase on the night. It has become a classy event in the world of cricket, superbly staged, and in its first two years at Lord's Fairfield Books were triumphant, with John Barclay's *Life Beyond The Airing Cupboard* and Anthony Gibson's book about his father, *Of Didcot and the Demon*.

The latter book, chosen by a panel chaired by Vic Marks, pipped *Golden Boy*, a biography of Kim Hughes by the Australian writer Christian Ryan, a book that was recently chosen in a poll of experts as the greatest cricket book of all time. Such is the unpredictability, the subjectiveness, of prize-giving in the arts.

My own books have been shortlisted for the Cricket Society award ten times, with that one victory with Geoffrey Howard. I am not sure if it is my best book, but I am glad it was the one that won. It was such a special day for Geoffrey, 93 years old and having that last moment of public acclaim.

I was asked to give the keynote speech in 2012, about the state of cricket writing. I told the audience what it was like as a shortlisted author to go through the ordeal, and I appealed to them not just to buy the winner's book. Then, at the end of it all, I opened the envelope and presented the prize to Chris Waters of the *Yorkshire Post* for his book on Fred Trueman. Chris is one of my favourite cricket writers, and I felt a glow when I sensed his joy.

I launched into the main body of my speech with a story.

Six or seven years ago I was playing for my wandering club, The Journeymen, at a college ground in Cambridge. I was brought on to bowl at the tennis court end and, as I peeled off my sweater, the umpire started up a conversation. "Tell me," he said. "Are you the chap who writes cricket books?" It's not often this gets mentioned when I play cricket. So I puffed up at his enquiry. "Yes, I am."

"I've got a question for you," he said.

"Right you are. Let me bowl a few balls first. Get loose."

After three or four balls I turned to him. "You had a question?"

"Yes. It's something I've been wondering for a while. Why are cricket books all so bloody boring?"

Those were his words. "All so bloody boring." Possibly the word wasn't 'bloody'.

I did my best to examine the issues, giving examples from the best of the game's literature, and I ended my speech with a rallying cry, aimed at the journalists and writers who were there.

Cricket's writers and reporters are not a marginal adjunct to the game. They are an integral part of its place in our imagination. And it's important that we recognise that and cherish it. And, in recognising and cherishing it, we should understand that the words themselves are so vital, so life-giving to the game – the game that we all love and want to hand down in a healthy state to future generations.

I'm not despondent. I'm still part of that great army of devotees you can find every Saturday afternoon on fields up and down the land – nearly 64 years old, captaining a third eleven that includes lads not even a third of my age, lads who are as in love with the game as ever I was. If they go on as long as I have done, they will still be playing in the 2050s. That's the lifeblood of it all. As Alan Gibson so wisely wrote forty years ago, the only sane test of the popularity of a game is how many people are playing it.

It's so important that our books don't stay too cosily inside a narrow niche of readers but that some of them reach out and inspire this wider audience. Cricket is the greatest game on earth. It will only remain so if we all look after it.

The next day I was fine-tuning a chapter of Micky Stewart's book and packing parcels. I had had my half hour in the spotlight. Now it was back to the solitary life of writing and publishing.

26

The readers

One of our readers arranged to visit us. He said he would be in our area and he would like to call in. It was unclear to me what the purpose of his visit was, but it has always been part of the ethos of Fairfield Books to be friendly towards our customers so I said it would be a pleasure to meet him.

When he arrived at two o'clock, I offered him a seat on the sofa and made him a cup of tea. He did not take the lead in the conversation so I asked him where he had grown up and, from that, I found some relevant cricketing topics to discuss: matches he had seen, cricketers he had known. Three o'clock came and went, then half past three, and I was no wiser what he wanted from the visit. There was no mention of buying any books.

It began to remind me of a story Sue's mother often told, of an elderly couple bursting through the unlocked front door of her house during a heavy storm. "Can we sit in here?" they asked, pushing into the front room, and she sat talking to them for nearly half an hour. Then one of them asked, "Will the dentist be much longer?"

By four o'clock I was running out of conversation, starting to sense that not only I but he was embarrassed. "I'd better get back to work," I said. "Can I show you the best way off the hill?" We walked to his car and, as he opened the door, he turned back to me and asked in bemusement, "But where was Fairfield Books?" Finally it dawned on me that he had thought we were a shop.

*

Nearly half the books we sell are bought direct from us, with no 50% discount for the retailer. Wih many of our titles, the extra income achieved by those sales is often greater than the final profit margin. Those direct sales are the crux of our viability as publishers. Some of those sales are generated by meetings, but the majority come from our mailing list, the loyal customers who have stayed with us, many for more than twenty years. They are special people, and we try to treat them all with a personal touch.

Many write with fascinating letters, sometimes revealing nuggets of cricket history that I have worked into books and articles. One that arrived too late for use came after I published Bomber's book *One More Run*. The denouement of the 1957 match at the heart of the book involved the Gloucestershire team scraping home by two wickets, only – amid the dressing-room celebrations

– to be told that the scoreboard had been wrong and they needed one more run. The field had to be cleared so that they could go back out. Sam Cook was next man in and, so the story goes, he had just downed a pint.

A reader wrote to say that he had been at Cheltenham that day with his grandfather, scoring in a little book as schoolboys used to do. At the match's first conclusion he had protested that the scores were only level. "Don't be so silly," his grandfather said, marching him out of the ground. "They have proper scorers. They don't make mistakes like that."

It was one of Frank Keating's 'tiddlers, adding to the whole gleaming weight of the catch'. If the book should ever reappear, I shall add it.

A man whose father had captained Northamptonshire after the Second World War invited me to his house to show me his scrapbooks. He had queried what I had written about his father which, though I still believe it to be correct, I would have phrased a little differently if I had understood more clearly what good work his father had done during the war.

A man who played for Middlesex 2nd XI often rings with delightful titbits of memory. In one match Danny Livingston, Hampshire's young Antiguan, got out trying to hit his fourth consecutive six, only to receive a fearful rollocking from the county's Secretary, Desmond Eagar: "We don't play our cricket like that in Hampshire."

A reader in Surrey spent his wartime boyhood in Bath and is full of vivid stories about the city in those years. To no avail I have tried repeatedly to persuade him to write it all down for a local history booklet. On the front cover he could put his photograph of a middle-distance race he won at City of Bath Boys' School, with a certain Roger Bannister coming in behind him.

He played for a club called Hampset for whom my neighbour Adrian got me to turn out sometimes. He had a story of a wartime match at Weston-super-Mare when they finished too late to get back to Bath and slept in an RAF hut. In the morning two airmen arrived on bikes to inquire what they were doing, followed soon afterwards by a farmer in search of some stray calves. "'Ave you seen any 'eifers?" the farmer asked and, struggling with his thick Somerset accent, they thought he was asking if they had seen 'airforce'. "There were two of them," they replied. "They went that way on bikes."

A reader in Dorset likes me to send him any surplus pages with photographs on them for the scrapbooks he makes up, and I am always happy to do so. He is in poor health, and sometimes he tells me about his problems. On one occasion he ordered some books that were not yet back from the printers, then three days later – at 7.30 in the morning – he rang to cancel the order. He had called the ambulance and thought he was not going to survive the day. I felt a cold chill for much of the morning, a telephone friend lost – and

I could not help wondering if, in his shoes, I would have gone to the trouble of cancelling an order for books. The following week the phone rang: "It's all right. You can send those books now."

In the year 2000 I performed in a farmer's barn in a local village's Millennium Pageant. Cloaked in a dyed dust sheet, in a monologue I wrote myself, I was a 14th-century mystic, seeing into the future by holding the eggs of all the birds. My vision was of men climbing the hill inside shells with wheels and engaging in a strange ritual with sticks and birds' eggs.

> There are hundreds of them up there. No farm work to be done. No half day to walk up the hill. They can spend their time visiting the eggs. There. I can see one bending to lift an egg out of its hole. He writes on a sheet of parchment, and he moves off again with his stick. Eighteen holes with eggs in them. It is a whole world of bird-worshippers.
>
> But I can't see the larks. Or the sparrows or the starlings, the dunnocks or the wrens. The sky is empty. I see it all, and I am wise. Because I know these birds. But these people that I see, they have no birds, only eggs. How will they be wise?

While I was getting into costume in an adjoining barn, a man asked me, "Are you the chap who writes about cricket?" He told me he had found his father-in-law dead in an armchair with *Runs in the Memory* open on his lap. It was a chilling moment, made worse a few moments later when I was waiting to go on stage. The woman organising us in the wings said to me, "You wrote a cricket book, didn't you? My father was reading it when he died." When I got home that night, I said to Sue, "You know, two people in Upton Cheyney have died while reading my book." It was only then that the penny dropped.

*

My all-time favourite correspondent has to be Tony Ward in Northampton. My books stirred him to write regular letters to me, full of wonderful vignettes of Northamptonshire cricket through the years. His memory of sights, sounds and snatches of dialogue was astonishing, all captured with a droll sense of humour, that same provincial humour that my mother's family had, looking with a wry eye at human pretensions. The pile of his letters grew and grew, every one of them a joy, till I decided that we had to make a little book out of them. *Typhoon Tyson to Twenty/20*, it was called, an £8 softback. With a rave review from Matthew Engel in *The Wisden Cricketer*, our print run of 500 sold out in double-quick time.

Tony still writes regularly, often with little gems that I wish he had come up with for the book. Here is one that still makes me smile:

In Northampton in the 1950s there was an old bookshop called *W. Musk and Co.* It was an institution. A lovely smell of new books, cartridge paper and Quink ink pervaded the nooks and crannies. I still have the occasional dream about it!

Like a lot of bookshops they had the occasional 'personality' to come and do a book signing. On one particular occasion we heard that a cowboy and adventurer by the name of Ross Salmon was coming to Musks. My mother was always intrigued by personalities so she took me down to see him. On approaching the shop in the Drapery, a slightly upmarket thoroughfare, we noticed a white horse tethered to the nearest lamp post. It belonged to Ross who sat inside wearing full cowboy kit with white stetson. My mother asked him for his autograph without buying a book. He was a bit sniffy about it but then signed one of his publicity leaflets. I was awestruck as you can imagine. A real cowboy!

A few years later I found out he was working as a statistician for *Test Match Special.*

*

I have sold books to a number of eminent people – including a winner of the Nobel Prize for Literature as well as men who have held the positions of Prime Minister, Head of the Civil Service, Head of the British Army and Manager of the England football team – but it is the quirky letters and phone calls from ordinary folk that have given me the greatest pleasure.

I was a great admirer of the eccentric author and self-publisher JL Carr. His novel *A Month in the Country*, a tale of lost opportunity set around a church in 1920, was short-listed for the 1980 Booker Prize and should have won. Another book, *A Season In Sinji*, told of a soldier in the last war, losing his girl to an officer and seeking revenge through cricket under the heat of a West African sky. That and *The Go-Between* are the best two novels that feature cricket.

Carr also published tiny books of wood engravings, poetry and all sorts. There was no sign of the corporate publisher trying to satisfy a pre-determined market place. Everything he did had a magnificent originality.

At the time I started reading him I knew nothing of publishing, but I loved the idea that he was going his own way, doing things the way he chose to do them: not making much money but staying true to himself. So one of the greatest compliments I ever received came when Graeme Wright, the former editor of the *Wisden* almanack, met me at a book launch at Downside School. "You're becoming the JL Carr of the cricket world," he said.

What a wonderful thing to be.

27

The last years of playing

The 'diary of a season' format is not uncommon in cricket. Peter Roebuck's *It Never Rains*, about his summer playing for Somerset in 1983, is generally considered the best, but he was a writer in a class of his own.

The great advantage of the diary is that it has immediacy. There is less room for the wisdom that comes with a more distant perspective, less sense of a text shaped into a measured and balanced narrative. Instead, there is a raw freshness that at its best can take the reader closer to the day-to-day experience of the diarist.

As somebody who was writing and publishing books about cricket history, I was surprised in September 2008 to receive a call from the Nottinghamshire batsman Mark Wagh. He had been spending that summer writing a diary for a Midlands-based publisher, Know The Score Books, and out of the blue they had dumped him. Was there any chance that I could come to the rescue?

Almost certainly I would have said no, had it not been for two things. He had been recommended to me by George Dobell, whose cricket writing I admired greatly. Also, by the oddest of coincidences, John Barclay had mentioned only a few days earlier that he had sat next to Mark at a lunch and found him a fascinating character – "not at all your typical county pro".

I agreed to read what he had written, I spoke to George, and soon enough there was another title on our schedule, our first venture into the contemporary game. A psychology graduate from Oxford University, Mark was starting to think about his life after cricket, with writing one option, so the book was important to him. We met several times, when I encouraged him to write some more general passages in which the diary entries could be set. He took it all most seriously.

After the book had been laid out and proof-read, I asked him to give the text one last read. The night before I was taking it to the printers, he rang in some alarm. His Search function was telling him that he had used the word 'pretty' 61 times, as a result of which we spent an hour and a half going through them all, substituting 'fairly', 'reasonably', 'undeniably', 'quite' and often nothing at all. I could not imagine most cricketers going to that trouble.

Two years previously, Stephen Harmison had 'written' a diary for a book, with Justin Langer, on the Ashes series in Australia. To publicise the book, he spoke to *The Wisden Cricketer*, becoming angry when it was suggested to him that he got depressed when he was away touring. "But it says that in your new book," the interviewer interjected. "Oh, does it?" Harmison said. "I haven't read that yet."

The great danger of the format is that the diarist, in his desire to be honest, upsets team-mates with his comments, but that was not in Mark's character. Rather, he wanted to explore his own experiences within some wider thoughts about the psychology of the game.

In one entry he was waking up the morning after a disastrous match in which, with rain approaching, he and his friend Bilal Shafayat had made a complete mess of a run chase, coming off to be greeted by stony silence from their team-mates and 'incandescent rage' from the coach Mick Newell.

> It feels like someone is just banging about in my head, hitting me with a hammer, except the hammer is images, feelings, words from yesterday. I wish it would stop, but my inner world is on constant loop, playing, replaying. It's just killing me.
>
> I can't stand the thought of seeing anyone; I feel like a condemned man, the accused, the wrong-doer. I can hear Mick, see him shaking his head, full of disgust. The feeling of animosity as Bill and I walked off in the rain. Mick's summing up, wanting to get out of the changing room, wanting the car journey to end, just desperate to be on my own.
>
> Self-pity is hardly going to help things, I suppose, and the hurt will fade over the next few days. The correct response is to come out fighting, score runs, field like never before and give Mick the finger, something at the moment I'd love to do. But another part of me just wants to crawl under the duvet, hoping it will all go away.

I thought that was superb writing. As someone whom Keith Andrew called 'a serious cricketer', I could relate to it completely. Mark's contemporary Robin Martin-Jenkins, reviewing the book in *The Wisden Cricketer*, related to it, too: 'On the surface it is a straightforward diary of a batsman's season. But delve in and you are taken deep into the psyche of the journeyman county cricketer, a place of fear, paranoia, self-loathing and, just occasionally, joy.'

It reminded me of the quote from John Arlott that Ken Taylor kept on a piece of paper, the quote that he felt was the closest to the truth he had ever read about the game he had played for a living each summer: 'Cricket is a game of the most terrifying stresses with more luck about it than any other game. They call it a team game but in fact it is the loneliest game of all.'

For me the book raised questions about the modern game, about the way the dominance of coaches can stifle characters such as Mark, intelligent men who fifty years earlier would have played as amateurs and felt freer to do things their own way.

I enjoyed working with Mark; at one point he was going to write a second book for us, about leadership in sport. Then he decided to become a solicitor, spending all his spare time, at home and in the pavilion, studying law books. In 2010, his last full season, when he was a key member of the Nottinghamshire team that won the championship, I found myself rooting for him.

Their victory came on a thrilling last day at Old Trafford, and five days later he was sitting on a newly-purchased bicycle in John o' Groats, starting a charity ride to Land's End, raising money for adult literacy work. He had done almost no training, his fellow cyclists had all dropped out, and he was doing the guidebook's 20-stage route in ten days. I met him for a meal in an Italian restaurant in Glastonbury on the eighth evening after he had set out from Worcester at first light and completed a gruelling 12-hour, 100-mile day full of hills. While he refuelled his body with large quantities of pasta, I was overwhelmed with admiration for his spirit – and his sense of independence.

John Barclay was right; he was not at all your typical county pro.

*

After hardly playing cricket in the summer of Tom Cartwright's death, I returned in 2008, though with no great success. I turned 60, my achilles tendons kept flaring up when I bowled, and I felt I was reaching the end.

The following winter, as the result of a chance conversation after a game in the indoor cricket league, I found myself being invited to join Winsley Cricket Club, up the hill from Bradford-on-Avon, and to take on the captaincy of the third eleven they were forming. My neighbour Adrian was now playing for them, hence the connection in the indoor cricket, and he advised me strongly against it. "They haven't got a third eleven. You'll spend all summer on the phone, looking for players, and you'll finish up cancelling most of the games." He then sent me an e-mail with 17 questions I was to ask the club before I made my decision: "Do NOT accept the captaincy unless you get satisfactory answers on all these points," he instructed me. "They're a village club with village club organisation."

At the meeting I only made one stipulation: that the team would not be the leftovers after the second eleven had had their pick but a stable mix of youngsters, with the right sort of older players guiding them. They agreed to this and, when I recruited an old friend David to join me, I was filled with optimism.

It was the friendliest of clubs, with a well-maintained home ground high on a hill, with a view across the fields of West Wiltshire, though, of course, the third eleven did not play there. They had an overseas professional – Terry Duffin, a Zimbabwean Test cricketer, who set a good example – and the club was on the up.

The Journeymen were always my first cricketing love but, of all the local cricket I played, that first summer at Winsley was by a long way the most enjoyable. In no time we seemed to develop exactly the team culture I wanted, with a pair of 18-year-olds in the first game soon recruiting their friends till we had just the blend of ages I had envisaged.

I took it all tremendously seriously, going to great lengths some weeks to take the field with a full eleven. I always started out with a plan of how I was going to work each of them into the game, even thinking through the field placings in bed the night before. At the end of one afternoon I apologised to Luke, one of the youngsters, that I had not given him a bowl, promising that he would open the following week, and I did just that. I thought nothing of it but Paul, one of the oldies, noticed, and he told me how impressed he was.

For some of the 18-year-olds, it was their first proper cricket. They had been drawn to the game four years earlier, watching England win the Ashes on Channel 4, and they all had sufficient ball sense to contribute to the team. One week I asked a lad called Jim to open the batting, and I was near to tears when he scored his hundredth run.

Our penultimate fixture was away at Norton St Philip, the other new team in the division. As the village's only eleven, they had match-winners well above third-eleven standard, notably an off-spinner and a seamer who was too fast at that stage for some of our youngsters. They had won all their games, and we needed to beat them to secure the other promotion place.

They made 227 for five in their 45 overs, more than I was hoping, and I gave my instructions at tea. The youngsters would come in from four downwards, and the top three – David, his son Tim and Paul – would see off the opening bowling, however few runs they scored. In the event Norton St Philip stuck to their two star bowlers for their full quota of 12 overs each, leaving us on 64 for one after 24 overs. It was a big field, and we needed eight runs an over from there.

We won in the last over by four wickets, a glorious game. Oli, the lad most intrigued by cricketing tactics, scored the winning run, coming off with a great beam on his face as we clapped him in. "What was so good," he said, "is that we had a match plan, we stuck to it, and it worked."

In truth, I thought our chance of winning at the 24-over stage was no more than 20%, and by then it would have been too late for a Plan B. But sometimes, as a captain, you deserve a bit of luck.

The lads did not often stay for a drink, but that night in the Fleur De Lys they sat with our scorebook, turning over the pages and reliving the highs of their first summer of adult cricket. Tom, a commercial designer in his mid-twenties, was off any day to live in Australia with his girlfriend, and he said his farewell to us in the car park, thanking me for everything. I am not sure that I have ever gone home happier from a match. And it got happier when I read the day's cricket results online and found that Mark Wagh had hit a century.

It was only third-eleven cricket in the bottom division of the Wiltshire League, but to us it was every bit as important as the matches the first eleven were playing. There were more moments of comedy, more oddballs we had to fit into the team at the last minute, more ramshackle venues, but we always played it properly – and we could not have had a better bunch of lads. They played for enjoyment, for recreation, never letting the tension of the game – or any aggravation from the opposition – get in the way of that. And, as far as my bowling was concerned, I was playing at a lower level on dodgier pitches, with a young team who were far better fielders than the ageing Journeymen had become.

It was 16 years on from my first coaching session with Ken Biddulph, and I was enjoying the game more than ever.

*

It was Ron Deaton, Bob Appleyard's friend, who suggested that I write a book about my own cricket. Whenever he rang, I would tell him of my latest match, I was full of it all summer, and he loved the funny stories I told, the glow I had about it all. So I started to think I might give it a go. But how?

So many people have written humorous books about low-level cricket and, though I wanted there to be humour in it, I was not sure I wanted to write that sort of book. The diary format of Mark's book set me thinking. Perhaps I could write a diary through the next summer. Then I realised that I would be 62 in June, the age at which my father played his last game. I was only eight at the time and have no memory of it, but Mum often told the story.

He had had a heart attack and a bad car accident and was very overweight; in her view he was making a fool of himself by going on. He wanted to bring up his fifty years for the village, having first turned out for them in 1906 at the age of 12. As he owned the field and employed most of the team, nobody was in a position to stop him. On the day when they celebrated his fifty years, he had a funny turn in the pavilion and could not go out to bat.

I have spent my life thinking about the radically different ways my parents dealt with dying. Dad fought death to his last breath, amazing the doctors by how long he lasted, putting an immense strain on everybody close to him. Mum, by contrast, hated causing any bother; once she was told she had cancer, she lost the will to live, dying within weeks. She was trying to be kind to us, to save us from what we had been through with Dad, yet her death left me with an emotional scar much greater than Dad's did.

That was the book I was going to write: the diary of an ageing third-eleven captain, the ups and downs of the summer with plenty of humour but interwoven with reflections on my own life, with that central question hanging over it all: "Should I go on playing, even to the stage at which I am making a fool of myself, or should I fade away before I become a nuisance?"

My birthday was going to fall on a Saturday, a cricket day, and it was Derby Day, too, just as it had been in 1948. I emerged from the womb as the race reached its climax – another of Mum's stories. Dad, staying late after his cricket match, did not come to see me till after ten o'clock.

The stars were aligned. I had to write the book. *Now I'm 62*, I would call it.

On the first of January, launching a fitness campaign, I went for a run and slipped on ice, limping home with blood oozing out of several parts of me. "Never mind," I comforted myself. "It will make a good first entry in the book."

I told nobody except Sue that I was writing it, and I tried my best to keep it in a separate part of my brain. Yet, when I showed the final manuscript to the team's most eccentric member, his response did not wholly surprise me. "When I was reading it, I did wonder if you've only been picking me because I was a character in your book."

It was strange to write a book in real time, with no idea how the story was going to unfold. A few times I found myself thinking, "I wish I'd written this in 2009. *Now I'm 61*. That was a much more uplifting season's cricket." The summer of 2010 had more bad days, but perhaps that made it a more realistic book.

Halfway through the year I decided to change all the names. Winsley became Loseley, the Victory Field became the Jubilee Field, I became Philip Stone. When I published the book, I made no attempt to explain what it was, whether it was fiction or fact. It was the one book where I struggled to write the blurb on the cover. At the time I thought, "It doesn't matter. Let the readers make of it what they will." With hindsight, that was wrong.

I showed it to several people before publication, and those first reactions gave me great hope that it was going to be a major success. They rang through their comments, and I scribbled down what they were saying.

"A very special book," David Smith, my most trusted reader, told me. "It has a terrific freshness and a tremendous honesty. Kindness and sympathy run right through it, and the writing is beautiful. Frank Keating will absolutely love it."

Ron Deaton also gave it a thumbs-up. "I enjoyed every word on every page in every chapter. I thought it was going to be a much lighter book. I had not expected the bittersweet emotional roller-coaster. It deeply affected me. I could not get to sleep after reading it."

There was Paul Coupar: "The personal material integrates beautifully with the cricket. It was very funny in places, but it wasn't a 'This is funny, you must laugh' book. You have created something exceptional."

After the book came out, the compliments flowed in. "I really laughed," John Barclay told me. "So much that Renira thought I had gone mad – well, madder." Then there was the Australian writer Malcolm Knox: "It pulls off that wonderful artist's trick of taking a small canvas and saying big things."

Simon Lister liked it greatly, too, but he was closest to the mark when he told me, "Some of your usual readers won't like it at all, you know." And among those who did not, to my great disappointment, was Frank Keating. "Why don't you get that book with Micky Stewart finished?" he chided me.

"Laugh?" Douglas Miller repeated in bemusement. "No. Was I supposed to?" Then he added, "I've put it aside for now. I got to about page 90, and I thought to myself, 'Does it just go on and on like this?'"

Usually I only hear from the readers who like my books, but this time it was different, the compliments mingling with brickbats, all contradictory till I hardly knew what to think. One reader said how well the different strands of the book integrated, another that it was very disjointed. "I can't get over how good your insights into the players are," read one letter, while another said, "I found the characters rather an amorphous lot. There was little psychological insight." One reader rang to say how deeply moved he had been by it, how he had felt it hitting right into his heart; another fretted over the absence of scorecards and averages. There were times when I wondered if I had sent them all the same book.

"I can't get over how good it is," said Chris of the Journeymen. "But what I can't work out is what the target readership is." When I wrote *Runs in the Memory*, I wrote the book I wanted to write, regardless of commercial considerations, and that is what I did with *Now I'm 62*. They were ventures into the unknown, and in that respect they are the books which are most special to me.

Worst of all was a reader in Norfolk who took exception to the portrayal of my eccentric team-mate, a character with whose personal difficulties he identified. He sent me three letters in a crescendo of anger that finished with him calling it "comfortably the worst book on cricket that I have ever read. Vicious, ill-researched and DULL, DULL, DULL."

*

My older brother Peter could not relate to the cricket in the book, but he did tell me, "After all these years I feel I understand you better."

A month or two after *Now I'm 62* came out, I called on him. He had just moved into a new house, and he showed me into his study. There on the desk was a silver pen-and-ink tray that I recognised from childhood. It used to sit on Dad's desk. "Who gave him this?" I asked.

"I'm not sure. Was it the Home Timber Trades Federation?"

I peered at the inscription. It was from the village cricket club – on the occasion of Dad's fifty years of playing for them. In July 1955.

"Hold on. That means he was only 61."

*

My cricketing death happened three times.

The first was in 2012 when, in a wet summer, Winsley hit a low. The first eleven had been promoted to a level too high for it, playing the first teams of big-town clubs such as Cheltenham and Swindon, and they hardly won a game. After an awkward season in which my five lads had insisted on staying down in the third eleven with me, most of them moved up to the second eleven that summer, and somehow, with the first eleven struggling and the rain never far away, I reached the situation that Adrian had predicted for me at the outset: with no core to my team and a constant struggle to find an eleven. In the worst week, having somehow recruited a full complement, I was travelling on Friday morning to a meeting with Micky Stewart, only to receive a text from the second-team captain: 'How many hav u got? I'm down to 5, and the 1s want 2 of them.' It was ten o'clock that night when I got up to eleven again, and it rained the next day.

We had to win our last game to avoid relegation back to the bottom division and, having announced my retirement, I had a dream day. Playing against the weakest of teams, I bowled 11.4 overs and took six wickets for four runs. It was the perfect ending.

Then I spoiled it by deciding in November that I was not ready to retire. I returned but, no longer captain, I enjoyed it all much less. The problems of the previous summer were still there, and in my frustration I said one or two things that I should have left unsaid. I had gone on too long, become an awkward fossil, and I regretted it.

That was the second ending, but there was a third in 2016. Scyld Berry, sensing that there was still a flame burning in me, persuaded me to play a league game for his Hinton Charterhouse second team. I had not batted or bowled for three years, and I was hopeless. I poked about with the bat; then, when I bowled, I never found my length and went for 19 runs in two overs. The captain was so unimpressed with me that he never got my name straight.

I wished I had not played. So, when a month later, out of the blue, the new Winsley third-team captain asked me to play, I said yes. Maybe I could end it all on a happier note.

When I got to the ground and saw our team, I could see that we were short of batting, but the captain was of a sunny disposition, ideal in the circumstances. When he won the toss, he opted to bat first. "Put me in at number eleven," I told him. "I'll go out and do the umpiring."

I was walking to the middle, bat in hand, in the 19th over of our 45, with the scoreboard showing 44 for nine. My partner Wayne, with whom I had played at a previous club, was a much better batsman than they gave him credit for at Winsley, and he was having the day of his life. My job was to keep him focused: "Let's see if we can get to 75 and a bonus point ... No risky shots, not yet ... Now let's see if we can get to 100 and another point." Then, when the score was in the 130s: "Do you know how many we had when I came in? We must be near a hundred partnership."

He finished on 95, I kept up an end for 24, and we came off at tea with the board showing 156 for nine. Though I had seen Higgs and Snow do it in a Test match at The Oval, I had never played in a game when the last pair put on 100. It just does not happen in afternoon cricket.

I could barely get out of the chair after tea, I could not bend in the field and, though I took two wickets, my bowling was stiff and ordinary. Several simple catches were dropped, and we lost by five wickets. Nevertheless, it was a much, much better ending for my cricket – though, of course, I had no thought of that now. I wanted to play again.

My next game was on the sloping ground at Bathford, when we bowled first. I fielded poorly, not liking it that I was a bit of a passenger to be hidden, but, when I came in to bowl, it was like the old days. Everything was working properly, my hips were rotating, the ball was swinging, and I started with a wicket maiden. It was 23 years since I had first visited Ken, and it was as if I had shed those years and was young again. I was filled with joy.

Running in to bowl the fifth ball of my third over, I ripped a calf muscle. I could not even stand to deliver the sixth ball. I hobbled from end to end at first slip till, a little later, the sky grew dark and there were distant rumbles of thunder. In no time the pitch was a lake, and I was carrying my bag back to the car, limping heavily, through the rain.

This time, I knew, it really was The End.

28

Micky

David Gower was a batsman I loved to watch. There was a graceful elegance in the way he timed the ball, and that hint of fallibility, the sense that an innings might not last, gave it all a greater thrill. I rooted for him always and, like many, was incensed when he was cast aside by England. The England manager at the time was Micky Stewart, and I saw him as a joyless sergeant-major type, rather stiff in interviews and unsympathetic to the freer spirits in the England team.

The truth, as I discovered when I met him, is quite different. Away from the probing questions of the press pack, he is delightful company, sharply observant of human nature and with an engaging sense of humour. Growing up in South London, the son of a professional gambler, he won a scholarship to Alleyn's, an independent school, where for part of the war he was evacuated to Rossall School in Lancashire. With that mixed background, the hurlyburly of Wimbledon dog track and the purity of the school choir singing Verdi's *Requiem*, he has a classlessness that has served him well in the world of cricket.

"Doesn't Micky speak nicely now," his mother said when he returned home after his first term away. Yet, some years later, when he rang his new girlfriend Sheila, he heard her brother calling to her: "There's a young cockney on the phone for you."

As a manager he took trouble to find out about his players' backgrounds, adapting his way with each of them accordingly. Only once did he make a bad mistake. Out in Australia, when the irreverent antics of the young Phil Tufnell got on the captain Graham Gooch's nerves, Micky handled him as if he were one of the rough-and-ready lads he had played football with in the South London parks. "It turned out his father was a silversmith, and he'd been to public school. If I'd known that, I might have treated him differently – not that I'd have been any less hard on him!"

We had a lovely day together in South London, walking round the scenes of his childhood. At one point we were in front of a wall, where he had spent hours throwing a ball and catching it on the rebound, the hours that turned him into the best close fielder of his generation. Then suddenly he spotted a traffic warden booking his car. Micky's pleading appeal to the chap was making no difference so I weighed in: "He grew up in this road. It's the first time he's been back for years." Then, growing desperate: "He's a famous cricketer. You're a West Indian. You like cricket, don't you?"

"No, I'm a tennis man," the warden said, stern-faced. But he did relent. "Well, don't stay much longer."

It was a book I had long wanted to write. There is nobody alive with a greater knowledge and understanding of the post-war English game at all its levels than Micky. Mindful of Frank Keating's compliment, that I never threw back 'a single tiddler's nuance', we met up more than thirty times, usually for four or five-hour sesions in Stockbridge, often with Sheila, that first girlfriend to whom he has been married since 1957.

That summer of 1957 Micky took 77 catches, one short of Wally Hammond's all-time record. In the last match, a festival game at Scarborough, a plan was hatched that Godfrey Evans would give him the catch that would equal the record. Micky's father, earning his living in a world with plenty of crooks, had instilled in Micky the importance of unimpeachable honesty, and Micky refused Evans' offer. In any case, as he likes to say, he had landed a 78th catch the previous Saturday, his finest one – getting married to Sheila.

Micky offered so many insights into the evolution of the game across his lifetime, and he did so with admirable objectivity. He was especially good on the invisible factors – how the culture of the game now is much more about winning than it was when he started, how there is so much more emphasis on the team, not just the individual performances.

As a manager he embraced those changes, raising the fitness levels of the England team, introducing more time together away from the matches. He was a crucial figure in the evolution of English cricket. Yet, when it comes to sportsmanship and good manners, he retains old values and I like that.

He can be very funny about the old world of amateurs and professionals. On the day he signed as a professional for Surrey, Peter May, who played as an amateur, was in the office. "Welcome to The Oval, Micky," he said. "Good luck in your career" – to which Micky replied, "Thank you, Peter." Minutes later, after he had signed the contract and they went to leave, he said, "Cheerio, Peter", only for the Secretary to reprimand him. "You mean Mr May. You're a professional cricketer now."

To us now in the 21st century it seems absurd, and it was worse in football where most of the so-called amateur clubs were paying their players more than the professional clubs. Micky, a quick-footed inside-forward with the properly amateur Corinthian Casuals, was selected to play for Great Britain in the 1956 Olympics in Melbourne. He reckons he was one of only three or four true amateurs in the side, and they would be up against teams from Eastern Europe made up of full-time footballers employed by their national armies. Yet Micky was banned from going because he was a professional cricketer.

His subsequent career as a professional footballer was brief, a few games in the old First Division for Charlton Athletic, but his thoughts on football were fascinating, understanding so clearly how the changes in sport reflect the changes in society. It was a tough game when he played, full of hard tackles on muddy pitches: "Over ninety minutes, if the referees had applied the laws as they are today, you'd hardly have had a player left on the field." But, in Micky's view, just as in cricket, the hardness came with an honesty, an upholding of a common sportsmanship.

"I remember watching a match in the early '50s at Stamford Bridge when the Chelsea full-back Stan Willemse kicked Stanley Matthews, and the crowd booed him. His own crowd. But twenty years later, when Ron Harris did the same thing to George Best, kicking him out of the game in the first twenty minutes, they cheered. Times had changed."

He was the first manager appointed to the England cricket team, when he had a fight to establish that he was the 'team manager', not the 'assistant to the tour manager'. For the people at Lord's, 'team manager' sounded much too like the dreaded football.

The job had been set up for Ray Illingworth, but Ray had turned it down, wanting more power in team selection. When some years later Ray did take over, his term in office went badly. The general view was that he was too old by then, too distant in age from the young cricketers. "He should have done it ten years earlier," the England bowler Angus Fraser said to me one day.

"That would have meant him doing it instead of Micky," I pointed out. "Would that have been better?"

"Good God, no," he said. "Micky was brilliant. I love him. He was like a second father to me." As I discovered when I researched my book, Angus is far from the only one to express such affection and respect.

From his years as manager Micky bore the scars of his run-ins with an unsympathetic press. He admits he should have established a better rapport; it was his one real weakness in the job. But some of the hard-nosed journalists at that time, fighting red-top circulation wars, were only interested in selling papers, not in helping the cause of English cricket, and that angered Micky.

The result of these scars was that he brought to the book a degree of carefulness about what he did and did not say. As a writer I find it much easier if the subject is open and trusts me to draw the line in the right place; then I have a proper grasp of what lies beneath and beyond the sentences I am writing.

Added to this, Micky took the view that, as a captain and manager, it was important never to show weakness, never to admit a mistake, where

I – coming out of a softer culture of psychotherapy and education – tended to see recognition of vulnerability and failure as a strength. Our views about what was and was not appropriate to put in a book were not always in accord.

It led to some difficult sessions after I had completed the writing. No doubt I would have had the same experience, probably even more gruelling, with Bob Appleyard if it had been me, rather than Ron Deaton, going through every line of his text. But it was tough enough with Micky. On our first day of reading it through, we managed just fifteen pages in nearly five hours.

The next time I set off, Sue told me that I had to be firmer. As soon as I arrived back home, she asked, "How many pages did you do this time?"

"Twenty," I replied.

"Oh well," she said rather wearily, with the heavy implication that I had still been much too feeble. "I suppose it's better than fifteen."

"I'm not sure about that," I told her. "The twenty included the fifteen we did last time."

It was, of course, greatly preferable to his not reading it properly, a tribute to his commitment to the book, and we got there in the end.

I interviewed a whole range of other people for the book, and I threaded in quotes from them. One former player spoke in a particularly lively way and, relishing the splash of colour his words introduced, I made the most of his testimony. Unfortunately Micky did not agree with anything he said, asking me to take it all out. Remembering how successfully I had got Bob Appleyard to respond to Ray Illingworth's comments, I suggested that a better alternative would be for Micky to reply to each of his contributions, creating a dialogue that would throw light on the issues. Micky agreed to this, and I inserted his replies.

The man in question had been one who had been pressing me to do a book with Micky but, after its publication, his attitude towards me became much colder. It was only then that I realised just how clumsily I had handled his contributions. Every time he spoke in the book, Micky had contradicted him, on two occasions starting his reply with the words: "That's rubbish."

My main regret, when I take the book off the shelf now, is that I allowed the printers to talk us into using a shiny paper for the text pages. It was in a summer when I was feeling a lot of pressure, my Winsley third eleven falling to bits, and, to add to the unwanted stress, our regular printers went bust, another casualty of the preference by many publishers to send their work overseas.

We finished up taking the book to Butler & Tanner in Frome, a firm which itself had closed down once but had been revived by a multi-million pound donation from Felix Dennis, a man who had made a fortune in computer magazines. He had achieved fame in the early 1970s, standing trial for obscenity at the Old Bailey after co-editing a schoolkids' issue of the alternative magazine *Oz*, and had fallen in love with Butler & Tanner after they printed a book of his poetry. By the time we went to them, the firm were back in trouble, the machines half-idle, and their salesman soft-soaped us into using a batch of paper they already had in stock. The look of a book does matter, and Micky's could have looked better.

The closure of our usual printers was a bad blow, especially as we had a lot of work, covering several books, on the computer of their pre-press man Rob. It was work that, with the receivers in, we would be unlikely to retrieve. I knew where Rob lived and found his telephone number in the directory.

"I was just about to ring you, Stephen," he said. "I've got your files here."

What a star! In the moment of losing his job, told to clear his desk and leave the building, he had found time to transfer all our files onto two computer discs. To this day we are using him for all the pre-press help we need. He is the most important person in our whole operation.

Scyld Berry said it was my best book, and there were excellent reviews from Mike Atherton in *The Times* and Steve James in the *Daily Telegraph*. Martin Chandler, doyen of book reviews on the online *Cricket Web*, reckoned it better even than my books about Geoffrey Howard and Bob Appleyard, to both of which he had given a rare five stars. Best of all, the *All Out Cricket* magazine's review was spot on about Micky:

> Stephen Chalke places Micky Stewart exactly where he belongs – sitting with the other giants of international cricket, a shrewd and talented operator and a man who saw the future at exactly the right time, realising the game had to change but maintaining the traditional qualities we all respect. A great read.

My friend Alistair said to me one day that he thought Micky was the Bobby Robson of cricket. Micky had been a close friend of the former England football manager and had spoken at his memorial service. So I was not surprised by his reaction when I repeated to him Alistair's remark. "Crikey," he said, gulping slightly. "That is a compliment."

I still see Micky from time to time. He is 87 now, but his memory remains sharp and he is always good company, with a fund of stories. Not long ago he told me of a morning at The Oval when a guest in the committee room asked him when he had started with Surrey. Micky explained how he had had to do National Service first, giving the man a long and laborious description of how the Royal Engineers was structured. "Then, when we went into lunch, to my horror, he was introduced as the Head of the British Army."

Laughter is never far away when you are with Micky.

29

Two offers

A fellow sports writer was talking on the phone one day. He told me about the sales of his last book, about the link-up with a television series that his agent was negotiating, about the advance he would be getting on his next project. They were numbers far beyond the realm of Fairfield Books and, after a while, I grew fed up with listening to him.

"To be honest," I said, "half of me is sitting here feeling quite jealous. And the other half is happy just to be this little chap out in the sticks whom nobody has ever heard of."

I doubt if he believed me, but it was true. Though we always wish with every book that we could sell another 500 or 1,000 copies, I have never felt any desire to be catapulted up to that world of agents and corporate deals.

In recent years we should have moved with the times more than we have. We should have embraced e-books, entered the worlds of Twitter and Facebook, maybe even had a design makeover to attract the next generation of readers. But we have stayed true to what appeals to us and, for the most part, it has worked well enough.

The market place has changed, with a great shift towards internet sales. In the early years we would ring all the high-street bookshops, pressing them to take copies of our books; now the effort yields so little, it is barely worth bothering. Where once our Waterstones in Bath had a great array of all the new cricket books, with several in piles on a table, now there is not half the space allocated to cricket. Most of the stocked books are paperback editions of old titles.

When we were selling Bomber Wells' book, I suggested to Sue that we should present it to Waterstones in Cheltenham as a local interest book. She left a message with them and, when the call came back, she persuaded them to take eight copies, passing the details to me. "Hold on," I said, "this is not Cheltenham, it's Tunbridge Wells." She rang back to apologise, and they said, "Oh, send them anyway." A few weeks later they ordered some more.

By contrast, when we published *Summer's Crown*, my magnum opus on the county championship, pricing it at only £20 in the expectation that we would place it in all the shops, Waterstones demanded a higher discount if they were to make a stock order. They insisted on 50% from my distributor, who in turn needed 60% from us. So we received £8 for a book that had cost nearly £6 to print, leaving aside the bills for the photographs, the proof-reading, the design work and the publicity. I agreed the deal on the understanding that their order would be substantial, but it turned out to be nothing more than a single copy of the book placed in each of 67 branches. The Bath branch took one which was sold immediately; they reordered, and that went within days; then nothing. After a while I asked why they were no longer stocking it, and the answer came back, "Well, we've only sold two."

There are at least three factors at work. One is the decline in interest in cricket. I remember years ago a man running a mail order firm, selling sports books, commenting on how cricket had reigned supreme in the 1980s but was now outsold by several other sports. Another factor is the impact of Amazon and other websites on traditional bookshops, with customers even using the shops to research books that they go home to buy cheaper online. A third factor, which I have increasingly noticed, is that shops are much less open to being approached by small publishers. There has been such a growth in self-publishing, with many of the books produced of indifferent quality, that outfits such as Fairfield Books, working outside the mainstream, are now viewed with more suspicion than they were in the days when Waterstones in Tunbridge Wells were happy to take eight copies of Bomber's book.

It would be much harder if we were starting now. Fortunately we enjoy three advantages: a strong mailing list built up over the years, a good reputation in the world of cricket and the fact that we are now on pensions and do not need to make as much profit from each book.

In the first ten years of Fairfield Books, up to Tom's death, I had largely focused on the cricket of the 1950s and '60s. But increasingly I grew frustrated that I was being type-cast: "He's that chap who writes about old county cricket." The creative, risk-taking side of me yearned for fresh pastures.

David Foot's autobiographical memoir *Footsteps from East Coker* was one such step into the unknown. David took some persuading to write it, feeling that words were coming to him less easily in his ninth decade. Scyld Berry and I cajoled and encouraged him, and the result was a beautifully written book, capturing his life in pre-war rural Somerset and his long career in journalism. There was only a little cricket in it, but he was well known in the cricket world and we sold out a modest print run of 1,000. When I asked him last year which of his books he was most proud of, I was delighted when he chose *Footsteps*.

A greater step beyond cricket came with Anthony Gibson. Our collaboration on the book of his father Alan's cricket writing, *Of Didcot and the Demon*, was a great success. We thought along the same lines, and our skills were complementary. So I was happy to help into print a slim autobiography he had been ghost-writing for a prominent West Country farmer, Fred Elliott. As Fred was paying the costs and exercising the final editorial control, it was not a proper Fairfield Books title so I brought it out under a new imprint, Charlcombe Books, named after a hamlet a few minutes' walk from our house. Anthony organised some first-rate local publicity including a five-minute feature on the BBC local news, there was a jolly launch in Fred's village Wiveliscombe, and in no time all 500 copies had been sold. It was a triumph of self-publishing, based on knowing exactly the book's target audience. Fred, who was 91, died the following year. At the launch of the book several of his friends said how good it was to celebrate his life with him among them.

On the way to Fred's farm one day, Anthony mentioned to me that he had written another book, exploring the relationship between landscape and literature in the West Country. It was with a publisher in Oxford who wanted to do it in a softback with black-and-white photographs.

"Oh no," I said. "A book like that has to be done properly."

I had no idea whether we could sell it, but it was right up my street, landscape and literature, and we took it on: *With Magic in my Eyes – West Country Literary Landscapes*, with a foreword by Michael Morpurgo. Six years later there was a sequel, moving north and further inland: *The Coloured Counties – Literary Landscapes of the Heart of England*.

I thought Anthony's approach, exploring how the landscapes inspired the writing and how conversely the writing made you see the landscapes afresh, was highly original. His background, as regional director of the National Farmers' Union, gave him an understanding of the countryside as a working environment that added an extra dimension, and we laid it out with his photographs, maps by Sue and portraits of the writers, all in colour.

I loved these ventures beyond cricket. By this time I was itching to extend the scope of Fairfield Books but, away from the niche we had developed, we found it hard to generate the sales that would pay for our 'doing the book properly'. When I went back to the National Portrait Gallery to purchase the images for the second book, the assistant asked if the publication was for commercial purposes. "Well, I haven't made a profit on the first one," I said.

"We'll put it down as academic," she said and gave me the images free.

These two books were Fairfield titles, but the success of Fred Elliott's memoir led us to take on other books under the Charlcombe imprint. The author took the financial risk and had the final say on the contents, but we only took on the title if we felt the author had a realistic sales plan. Some had cricketing themes, but among the others were a portrait of a North Country stationmaster in the 1920s, a semi-fictionalised account of a family's flight from Burma during the Second World War, a Who's Who of Welsh rugby players and a children's story introducing the topic of dementia to eight to eleven-year-olds. We are still hoping that the children's book will have the success it deserves, it is so sensitively written, but that is such a hard market to sell in. By contrast, the rugby book, with its obvious target readership, has almost sold out.

In laying out the rugby book, I was intrigued to discover that, among those who have represented Wales in the past hundred years, five – maybe six – are thought to have committed suicide. This compares with a figure of two for England Test cricketers in the same period, reinforcing my long-held suspicion that it is a myth that the suicide rate among cricketers is abnormally high. The theory stems, I suspect, from cricketers having, until recently, had their lives more comprehensively researched than players of other sports.

As Fairfield Books we undertook two books for charity. The first, edited by Anthony Gibson and me, was *Gentlemen, Gypsies and Jesters – The Wonderful World of Wandering Cricket*, profiles of some 100 or so cricket clubs without their own grounds – though, somewhat to my confusion, the Hampshire Hogs, who have had a home ground for fifty years, managed to get in on the basis that they have 'the ethos of a wandering club'.

It was all very English, with social class much to the fore among the older clubs. The Gloucestershire Gipsies, when they formed in 1921, confined membership to 'men who might be regarded as acceptable guests in the average country house'. But, away from the world of league cricket, there was plenty of humour, too. I am not sure why, but the story that made me laugh more than any other concerned the former Derbyshire cricketer Alf Pope, playing for a now-defunct side called the Pioneers:

> In Berlin they ended up one evening in a brothel, being entertained by a sexual exhibition by two girls. Much raucous noise accompanied the performance. Then in a brief lull the voice of Alf Pope, from the back, could be heard: "I remember getting four for 26 at Old Trafford on a day when it was doing a bit."

The book was the brainchild of Simon Dyson, then chairman of the Cricket Foundation which ran the Chance to Shine programme, taking cricket into primary schools. He found six benefactors to put up the cost of producing the book so that all the money from the purchases went to Chance to Shine. As a veteran salesman with IBM, Simon was ferocious in persuading the various clubs to buy the book, getting me to produce league tables of how many each club had ordered, shaming the ones who were near the bottom. We sold out a print run of 2,000 and generated £50,000 for the charity.

241

By then our printers, Midway Colour Print, had gone out of business and, after the unsatisfactory job with Butler & Tanner, we were back where we had started with Antony Rowe, the Chippenham printers who had made such a mess of our first book. Now they were part of CPI, an altogether more professional operation, and this book, being in full colour, was sent to their Croydon branch for printing.

Black-and-white litho printing still requires a machine minder with an eye for ink levels, but the modern four-colour machines are so computerised that the inks look after themselves. On this job, unfortunately, one section of pages was printed with the yellow and magenta sheets mixed up, a mistake that we only spotted after binding. There was only one picture affected, where the team all had ghastly complexions as if they had been drinking for days. And who should they be but the Ravers, a team of jazzmen, with dear old Frank Parr sitting in the middle of the front row?

John Barclay wrote a third book, *Lost in the Long Grass*, a whimsical collection of essays on twenty-odd people he had known in the world of cricket, and from that we hatched the idea for a book to raise funds for the Arundel Castle Cricket Foundation charity: *Team Mates*, profiles of two dozen or so cricketers, with each contributor choosing a favourite team mate from their playing days. Benefactors would put up the money, just like *Gentlemen, Gypsies and Jesters*, and all the proceeds would go to the Arundel Foundation.

John was brilliant at working out who would write well and persuading them to do it free of charge. The result was a high-class collection, with five former England captains alongside some village cricketers. I was struck how many of the contributors chose people of very different backgrounds from their own, once more underlining the power of cricket to transcend the divisions of class, race and nationality.

John, as always, made the venture enormous fun. When we received the entry from Angus Fraser, John was in raptures about its opening line: 'It was not a day during which I was expecting to be surprised.'

"It's up there with the first lines of *Rebecca* and *The Go Between*," he said several times, somewhat to the bemusement of Angus.

The book sold out two print runs, raising £25,000. There was talk of creating a series, using the 'Team Mates' formula with other sports, but I was not confident we had the right contacts, either to write or to buy the books.

*

Amid so much publishing, there was less time for my own writing, so much so that, after one circular to our mailing list, I had a disgruntled letter from Tony Vann in Yorkshire: "When are we going to have a new book by you?"

I was no longer maintaining the monthly routine of writing for *The Wisden Cricketer*. My irregular contributions came to an end when, after a change of ownership, the editor John Stern left the magazine in early 2011. His replacement opted for a new approach, printing multi-page features on Shane Warne's progresss at the poker tables of Las Vegas and on the speculative monetary values of the world's top cricketers.

In 2010 I agreed to take over the writing of cricket obituaries for *The Independent*. Unlike with a monthly magazine the turnaround time was short, especially when the cricketer was famous, and that added to my anxiety. I am not a fast writer; I like to do my research and mull over how best to put it all together: the high points of the career, the descriptions of playing style, the little humanising stories, the sense of the man at the heart of it all. Each obituary had a strict word limit and, as the deadline neared, I always seemed to have 50 or 100 words too many.

Fred Titmus was a challenge. In mid-morning I told Chris Maume, the obituaries editor, that Fred had died, and he wanted my copy for the edition next day. To make matters worse, it was Budget Day and the obituary pages were going to press early. Could I submit by three o'clock? I was in a panic, unable to see how I could do Fred justice with so little time, but relief was at hand. Late in the morning, news came through that Elizabeth Taylor had died. She took priority over Fred, and I was given another 24 hours.

The Independent had pre-written copy on Don Wilson so there was no conflict of interest when the *Daily Telegraph* asked me to write his obituary. My favourite story in the piece was one Don had told me about Peter O'Toole in the Lord's nets facing the bowling of Imran Khan but, for some reason which I never understood, when the piece appeared in the paper, a sub-editor had changed the story so that it was Don facing Imran. I rang to complain, saying that *The Independent* never altered my copy like this, only to get the reply: "That's because they can't afford sub-editors."

Two years later, when the *Telegraph*'s cricket obituarist, the delightful Robert Gray, stood down, he recommended me to take over from him. Remembering the episode, I stayed loyal to *The Independent*. As things turned out, it proved an unwise loyalty.

*

In January 2013 Frank Keating died. He was, I suppose, the patron saint of Fairfield Books, always looking to do what he could to support us.

Scyld Berry, cricket correspondent of the *Daily Telegraph*, is a different character, more cerebral, less given to romanticism and to gushing praise than Frank. But he, too, has been a great help to us over the years.

It was Scyld who encouraged me to work with Geoffrey Howard, and more recently he set the ball rolling for books with Geoff Cope and Brian Rose. He persuaded David Foot to write *Foosteps from East Coker*, and during his four-year tenure as editor of the *Wisden* almanack he commissioned me to write a 4,000-word article on how English cricket survived the Second World War. When I sent it to him, he came across from Bristol, took me to the pub for lunch and talked through a few changes he wanted me to make: a discarding of my first paragraph, a sentence turned round the other way, little touches all of which strengthened the whole. I have never experienced such sensitive, intelligent editing.

As 'this little chap out in the sticks whom nobody has ever heard of ', I have no idea of the sequence of events which led to his being replaced as editor of the almanack. He seemed a perfect fit for it: a man with a deep understanding of the game's history, equally in touch with the present day. Maybe Bloomsbury, who own *Wisden*, wanted a younger editor, with more feel for the social media.

In late 2012 Chris Lane, the managing editor of *Wisden*, rang with a proposition. Would I sell to *Wisden* the e-book rights to my titles, the names on my mailing list and all my unsold stock? In exchange they would pay what seemed to me to be a large sum if I would write four books for them. He even said they would pay for me to employ a lawyer to negotiate the contract.

When we met, he was very taken with my two monographs about George Hirst and the 555 partnership, and he floated the idea of *Wisden* launching a readers' club, with one of these each quarter. I would not have to write them all but, if I ran that for two years, that could count as two of my four books. I was excited by this, ringing the young journalist Andy Bull that evening. He had told me how he had been the last person to interview Harold Pinter, all about cricket, and he wanted to expand on the article the *Guardian* had published. Here was the perfect outlet for it, I said.

Coming at the end of the year when I had given up the captaincy at Winsley, when I was struggling to find a good printer, when recent books had not sold that well, the timing of the offer made it appealing.

I sent in all the paperwork he requested, with proposals for eight possible books. They included the readers' club series, a third *In The Memory* book about the 1970s, a history of the county championship, a set of essays called *Cricket's Non-Conformists*, a portrait of the summer of 1963 with the title *The Year That Cricket Changed* and this book that I am writing now, the story of my journey from Ken Biddulph's coaching to my cricket writing.

After a long delay Chris rang to say that the deal was off. The key woman at Bloomsbury thought that none of my ideas had commercial merit. "None of them?" "No, none."

It was a shock, but it did not upset me that much. If they had any doubts, then it was better we left it than that I was answerable to people who had no confidence in my work. In any case, part of me was too set in my ways, wanting to carry on doing things to my own standards.

One Friday afternoon a month later, I was in the thick of laying out *Gentlemen, Gypsies and Jesters*, my head lost in the fiddly task of reproducing the club colours of the Band of Brothers and the Stragglers of Asia, when the telephone rang.

"Stephen? It's David Collier. We haven't met for a while. How are you?"

David Collier? David Collier? The name seemed familiar.

"I'm very well, David. How are you?"

"Very good. I'm just back from New Zealand."

David Collier? If I kept the call going, perhaps I would work out who he was. Was he that man who wrote a book about cricketing pub signs? Or the Surrey member I met in Menorca? As the conversation went on, I started to wonder if it was a cold call, maybe a printing firm touting for business.

"Anyway, to get down to the point of my call, I've been talking with Giles."

I could not let it go on any longer. "Giles," I repeated. "Giles who?"

"Giles Clarke," he said, rather taken aback.

The penny dropped. It was the downside of being 'the little chap out in the sticks'. Giles was the chairman of the England and Wales Cricket Board, David the Chief Executive. They had heard I was struggling a bit, and they wanted to offer me some support. How could they help?

I suggested underwriting my next book, covering my costs if I made a loss. "I was thinking of writing a history of the county championship," I said off the top of my head, plucking out one of my *Wisden* proposals.

"Perfect," he said. "We're keen to promote the county game."

I prepared some costings – "Oh, that's well within budget," he said cheerfully – and soon enough he reported back that the board had allocated £25,000, the only condition being that I would give them 500 free copies.

"Now what about this underwriting business? Would you like us to do that or just to give you the money?"

It was a no-brainer, but I held back. "That's up to you," I said.

"Well, I'd just as soon we paid you the money."

It was a wonderful break, suiting me much better than the *Wisden* offer.

Out of courtesy I rang Chris Lane to assure him that I was up and running again, and his reply rather startled me: "The county championship book? We were going to ask you to do that for us."

I learned later, from a third party, that it had been Scyld Berry who had spoken to Giles Clarke about me.

30

Summer's Crown

Day after day, month after month, from November 2013, I immersed myself in the history of the county championship. The summer of 2015 would mark the 125th anniversary of the competition's birth, and I promised the ECB that my book would be ready in time for their celebration of this landmark. There were times when it seemed an impossible deadline, but I battled on.

I delved deep into the old newspapers that were available on my computer, I read books aplenty, and I drove all over England, interviewing players and administrators past and present. It was a monumental task, on a scale far greater than anything I had tackled before. Not only was I researching and writing the text but I was tracking down images, then fitting everything into complicated double-page templates.

For each decade I spotlighted five players in a double-page spread. My first choice for the first decade, the 1890s, was Bobby Abel of Surrey, about whom I knew little when I settled to the task one morning. I speed-read a biography by David Kynaston, I consulted other books, finding a good description of him in Harry Altham's *History of Cricket*, I went online to pick up little phrases from newspaper reports, and by mid-afternoon I had written a short pen portrait, with some humanising details (early to bed, careful with money) mixed in with the cricket. Then I had to spend another hour or two, fiddling with the text till it fitted the space I had allocated for it. It was a full day's work, and it took up just half a page in a 352-page book.

In a feature on the Yorkshire captain Lord Hawke, I set aside half a page to write about Bobby Peel's last match for Yorkshire in August 1897. It had become the stuff of folklore, how he had gone onto the field so inebriated that, when he went to bowl the first ball, he was facing the wrong way and hit the sight screen. In some reports he urinated out in the middle. Lord Hawke sent him off, and he never played for Yorkshire again.

Though 43 years old, Peel was still a key member of the side, and Yorkshire struggled to find a replacement, settling at the start of the next summer for a lad called Wilfred Rhodes from a village outside Huddersfield. He had been for a trial with Warwickshire, who had not been impressed, but Yorkshire, in their desperation, gave him a go. He took 13 wickets in his first match and went on to become the greatest wicket-taker in the history of the first-class game. It was a story I had to include.

"Nothing ever gave me so much pain," Lord Hawke wrote of the dismissal of Peel, and a 1990 biography of Hawke began with the sad story. The author placed the episode at the start of a match against Derbyshire at Bradford, a match in which – presumably because he was sent off before the start – Peel did not appear in the Yorkshire eleven. Much of the story, though not the sight screen or the urinating, was drawn from George Hirst's memory of the incident, retold thirty years later.

I went online to the British Newspaper Archive to see if I could find anything fresh to add to the story, and immediately most of the detail unravelled. It had not happened before the start of the Bradford match; it had happened the previous day at Sheffield, on the last afternoon of a match against Middlesex, when Peel bowled well below his best and was sent off. There were hints in the reports that he was not in a fit state, and in a lengthy interview he defended himself against this, saying he had had only two small glasses of gin and water before coming to the ground and nothing during lunch. He admitted to falling over but only because there were three spikes missing in his left shoe.

As for the ball against the sight screen and the urinating? There was no trace of either. His bowling figures, before being sent off, were seven overs for 16 runs, with no wides or no balls. Furthermore, there were only two matches left in the summer and, if Peel had not gone off in high dudgeon and signed to play for Accrington the next year, Yorkshire would have taken him back. All this I established inside an hour, sitting at home in front of my computer.

*

Still in the 1890s I gave a double-page spread to Hampshire's amateur ethos, with servicemen from Aldershot and Portsmouth dipping in and out of the side. One such was Major Bertie Poore, home on leave from South Africa in 1899. One week he was the Best Man at Arms in the Royal Military Tournament and the scorer of the winning goal in the final of the Inter-Regimental Polo Cup. The next week he was hitting three centuries for Hampshire. He scored 1,399 runs in the championship that summer, at an average of 116, then went off to fight in the Boer War.

In my search for old photographs I was directed to Roger Mann, a retired wholesale greengrocer who had built up a magnificent collection over a lifetime. He invited me down to his house in Torquay, where he asked me, "What topic are you working on at the moment?" I said Bertie Poore, and immediately he was on his hands and knees, pulling out from under a table an old leather kitbag. On it was written 'Major R.M. Poore, 7th Hussars'.

Roger proved a great help, not only supplying photographs when I asked for them but offering ideas for features. At his suggestion I wrote a page, with an excellent picture, about William Whysall's funeral when several thousand people lined the streets of Mansfield to pay tribute to the stalwart Nottinghamshire cricketer. I also wrote a fascinating page about the cricketers who died in car accidents in the 1930s, a topic it would never have occurrred to me to explore.

*

I had fallen in love with cricket in the 1950s, when the county game attracted reasonable crowds. I had this idea, like many of my generation, that it had always been healthy and had only fallen into crisis in the 1960s, when people's leisure activities were changing. So it was quite a shock, researching the book, to discover that, throughout much of its existence, county cricket has been in a parlous state. As early as the 1900s, there were complaints that there were too many counties, too many matches, not enough people watching them, not enough money – and, worst of all, some of the counties, in their desire to win the championship, were importing 'colonial cricketers'. In 1906 *The Times* published an editorial deploring this development:

> The one object of the county championship competition is to see which county can produce the best cricketers, and not which can purchase the best cricketers. Under the present system a millionaire with a hobby for cricket could make Rutland the champion county in about four years' time, and there need not be a Rutland man in the winning eleven.

Had that ever happened, I found myself wondering. Had a county ever won the championship with no home-grown players in their first-choice eleven? And indeed it had, the first time by Leicestershire in 1974. And would you believe it? The previous year, in a local government reorganisation, Rutland had become a part of Leicestershire.

Writing an overview history gives you the chance to make these connections across time, and one that especially appealed to me involved two Middlesex captains, each playing for the last time at Lord's.

The first was Pelham Warner in 1920, a victorious England captain in Australia but never a championship-winning Middlesex captain. Victory in his last game against Surrey would change that. On the second evening it looked unlikely that they could win the game, which meant that Lancashire would be champions. At that time counties chose how many games they wanted to play, with percentages determining the championship table, and

Middlesex, with a larger reliance on amateurs, opted to play only 20 to Lancashire's 28 – so Lancashire's percentage was boosted by wins against the lesser sides that Middlesex chose not to play. On the last morning, as a result of this anomaly, there was a letter in *The Times*, under the nom de plume of 'Fair Play', arguing that MCC should step in and award the title to Middlesex. As it worked out, they did win, a match that turned on a wonderful catch in the deep by Patsy Hendren. 'His arms were stretched almost out of their sockets,' a team-mate wrote. 'Had he started smoking a year earlier and been a fraction of an inch shorter as a result, he would not have made it.' It was Warner's finest hour in cricket, and 'Fair Play' was forgotten, only revealed years later to be Warner himself.

Fast forward to 1982, to Mike Brearley's last match at Lord's, another victorious England captain in Australia, another Middlesex captain looking to beat Surrey to secure the championship – though not Brearley's first. I sat in his front room, and he told me the tale, how on the first morning before play the 49-year-old long-retired Fred Titmus, on his way to collect a visa from the American Embassy, called into the dressing room to wish them good luck, only to find himself being offered Clive Radley's spare flannels and Mike Brearley's spare socks and boots. They had a hunch they might need a third spinner, and so they did. On the final afternoon the slow left-armer Phil Edmonds ricked his back, and Fred Titmus, stepping into the breach, took three crucial wickets. He had played his first game for Middlesex as a 16-year-old back in 1949, alongside Mike's father Horace in one of his only two appearances for the county. As he left that night, he turned to Mike, saying, "I came in with the father, and I went out with the son."

They were wonderful stories, both of them.

After the book was published, I was asked to speak to the MCC History Group in the Long Room at Lord's, and for fun I chose my all-time best county eleven. For captain, given the venue, it seemed best to opt for Mike Brearley. Shortly afterwards, I repeated the talk at The Oval, and this time I decided it was more politic to choose Stuart Surridge, who led Surrey to the title in all his five years at the helm. And when I was up in Headingley, I switched to Brian Close. Before writing the book, I had been under the impression that Brian had captained Yorkshire to four titles starting in 1963 but, in an interview for the book, he explained to me that, when Ronnie Burnet had led them in 1959 and Vic Wilson in 1960 and 1962, it was his input to the decision-making that had been the decisive factor – or, as he put it, "I did all bloody seven really."

I wanted to write about Brian again, and the book gave me an opportunity to do so. We met in the Hawke Suite at Headingley one morning while

Yorkshire were playing, and he talked for two hours, inevitably returning to the painful subject of his sacking by the county.

Throughout our conversation Geoffrey Boycott was close by, at one point interrupting to ask what the purpose of my interview was. After lunch, when Brian had gone, I returned to the room to be greeted by Geoffrey whose first words to me were, "You're not going to print all that rubbish he was telling you, are you?"

I was a bit taken aback, but I stood my ground. "I think I can work out what's rubbish and what isn't," I said.

"Well, sit down and I'll put you straight about why he was sacked."

"No, I don't want that," I said, trying not to show that I was gulping. "I'd rather hear your views about the state of the county championship."

"Right, I'll talk about that then," he said, and he instructed me to sit down and to turn on my tape recorder. Then he addressed me, rather as if I were the nation, with clear, well-expressed thoughts in well-formed sentences, much of which I reproduced in the book's introduction. After about twenty minutes, he suddenly got up and, with barely a "That's your lot", walked into the next room. My nerves were jangling, but he had spoken great sense and I was immensely grateful to him.

I cannot think of another sport where captaincy plays such an important role. I have a piece of paper on which I have written two pieces of advice for captains at all levels of the game. One is from Richie Benaud: "Stay two overs ahead of the game and be lucky." The other is from Viv Richards: "Get ten great players around you, man."

Mike Smith, the former England captain, said to me once: "A good captain can't make a bad team good, but a bad captain can make a good team bad."

The best words I have ever heard on captaincy came from Brian Close when I interviewed him for Yorkshire's film tribute to Fred Trueman. Fred always said that his proudest moment in cricket was when, with Brian out injured, he led Yorkshire to an innings victory over the touring Australians. I asked Brian whether Fred would have made a good captain of the county.

"To captain a side over a summer," he said, "you've to look after four things, and you've to look after them in the right order. First, there's the game you're playing. Then the team. Then the individuals in the team. And lastly yourself." He chuckled. "I'm not so sure Fred could have put them in that order."

I read those words to Mike Brearley, and he asked me to repeat them. "And Brian said that?" Brian had such a mad streak to him that it was easy to overlook what a good brain he had. What was it Ken Biddulph said? "He could be a brilliant genius and thick at the same time."

Near the end of Brian's life he was interviewed in *The Cricketer*. He was asked, "What would you say in a meeting with the team's computer analyst, nutritionist and mental performance coach?"

"I'd sack 'em," he replied. "Players used to talk between themselves to learn the skills of the game. Bomber Wells from Gloucestershire used to take his players into the bar after a game against Yorkshire. They'd have ten minutes with Freddie, ten minutes with me and so on. He said they learned more about the game that way."

I thought to myself, "Hold on, that's a quote from my book." So I looked up what Bomber actually said. It went as follows: "It was lovely playing against Yorkshire when Fred and Closey were young. You'd split up into two parties. Fred would be at one end of the bar, Closey up the other. You could have half an hour of Closey lambasting Fred, then when you got fed up with that you could go and hear Fred lambasting Closey."

*

Stories from the past have an extra charm, that sense of 'a foreign country' to which LP Hartley referred.

I loved writing up the innings of Derbyshire's Ted Alletson at Hove in May 1911: how he was a county cricketer of no distinction, how on a cold day he had gone for an early-morning swim to help a sprained wrist, how in later life he worked in a colliery. Yet on that day, batting at number nine, he went out after lunch and, off just 52 balls, took his score from 42 to 189. John Arlott, devoting a monograph to the feat, called it 'the most remarkable sustained hitting innings ever played in first-class cricket.'

Yet, as I discovered when writing *Summer's Crown*, there are just as good stories in the modern game and, when they become part of the distant past, they will acquire the same charm. Sitting with me at Chelmsford, Graham Napier relived for me the day at Whitgift School in May 2011, one hundred years on from Alletson, when he blasted his way from 83 to 196 in just 33 balls. It was his first game back in the championship side after a year out with a double-stress fracture of the back. He said he realised, during his long lay-off, how much he loved the game. "I told myself, if I ever played again, I was going to enjoy every single moment, the bad days as well as the good."

It is in the nature of cricket that it will always generate great stories.

*

John Barclay reckons that it is much more fun to write about failure than success, and I know what he means. While writing *Summer's Crown* I kept an eye open for the disasters: a pre-war Northamptonshire cricketer who played 54 championship matches without ever being on the winning side, a Leicestershire batsman ruled 'out, absent' at The Oval because he took the tube to Kensington, not Kennington, and a Nottinghamshire bowler, John Howarth, who appeared in a record 13 matches without scoring a run. When I rang him, he was full of beans, reliving his batting failures in great detail; he even asked me to send him a copy of the book when it was published. But humour can be dangerous territory; you never know where you are with it. I tried to get another cricketer to tell me about the summer when he finished with a batting average of 0.5, and he snapped my head off: "I don't think it's very nice to laugh at a thing like that."

*

The ECB grant gave me confidence to splash out on photographs, making the book a more ambitious project than it would otherwise have been. It also allowed me to buy some assistance when, during the summer, I realised that I had too many interviews still to do – and I found an ideal helper straightaway. *The Cricketer*, in a cost-cutting exercise, were making Benj Moorehead, one of the editorial team, redundant, and by a happy coincidence I was talking to him within an hour of his hearing the news. It was perfect timing, raising his spirits when they most needed a boost and giving me a capable research assistant with time on his hands. He took on some of the modern features, sending me interview transcripts and background notes that were superb. As a result the book went to the printers in early February, just as I had planned.

After a year and a quarter when I had done little else but research and write *Summer's Crown*, that should have been the cue for a breather, but there followed the most demanding two months in the history of Fairfield Books.

Chris Saunders, the specialist cricket-book dealer, had come up with the idea of producing for each of the eighteen counties a special edition of *Summer's Crown*, in appropriately coloured cloth with the club's crest and a slip case, with the signature of a prominent player and a bound-in, eight-page supplement with fresh material on that county. So, after writing a 352-page book, I now had to produce in double-quick time 18 eight-page supplements.

I had extracts to sort out for Scyld Berry for the *Sunday Telegraph*, a circular to my mailing list to prepare and post, a launch in Bath to organise and, in the middle of all this, Bob Appleyard died. I needed time not just to grieve but to write an obituary for *The Independent* and to attend his funeral in Yorkshire.

With half the supplements still unwritten, the printers rang, ahead of schedule, to say that the books were ready for collection, all 4,500 of them: 4,000 for me and 500 for the ECB. I had opted for a higher-quality paper, to get the best definition from the pictures, and I had not fully grasped how large and heavy the book was going to be and that consequently there would be only eight, not 16 or 20, books in each box. I went across on Friday afternoon, planning to bring home a first carload, and I was confronted by 14 large pallets, each weighing half a ton. They were taking up most of the space in the entrance to the despatch area, and the man in charge told me firmly, "I want all of these out of here by Monday lunchtime at the latest."

I arranged for one pallet to be sent to my distributors in Eastbourne. I had hoped that I could send a second to the ECB but, when I rang, I found that all the three people with whom I had been liaising – Giles Clarke, David Collier and Colin Gibson, the director of media communications – had gone, and nobody in the building seemed to know anything about the book. When finally somebody took responsibility for dealing with me, they were horrified by the idea that I would be sending them 500 books. I was asked to bring 50 copies to the pre-season launch at Worcester, and later, with some reluctance, they allowed me to deliver a further 100 to Lord's. There was no 125-year celebration.

Our house is in a late Victorian terrace, essentially a workman's cottage with its loft converted into an extra bedroom, and there was no way the upstairs floors would bear the weight of all these books. We hired a commercial storage unit, which left us six pallets to bring into the house on Monday: 240 boxes on top of all the boxes of our other titles. There was no question of the pallets being left outside, each box would have to be 'handballed' from the lorry into the house and up either one or two flights of stairs. The hauliers agreed to do this and to deliver at 1.30. We arranged for Martha and her husband Steve to take time off work and to join us, to set up a relay chain.

Just before 12 o'clock, long before Martha and Steve were due to leave Bristol, a large lorry drew up, with two men in the front seat. One said he had diabetes and could not do any lifting, but the other was keen to help and he, Sue and I set to work. It was a massive task: each box weighed 13 kilograms, more than the heaviest sack a Royal Mail employee is allowed to carry, and Sue and I were old-age pensioners. I took the first box and, keen to show enthusiasm, ran up the stairs with it. "That's not a good idea," the driver said. "You won't keep that up for long." Of course, he was right.

Then, when the books were all in, it was back to writing the supplements for Chris Saunders.

*

The reviews and the letters I received from readers overwhelmed me.

First up was a deeply moving postcard from John Woodcock, the former *Times* cricket correspondent whose prose style has always been a joy to read: 'I am, quite simply, lost in admiration! *Summer's Crown* is a really wonderful effort, and I see you designed it as well. Your selection of pictures and their quality match the text. My own favourite decade is still the 40s, and you cover it beautifully: the innocence, the sense of relief and reclamation, all the old anecdotes and a thousand others. It really is a terrific book.' Then I had a letter from Doug Insole, saying he had read it from cover to cover and loved all the stories. Having my work appreciated by people like this, men who had spent a lifetime in the game, was extra special.

The greatest boost for sales was being included in most of the 'books to buy for Christmas' lists in the major national newspapers, something we had never experienced on this scale before.

Enthusiasm for the book was not universal, however. To my surprise I found that I had walked into a hornet's nest, a long-running sectarian battle between factions of statisticians. The dispute centred on the start date of the championship. I had written a double-page spread on the subject, summarising the problem as wittily as I could. By settling for the date of 1890 that is currently used by *Wisden* and the *CricketArchive* website, I thought I had avoided controversy. I should have known better.

At one time *Wisden* had the start date as 1873, leading to centenary celebrations with commemorative postage stamps in 1973. At another time it was 1864, which conveniently coincided with the first edition of *Wisden*. Since 1995 it has been 1890. Supporters of Gloucestershire who in 1994 could pick up their *Wisden* and discover proudly that their county had won three outright championships now find themselves reading that 'Gloucestershire, Northamptonshire and Somerset have never won.'

The problem with the years before 1890 is that the championship tables published in newspapers, magazines and annuals had no commonly agreed method of ranking the counties. 'Most wins', 'fewest losses' or 'wins minus losses', all were problematic as the counties played differing numbers of matches. Nor did the publications always agree what matches counted, with the table for 1886 in the magazine *Cricket* including the touring Australians. That gave the title to Surrey, where other publications put Nottinghamshire first, a difference that may have been due in part to the editor, Charles Alcock, being Secretary at The Oval.

The summer of 1890 was the first when the eight counties agreed a system for the points table, hence the current preference for that date.

Roy Wilkinson, the Yorkshire statistician, was dismissive of my book, saying that I had wiped out all the achievements before 1890. Peter Wynne-Thomas, the Trent Bridge librarian, was another who said I had got the whole thing wrong. I had listed Nottinghamshire as being county champions six times where his Notts yearbook had the figure at 21, the first of which was in 1853, a full decade before the formation of the Yorkshire and Lancashire clubs. In that year, according to *CricketArchive*, there were four inter-county matches, three of which involved Nottinghamshire, who won two and lost one.

Statisticians seem to be prone to such disputes. When a meeting was called in 1973 to form the Association of Cricket Statisticians, they even managed to have a furious argument about that, agreeing to go ahead only by 13 votes to 12.

Fortunately Major Rowland Bowen, the cricket historian who had persuaded *Wisden* to switch to 1864, was long dead and not able to add his fury. Bowen, an irascible eccentric who sawed off one of his own legs, brooked no opposition, banning those who queried his judgements from subscribing to his privately produced magazine *Cricket Quarterly*. On one occasion he returned a cheque to a man who knew nothing of all this, accusing him of being a blackballed subscriber trying to get back in under a false name.

*

What a journey it had been from Ken's coaching sessions to *Summer's Crown*. I had started out recording the voices of old cricketers, an oral-history project that threw a light not just on the first-class game but on the English way of life in the years when I was growing up. For *Summer's Crown*, I had stepped back and tried to capture a longer view, a social history from Victorian times to the present day, looking to bring alive characters who had died long before I was born.

It was never my intention to write a book that fitted it all into an overriding thesis, rather as Derek Birley did in his *Social History of English Cricket*. As Hazel might have said, that is how they encourage you to write in universities. Rather, I wanted to capture the humanising detail and the strange, improvised way the county game has survived its repeated crises.

Was it Andy Warhol who said that everybody has their 15 minutes of fame? Mine came when I drove down to the Ageas Bowl in Southampton to be interviewed by Helen Castor for Radio 4's *Making History* programme. In fact, it was only seven minutes, and very few of my friends heard it.

The feature ended with Helen summing up what I had said: "So, for all its traditionalism, cricket has actually been quite adaptable, quite willing to look for change in the effort to survive."

"Yes," I replied. "I think cricket has got this image of being very stuffy and the last to change. But look at the county championship; it's completely the opposite. It's a triumph of innovation and imagination with a competition which has been structurally unsound almost from day one."

I would not have said that twenty years earlier, on the balcony of the Stratford Park Leisure Centre with Ken. I doubt if I would have said it like that when two years earlier I had started out on *Summer's Crown*.

It was an extraordinary journey of discovery.

31

Last books

Over the years we have been offered for publication several hundred books, almost all of them cricket titles. Sometimes, in my cynical moments, I wonder if there are more people writing cricket books than there are reading them.

Many are insufficiently commercial even for us, but there have been a few where we have told the author that their book needed a bigger publisher. One such, looking at recent Ashes series and drawing on in-depth interviews with the various captains, was by the journalist and former Kent captain David Fulton. A well-written, well-researched book, it would have enhanced our list, but I did not think we could do it justice. "A bigger firm will get you much more coverage and a much wider distribution than we can," I told him. In the event it was published by an Edinburgh-based subsidiary of Random House, and it did not get half the attention it deserved. It may not have been true, but I found myself thinking, "We could have done better than that."

Some proposals arrive when we are too busy; some are too close in subject to other books. Then there are those that we agree to publish but which never materialise.

In the summer of 2013 Fred Rumsey, the Somerset and England fast bowler of the 1960s, approached me about publishing his autobiography. He e-mailed a few short samples of writing, then came down to Bath. For four hours, sitting on the sofa, he entertained me with a welter of terrific stories from his life, but he came at a bad time. I did not want to lose the chance to publish it, but I was just about to embark on researching and writing *Summer's Crown* so we left it that he would get on with the writing and come back to me when he had made more progress. As I helped him up, a big man, from our sagging sofa, I did wonder whether I had shown enough enthusiasm.

I heard no more from him till we met at Bob Barber's 80th birthday party on *HMS Victory* in September 2015, more than two years later.

"What's happened about your book?" I asked him.

"Oh, I haven't bothered with that. You put me off. You didn't seem much interested."

A pang of regret ran through me. But, when I started to express my surprise, Fred's long-suffering wife Coleen stopped me. "Don't take any notice of him," she said. "He's just lazy."

The following summer the committee of our re-formed Cricket Society in Bath met to discuss possible speakers, and Anthony Gibson suggested asking Fred. The book seemed to be dead, and Fred had long retired from the speaking circuit. But he seemed to feel he owed me a favour, and he did not rule out coming down to Bath. He was wintering in Spain so, if he did come, he said, it would have to be in September.

In July I bumped into him at cricket at Cheltenham, and he was still prevaricating. "I'll let you know about that meeting soon," he said. But August came and went, and there was no word. Then, as I was starting to give up hope, our speaker secretary contacted him one last time, and he said yes.

It was a fabulous afternoon. Already 80 years old, he spoke from two o'clock to 4.30, with a 20-minute tea break, and we would happily have listened to him for another hour. In fact, Fred would happily have gone on for another hour. The stories tumbled out. The punchlines of the funny ones were delivered with superb comic timing, causing the room to erupt with laughter, and the serious ones had us spellbound.

"You must write that book," I implored him as he left.

His next contact was an e-mailed Christmas card from Costa del Sol. It featured a film of his four-year-old granddaughter singing *I'm Dreaming of a White Christmas* in Spanish. There was no mention of the book.

*

By this time I was in the thick of writing a book with Geoff Cope, the Yorkshire and England off-spinner of the 1970s. I had had a session with him for *Summer's Crown*, and I had been most impressed not just by the quality of his memory but by the way he brought people and situations to life when he talked. So, when Scyld Berry suggested him as the subject for one of my books, I did not need any persuading.

It was the easiest book I have written. On the first afternoon, when I arrived at his house in Guiseley during a walking holiday in the Yorkshire Dales, he was ready for me, with a pile of documents on the dining-room table and a list of thirty or so subjects he wanted to cover in the book. Later in the holiday I put in a full day, covering his childhood, and it was clear that he was happy to open his heart, bringing a tear to my eye on two or three occasions. A man of great warmth, he did not hold back.

The rest of his life was covered during four two-day visits. I would arrive late on Monday evening and leave at teatime on Wednesday, and we would sit at the dining room table from nine to five, with Ron Deaton joining us each time. Ron knew the process well, from his involvement in the books with Bob Appleyard and Ken Taylor, and he also knew the history of Yorkshire cricket better than I did so his presence was crucial in several ways: as a fact-checker while we were talking, as a wise point of reference when we tackled a tricky subject and as a reassurance to me about the book's worth. "I'm loving every minute of this," he said more than once. "There's so much you're saying, Geoff, that I haven't heard before."

Geoff suffers from retinitis pigmentosa, an eye condition in which his field of vision has narrowed to the point that he now sees the world as if through a keyhole. Over Christmas and New Year we had a break of nearly three months while he changed guide dog, a major event in his life. But otherwise he was keen to keep going. Cricket gave him a busy round of activities each summer, but in his condition winters could seem long and rather empty.

We worked through Geoff's life in an orderly way. Often, as he talked through an episode, I could visualise it falling onto the page exactly as he spoke it. He could recreate conversations and emotions, and he had perceptive insights into his fellow cricketers, often with a different angle from what I expected.

He captured Fred Trueman's kindness towards young players, recalling a match when he had to drive to Bath from a second-team game in Harrogate.

> I got there at half past two in the morning, and Fred was asleep on the settee in the lounge. The night porter said, "Mr Trueman's been waiting up for you. I'm to wake him when you come."
>
> He woke him up. "Where am I? ... Oh, you're here ... It's stupid they didn't let you go earlier." A few expletives as well. "Now you get yourself to bed. You're supposed to be at the ground for ten o'clock. You be there for a quarter to eleven."
>
> The next morning it was "How do you feel? Are you tired?" "I'm OK. I want to play if you want me." "I want you, sunshine." And I played. I thought, "Who else would have waited up?" They're the little things you don't see on the outside.

He did not get the same treatment from Brian Close when he was sent down to join the team at Hove.

> I had a letter from the committee that I had to give to Closey before play. He read it and said, "Put that back in your pocket. Tell them you gave it to me at lunchtime. Oh, and you're twelfth man today."
> I was intrigued by this so I read the letter. It said, 'The committee request you play Geoff Cope in this game to give him experience.'

Many of his years with Yorkshire were played under the captaincy of Geoffrey Boycott, and inevitably there were stories. On one occasion, playing at Lord's, he was summoned to Boycott's hotel room after play, giving up a dinner date with friends. At the time Geoff was inspecting the pitch before play each day, trying to figure out how it would behave. When he arrived at the hotel room, he was left standing in the doorway while Boycott wrote notes on the day's play in a book.

I said, "You wanted to see me?"

"Oh yes. Why do you go and see these pitches?" And he's still writing.

"I just want to see if I'm right in my thinking. I can perhaps get to know the game a bit better."

"Right. Well, in future don't let anybody see, but go out and do the pitch. Come and tell me what you think. And I'll put you right."

That's Geoffrey, that's how he spoke. I'm stood there, and he's writing up. He said, "Yes?"

I said, "Well, you wanted to see me."

"That's what I wanted to see you about."

"But I was going out for dinner."

"Well, you're far better going to find a restaurant on your own, analyse how you bowled today."

No one is suggesting that the words are verbatim as they were spoken, but they give such a vivid sense of the situation, the relationship, the character of Boycott. There were other stories in similar vein, and the portrait that emerged of his captain did not seem flattering to me. Yet, when the book came out, several readers said to me, "He's been very fair to Boycott, hasn't he?"

Both Ron and Geoff love their football. Ron has been a season ticket holder at Leeds since their glory years in the 1970s, and inevitably some of the lustre has gone for him. During one of our sessions he left early to attend a match, saying a little wearily, "I'll be glad when I no longer feel the need to go."

Geoff, a promising footballer in his youth, knows the stars of the great Leeds team well, but he had grown alienated from the modern club, finding it soulless and detached from its community. He had transferred his allegiance to the down-to-earth, friendly AFC Halifax, where he and his guide dog are the club's joint vice-presidents. During two of my visits I drove him to evening games, enjoying the banter of the pre-match meal where the directors' table was in among all the supporters. It was easy to see what Geoff loved so much about the place.

In the car on the way there, away from our structured sessions around the dining-room table, he came out with one of the best stories in the book, about the Headingley Test of 1963 when, as a 16-year-old, he and two friends spent all match as attendants in the dressing room of the West Indies team, with their impressive captain Frank Worrell.

> Big Wes Hall would pick up a paper, turn to the racing results and he'd be mimicking Peter O'Sullevan, commentating. Big Charlie Griffith was there, of course. "Charlie, it's time to work," Wes would say. And they'd go across to little Deryck Murray, pick him up under the armpits till he was about two foot off the ground, and they'd walk him out of the dressing room, down the corridor, onto the field of the Test match. We looked at this and we thought, "Gee, don't they enjoy life!" ... It was the first time in my life when I realised that it doesn't matter what colour you are, it's what's underneath that counts. And Frank Worrell was the man who did it. He really brought home to me what you can gain in life through friendship.

Geoff's life story was a bittersweet one, with more than its share of setbacks, knocks that he did not flinch from describing, but at the end of the book the message he wanted to convey was a positive one.

> Above everything, sport is about friendship. It's about the people who play and the people who support. I've been blessed because I've made friends among both groups. And when you put the two together, the players and the supporters, all it boils down to is that we're just ordinary people – and as ordinary people we can share with each other the pleasures we have. If I've been able to play a small part for somebody not as fortunate as me, then I'm grateful that that person has got that little bit of pleasure. I sit here now at 70 years of age, and I think, "Was there a better way to have a living?"

We launched the book at a Yorkshire match at Scarborough, and it was soon clear that the reader reaction was positive. One man was on the phone to me for twenty minutes: "What a fabulous book. Geoff Cope's warmth really comes through. There were parts where I felt as if I was sat in the dressing room with him – and parts where it made me want to cry. I read so many cricket books that have the same stories in them, but this was so fresh. I learned so much that was new. I can't rate it highly enough."

'Again you have succeeded in leaving the reader feeling they know and like your subject,' one man wrote, 'not because the picture has been contrived or touched up but because you let him speak for himself.'

From beginning to end the book was a joy to work on.

*

One day in May I was making the last corrections to Geoff's book when, in a lull in the calls to Geoff and Ron, the telephone rang. "Stephen, it's Fred ... I've been working on my book over the winter ... I've written 60,000 words so far." His call was a complete surprise, and my heart leapt. Not only had our Cricket Society meeting renewed my enthusiasm for his book but it had inspired Fred. It had given him the realisation that there was still an audience for his story.

He sent it through by e-mail, and in my diary I recorded my verdict after reading it: 'I enjoy it greatly. Fred has a vigour, a love of life, a natural curiosity, that engages me throughout, and I laugh aloud many times. I shall have great fun publishing it. I'm sure it will go down well.'

Fred and Coleen had sold their home and were staying with a friend south of Worcester. Her husband had died and, with a large house with 'spare rooms', she welcomed their company. When I arrived, I found myself standing in front of the great oak door of a 16-bedroom Elizabethan manor house surrounded by 50 acres of land.

"Have you come to see Fred?" Brenda asked. "I'll take you down to his office." We walked down a dark stone corridor to find Fred's great frame perched on a swivel seat in front of a computer. The room around him was packed with all sorts: a piano, an assortment of sofas, a large stack of chairs and a full-size billiard table. Brenda and her husband had been letting the house for wedding receptions and parties.

Fred and Coleen had been married for 51 years, both strong personalities who gave as good as they got, and now they were living with Brenda, an arrangement they were thinking of continuing when Brenda downsized. "For the rest of my life," Fred told me cheerfully, "I'm going to be nagged in stereo."

Fred's life has had something of the quality of an 18th-century picaresque novel, full of different adventures, and this extraordinary manor house seemed a perfect location for finishing his book. I stayed for eight hours that day, and I left expecting Fred to crack on with the writing while I was launching Geoff's book.

His progress was slow. A lot was going on in his life, and he did not find it as easy to focus on the task as he had in Spain. He was due to fly out at Christmas and, in the weeks before he left, I drove up to the manor house four times to talk through with him the remaining sections and to give him a fresh stimulus. Each time I arrived at eleven, planning to leave around four, but his company was always so enjoyable, his conversation so rich, that I never left before seven.

Here was a man who had single-handedly pioneered the idea of a union for professional cricketers, using his natural charm and his organisational skills to overcome opposition from the establishment at Lord's. He had been the first man to see the potential for commercial sponsorship in cricket, setting himself up one winter at Taunton in a public relations role, then doing the same job all the year round at Derby. He had been a major force in modernising the Lord's Taverners charity. As a travel agent he had organised a long-running cricket festival in Barbados, even establishing on behalf of Shell the region's first inter-island football tournament. He had run a multitude of other business ventures, written a best-selling book for Fred Trueman and had an army of friends: from Eric Morecambe and the comedian Dave Allen to David Gower and the anti-apartheid campaigner Donald Woods. And his conversation reflected this breadth. One minute he would be explaining the economics of developing petrol stations; the next he would be comparing the melodies of Beatles and Hollies songs.

His stories were full of fun, none better than the one about the Test at Lord's when he shared a hotel room with Geoffrey Boycott. With Sunday a rest day in the match, Boycott headed back to Yorkshire, leaving Fred free to invite Coleen, by then his fiancée, into the room. When Boycott returned on Sunday, he could not get into the bathroom, a fact that he duly reported to the match manager Alec Bedser. So on Monday morning Fred found himself on the receiving end of a lecture from the former England bowler:

"I understand that you have had a woman in your bedroom."

I said, "Yes, Mr Bedser."

"That's not good, you know."

"Who's told you?"

"It doesn't matter who's told me. You are a bowler, you need your strength to be bowling in the match."

"Yes, Mr Bedser."

"In my day," he went on, "it was beer for the bowlers and women for the batsmen."

So I said to him, "Well, God bless the all-rounders."

What I soon came to realise is that, beneath his infectious enjoyment of life, he has a strong moral fibre, a sense of right and wrong that he learned from his mother in the East End of London. He never took a penny, unlike some, when he gave his time to the Lord's Taverners and, again unlike some, he resigned from the Professional Cricketers' Association when his job at Derby put him on the employers' side of the table.

One afternoon we discussed the title of the book, and we played with various phrases that captured both the fun of Fred and his sense of right and wrong. They were all a bit clumsy, and I rang Sue for her opinion. She suggested *Sense of Humour, Sense of Justice*, which Fred loved. "If I saw a book with that title," he said, "I'd buy it." It was just right for what he had written, and a number of readers have told him so. Every so often, when he rings, he says, "Give Sue a kiss from me for thinking of the title."

Fred has good attention to detail, making him a capable organiser, but at heart he is a visionary, a man who has been at his best coming up with new ideas, then moving on. For that reason he has probably not had the recognition that he should have had.

Perhaps the progress of the book reflected this side of his personality. He had broken the back of the writing, but it took a long time for him to finish it. I suppose I could have taken over the project, recast it in the format of one of my books or even ghost-written the remaining sections, but I did not want to do that. Fred cared about the writing and, when he got down to it, he was doing it exceptionally well.

While this was going on, I acquired two further titles for publication. Scyld Berry suggested that Brian Rose, captain of Somerset in their glory years in the early 1980s, should collaborate on a book, and I set up Anthony Gibson to work with him. Then Pat Murphy, whose updated edition of *The Centurions* I had published, got me on board with a book about Warwickshire's *annus mirabilis* of 1994, a project that he was the perfect person to write and that the county was keen to promote.

They were both books that I wanted to publish to a high standard but, at this point, my great passion was to see Fred's book into print. My assumption was that it would come out some time during 2018, but Fred's health, with three serious scares in the year, made that impossible.

In January he rang me from Malaga Hospital where he had been for over a fortnight, suffering from a kidney problem that the doctors had not got to the bottom of. For four days he was deprived of water – "I can't tell you what hell that was" – and he asked me, "If anything happens, have you got enough to finish the book?" It was not the only time he asked me this.

In June I arrived at the manor house one day to find him still at the breakfast table, with Coleen and Brenda having just realised that he had had a mini-stroke in the night. He was struggling for words, but he got up from the table, ignoring their concern, and led me into his 'office' where he pulled out a box of photographs for us to work through. The first was of a pair of men at a bar, neither of whose names he could remember. I recognised Denis Compton, but it took me a while through a kind of Twenty Questions with yes/no answers ("Cricketer? ... Entertainer? ... Actor?") before I twigged that the other man was Oliver Reed. Then the ambulance arrived. "Which one of you is it?" the man asked. Then "What's your name?" which Fred could not answer. It was a harrowing moment, but Fred recovered remarkably quickly, being almost back to normal when I returned ten days later.

In early December he went into hospital for keyhole surgery on an enlarged aorta. The operation was a success, but he picked up two infections, one of which led to his being told by a junior doctor – to the astonished anger of the man's superior – that he was going to die. I asked Fred how he had reacted to that, and he said he had stayed calm, making arrangements with Coleen and the children. "Make sure Stephen gets the book published," was one instruction. When he was through that scare, it emerged that he had lost much of the use of his right leg. In all, he was in hospital for eleven weeks.

To write Geoff Cope's book I spent ten days in his company. Though Fred wrote his own book, I spent fifteen days with him. I recorded his conversation, just in case I had to complete the book for him; I teased fresh memories out of him; and we worked through his enormous collection of papers and photographs.

The book would have been so much more successful if he had written it fifteen years earlier, when so many more of his contemporaries were alive and he was not so long out of public view. But, as with Geoffrey Howard and Bob Appleyard, there was a magic in capturing his memories now.

Fred's years as a cricketer were a relatively small part of a full life, yet they were the part that would be of most interest to the book's main readership. It was a dilemma I had faced with several of my books: how much to write about Bob Appleyard's career in the print business, Geoffrey Howard's wartime service, Geoff Cope's years in the paper trade. Fred was writing his own book, and I felt that his later chapters were too long. If I had not believed so strongly in the book, I might have let his text go as written, but I felt a duty to prune back the last third of it. Whether I was right to do so, we will never know, but earlier in the life of Fairfield Books I had occasionally erred on the side of under-editing, which I suspect is the greater fault. So, to Fred's disappointment, his readers never discovered that he had a brief business partnership, though they never met, with Nick Mason, Pink Floyd's drummer.

Fred was a Cockney, the son of a stevedore, and his description of growing up during the Blitz was vivid and moving. He won a scholarship to a good school and was doing well in business before he became a professional cricketer. His years as a player were the last when MCC ran the game, and he had little respect for their pompous snobbery. At Lord's, when he joined a public relations sub-committee, he was accused of being 'a young upstart coming into the game, believing you can change everything overnight'.

He wrote how he regretted agreeing to become an MCC member and what a struggle it had been to resign: 'I don't admire them. They think they own the game, and they are not good when they go abroad.'

Yet, at the last minute, when the text was agreed and the book was ready to go to the printers, he added a paragraph to the last chapter:

> From the day, prior to the Second World War, when my father gave me the coal shovel and a worn tennis ball, only the well-being of one thing has run through the whole of my active life – Cricket. As you are aware, I have had my differences with the MCC and my criticisms still stand, but I must admit that I admire them for their age-long devotion to all that is cricket and their desire to oppose unnecessary change.

Fred has never been interested in politics in the way that Tom Cartwright was, but this paragraph reminded me of what Tom had said: "I'd rather see the thing go back to being controlled by the MCC of yesteryear, that type of person, rather than the hard-bitten professional who's come out of the City."

*

It had been a long journey from the day in August 2013 when Fred had sat on my sofa, asking if I would publish his book, to the day in late March 2019 when he sat in an upstairs room in the manor house, signing the first printed copies. His leg was still feeble from the operation, preventing him from going up and down the staircase, but his mind was as alive as ever with sharp observations and stories that, for all my visits, I had not heard before. One involved the comedian Jasper Carrott, a great Birmingham City football fan, getting a lift in Fred's car. He invited Fred to identify the three football clubs with rude words in their names. "Arsenal," Fred said, then after a while "Scunthorpe", but he could not think of a third. The answer was: "Aston Fucking Villa."

He told the story with impeccable timing and a relish for the words. It was impossible not to enjoy time in his company.

*

The weeks that followed stretched me to my limit. I was bringing out three books at the same time – Fred, Brian Rose and Warwickshire 1994 – and I had ordered 2,000 copies of each. I filled the car 15 times with boxes, carrying them all upstairs, then driving here, there and everywhere to make deliveries and get copies signed.

I went down with a heavy cold and was almost voiceless for a meeting of our Cricket Society at which I had to interview Fred and Brian Rose. Afterwards, I received an e-mail of congratulation from a member: "If I may say so, it was excellently chaired. So many chairmen butt in and don't leave the pauses. In fact aside from a few prompts you were almost silent, it appeared."

If I had had any doubts about retiring from publishing, they were dispelled. I was 70 years old, and I had run my course with it.

32

All change

I often think of that story Ken Biddulph told, of the ball the Somerset Secretary gave him at the start of his time with the county, an old ball that he was expected to bring with him to the nets, how he took it home each night and polished it up. It landed in the river a few times, got tatty, and he went back in midsummer for another. "Another?" the Secretary thundered. "What have you been doing to it? You've only had that this summer."

On a similar theme I was told of a game at Leicester when David Sheppard, captaining Sussex, became frustrated by Leicestershire's failure to declare. When the new ball became due, he took it but he instructed his bowler not to take it out of its greaseproof packet – "and whatever you do, don't drop it." Slowly he adjusted the field. Then Charles Palmer, who doubled up as the cash-strapped Leicestershire's Secretary and captain, tumbled down the pavilion stairs, frantically waving the batsmen in. As they walked off, David Sheppard turned to his team: "I knew they couldn't afford a new ball."

Was that really the state of county cricket's finances in the early 1950s?

I think, too, of the story John Pretlove told me. Educated at Alleyn's and Cambridge University, John played as an amateur for Kent where, soon after arriving, he was approached to fill in a membership application for the Band of Brothers, an exclusive wandering club. "You're just the sort of chap we're looking for," the man said. Six weeks later, with no reply, he raised the matter: "I filled in the form for the BB, and I haven't heard anything." After an embarrassed pause, the man told him he had been rejected: "I'm sorry, John, but your father's in trade."

Was that really how England was in the 1950s? Sometimes I find it hard to take in how much has changed in my lifetime.

Money and social class. How the tension between the two dominated the English game in the post-war years.

In the 1950s the English class system was at the heart of our cricket, with power in the hands of men who for the most part were marked out by their birth and private education. They played as amateurs, finding ways to keep up the pretence when they needed to be paid, and they ruled as MCC, a private members' club. They cared deeply about the game, but in that post-war world they struggled to find ways to keep it solvent.

Some of the less proud counties raised money through football pool schemes. Warwickshire were the most successful, with 650,000 subscribers, many of them recruited in the local car factories. The proceeds funded major ground developments that brought Test cricket back to Edgbaston. Northamptonshire generated more than half of their annual income from their scheme, allowing them to run a playing staff of 29, the largest in the country. Keith Andrew gave me a copy of an unpublished memoir by Ken Turner, their Secretary, in which he said that, with 79,000 participants, 'It was equivalent to Wembley Stadium being three-quarters full every Saturday.'

This was a new world for cricket, a popular alternative to the donations of rich patrons such as the Duke of Devonshire, to whose Chatsworth House the Derbyshire Secretary made an annual pilgrimage. But MCC did not approve, their Secretary calling it 'easy money, which I believe to be a dangerous thing.' The grander counties, not wanting to sully their reputations, did not take part, and by the 1960s some were in financial distress.

In 1949 Geoffrey Howard left The Oval to be Secretary at Old Trafford, and he told me how shocked he was when he returned as Surrey's Secretary 16 years later. The county had been the great team of the 1950s, winning seven successive championships, but the ground had seen no improvements in all that time, was distinctly shabbier, and the balance sheet made disastrous reading. The old clock at the Vauxhall end had become too expensive to repair, and soon after Geoffrey's return the committee considered an offer from Guinness; they would pay for a digital replacement if the clock had their name on it. No, the committee decided, that would be advertising, and Surrey County Cricket Club was above that sort of thing.

Geoffrey encouraged new blood onto the committee, and the first advertising hoarding, for Excess Insurance, duly appeared. During the Oval Test of 1968 Gubby Allen, the most powerful man at Lord's, reacted with horror when he spotted it. "What the devil's that?" The reply came back: "We're broke, and that's £500." Three years later, Surrey were staging a pop concert, with The Who and Rod Stewart performing. 'Pop goes the Oval' was the newspaper headline, with the income of £4,210 lifting the county into a rare annual profit of nearly £600. The world was turning.

The enterprising Fred Rumsey was in the thick of this change. When Somerset reached the Gillette Cup final in 1967, their players received no bonus so he produced a commemorative booklet, sold advertising for it and raised nearly £1,000 for the team. Then, for the duration of that winter, he became county cricket's first PR man, tapping into the previously unexplored world of commercial sponsors: "It was obvious to me that sponsorship money was there for the taking, yet nobody was doing the asking."

In 1968, under pressure from a Labour government that would not give money to a sport run by a private members' club, MCC relinquished its control of the English game. The Test and County Cricket Board, the TCCB, was formed and, though it was run by many of the same people as MCC, it was soon embracing sponsorship and looking to increase the revenue received from the televising of cricket.

Now, fifty years on, the game is awash with money as never before, and that money has brought a much greater professionalism.

Gone are the days when the county cricketers said their farewells at the start of September, then gathered in April for some gentle pre-season practice. Martin Horton recalled how it was at Worcester: "Two hours or so of nets in the morning, another two in the afternoon. At lunch we'd walk up to the pub and have a couple of pints and a pie. If it was too wet, we might go to Edgbaston – though I remember Reg Perks, when he was captain, taking us up on the Malvern Hills, smoking his inevitable cigarette all the way. He stopped off for a cup of tea at St Ann's Well while we went on up."

The coaching barely existed after pre-season. If the county retained a coach for the summer, he rarely saw the first team. "We used to rely on the senior batsmen and bowlers," Martin said. "Or the umpires. You'd edge one through the slips and, when you got down to the other end, there would be Jack Crapp or Emrys Davies. 'Do you realise you're lifting your head?'"

Some of the counties were lucky in having perceptive coaches, such as George Hirst at Yorkshire before the war and 'Tiger Smith' at Edgbaston in the '50s and '60s. But coaching, as a career involving specialist training, was in its infancy.

At Somerset their former player Bill Andrews was left to interpret the role in his own cheerful way. "He gave so much to Somerset cricket," Peter Robinson said. "Going round the schools and the clubs, speaking every night at meetings and raising money. He had such a tremendous love of the game." But his supervision of the second team was of little help to the upcoming players. "I remember we were playing Wiltshire down here at Taunton, and we were getting a bit of a smacking. A few minutes after the start Bill would nip out the back and go into the Ring O' Bells. He came back just before lunch, saw the score and started having a go. John Martin was the captain. 'John, you bowled like a pr-pr-proper idiot.' He used to stutter. 'But I haven't had a bowl yet, Bill.' 'Don't you argue with me.' We saw him a bit later, and he'd nodded off."

"He was a big-hearted man, full of enthusiasm," Peter Roebuck said, "but he was chaotic. The Under-19s would have no matches for three weeks, then somehow there'd be three in one day."

"I used to say to people," Micky Stewart recalled, "I don't know why cricket is called a professional game. A, There's no money in it, and B, The general approach isn't professional at all."

It is all so different now. The cricketers are properly paid, employed all the year round, with specialist coaches on hand to fine-tune their skills, with expert guidance on diet and physical conditioning, with psychological support and post-playing career advice. Nothing, it seems, is left to chance.

The technology has advanced in leaps and bounds. Where once the bats possessed a small 'sweet spot', requiring perfect timing, now the mishits can fly to the boundary. There are helmets to protect the head, comfortable boots providing specially designed support, wicket-keeping gloves with a wider catching area. Bowling machines, slow-motion video playbacks, computerised statistical analysis; floodlights to allow play in gloomy light, improved drainage systems to reduce the time lost after rain. What a triumph of human inventiveness it all is.

In so many ways it is a better game for all the money that has been spent on it: more dynamic, more athletic, more exciting. Just as our way of life is better for our greater wealth: the labour-saving devices, the ease of travel around the planet, the dramatic advances in medical care. Crucially we are a more open, less class-conscious society, better informed about, and more tolerant towards, people different from ourselves.

It has been a wonderful time to be alive.

*

Yet even the best of changes are rarely without unforeseen side-effects. The technological advances have created dramatic change in the climate of our planet. The labour-saving devices have brought an alarming rise in obesity. Our greater mobility – moving from job to job, from place to place – has weakened our sense of community.

And so it is with cricket. In so many ways it is a better game than it has ever been, but I cannot shake off an unease that, in its professionalisation, in its drift towards a centralised, top-down corporate structure, it has lost a little of what made it so special.

When I was young, there was a saying in common usage: "It's not cricket." It meant quite simply, "That's not fair." It is a long time since I have heard anybody say it. In those days cricket was a much more central part of our national culture, and it had this association with fair play, with an ideal of sportsmanship and good manners. Yes, there was a hint of social class in that, and yes, of course, the game sometimes fell short of its lofty ideals. Nevertheless, that code of good sportsmanship and fair play was shared throughout the country in every level of the game.

Much of that spirit still survives in cricket, perhaps more so in the first-class game than at club level. But it has been eroded to the point that it has become necessary not only to spell it out in a preamble to the laws of the game but also to put in place penalties for its infringement. Who could have imagined fifty years ago that cricket would need to introduce a system of red cards for umpires to send off badly behaving players?

*

We are a more result-driven society than we used to be. We live in a more competitive world, where almost every activity is measured and ranked. We have much less tolerance for mediocrity, for rubbing along as best we can. Success is impatiently demanded.

"When I was a boy," Dickie Dodds told me, "cricket was a pleasurable activity. A game. You had a game of cricket. You didn't play in order to win. When I went home to my father, it wasn't a question of 'Who won?' It was 'Did you have a good game?' Now, with all this one-day cricket, the result has become the great thing."

'You didn't play to win.' What a strange remark that now seems.

Up to the late 1960s there was no league cricket in the south of England. Though teams played to win, the result was not everything. "It was more about testing your individual skills," Micky Stewart remembers. "The enjoyment of scoring runs and taking wickets, and how that was achieved, that was what mattered most."

It was a vestige of the Victorian ideal of the sporting amateur, playing purely for enjoyment, disdaining 'pot hunting'. In many places it had more than a hint of snobbery: exclusive clubs with the right sort of chaps wanting to play against other such clubs. But that form of cricket – playing to time, with a draw possible, with no leagues – was played in towns and villages, in school and army sides, throughout much of England.

It started to change in the 1960s, as so many things did.

In 1963, in the same year that the amateur/professional distinction was abolished, the counties introduced a one-day knockout cup, with much more emphasis on the result than the traditional three-day game. Then in 1968, in the year that MCC passed many of its powers to the new TCCB, the Surrey Championship was established, the first major league in the south.

Cricket became a more urgent game, with more emphasis on athleticism in the fielding and the running between the wickets. Micky Stewart recalls how it had been: "People used to say, 'I can't keep running these singles if I'm looking to bat all day.' Running between the wickets was bracketed with dashing around in the field. It wasn't part of the English game."

The one-day game led to a greater risk-taking in the batting, with the development of exciting new shots, but it also created a more defensive mindset among the bowlers and to a decline in the role of spin. "When I was 14 or 15," the Gloucestershire and England off-spinner David Allen told me, "I started playing with the men at Stapleton, and we played all time matches, not over-limit. I used to get slogged out of the ground, and they'd say, 'That's all right. We'll put another man out there. Pitch it up, he'll get out in a moment.' They had that lovely, optimistic attitude. But then there wasn't the fear of losing."

Tom Cartwright, a craftsman who had learned his trade in the older game, was disturbed by the changes. He thought cricket was losing its subtler skills, becoming more brash, more macho, more geared to providing instant excitement for a noisy crowd. For him the changes were a dumbing-down, driven by businessmen more concerned with the marketing than the product. "It's like so many things that you buy. All the emphasis is on presentation and packaging. Nearly always the thing itself is inferior in hand-crafted quality."

Raman Subba Row, the former England batsman, said to me that he thought there were now three different games: traditional two-innings cricket, the one-day game and Twenty20. He called them Cricket, Cracket and Crashet. Now we are to have The Hundred, a shorter game even than Twenty20.

We live in a commercially driven world, and it all comes down to a financial bottom line, the serving up of a product that people will buy. We have created a culture in which people want instant gratification more than ever before and, because things are more easily within reach, we have eroded that sense of fulfilment that comes with slow, painstaking achievement. Just as cricket needed to change in the 1960s, to shake off its Victorian amateurism and embrace sponsorship and the one-day game, so it needs to change now, to meet the needs of today's audience. Or so the argument goes.

'Cricket purists may scoff,' Henry Wear, an Australian academic, has written, 'but today's consumers are a time-poor, technology-savvy audience who demand constant stimulation.'

Constant stimulation. Is that the future of the human race?

Sue Grainger, the long-serving Lancashire committee member, taught for more than thirty years in the same primary school in Liverpool. When I asked her what changes she had witnessed in that time, her immediate response was to say that modern children cannot concentrate for so long. Their attention spans are shorter; they need the day to be broken up into a series of shorter activities.

271

I often think about that. We are starting to tackle the alarming rise in obesity, but this decline in attention spans? Are we really happy to accept that, to adapt everything to cope with it?

For me cricket has a specialness that is everything to do with being slow and drawn out. It is a team game played by individuals, when one moment you are an idle bystander, the next all eyes are on you. That tests character, and it reveals character – and from that comes so much of what I love about the game: the drama of it, the humour, the friendships.

It has a magical rhythm, an ebb and flow in which the quiet passages can be every bit as intense as the moments of action. As the Scandinavian girlfriend of a team-mate once observed, "I sense, beneath all this English calm, there beats a great passion."

The cricket I played was mostly afternoons, with the occasional all-day fixture. At our level of ability, that was long enough for there to be a proper contest between bat and ball, for the game to have twists and turns, for the batsmen to build innings and to feel the pressures of responsibility. Those elements were less in play in the 20-over evening games, less still in the 10-over helter-skelter of the indoor cricket league. I loved it all, but it was the longer game that was the real cricket for me.

*

Of all the cricketers I have interviewed, none has had a story that moved me more than Geoff Edrich. From a Norfolk farming family, brother of the great England batsman Bill, he spent much of the war as a prisoner of the Japanese, building the bridge over the river Kwai. He returned home, a six-stone weakling, to discover that his wife, assuming him dead, had moved on in her life. It took a year for them to get back together, and in that time he tried to establish himself in county cricket.

Lancashire gave him two matches to show what he could do, and in the first he was given lbw to a ball he had hit. So in the second, at the old Wagon Works ground in Gloucester, when he edged a ball from Tom Goddard to short leg and the umpire said "Not out", he batted on. What followed stayed with him vividly for the rest of his life.

> He bowled another couple of balls which I played, and the umpire called 'Over'. Wally Hammond was at first slip. He used to walk from first slip to first slip like a prince, swinging his arms. He didn't look at me. I wouldn't have minded if he'd looked. He just walked, and I heard this voice, 'Your brother wouldn't have done that.' And I thought, 'This is no good.' I got down the other end, and I waved my bat at one of George Lambert's and the castle went down. I didn't play at it. I wanted to get out. I wanted a tunnel to crawl into.

From that day to the day I finished playing cricket I never stayed when I got a touch. If you cheat to win a game of cricket, it's not cricket, is it?

David Green, the son of Burton-on-Trent's Ind Coope groundsman, told me about a Sunday match when he did not walk for a catch to the keeper. Cliff Gladwin was Derbyshire's senior professional, a tough, plain-speaking man who could put the fear of god into the junior players. At tea he took the youngster by the lapels. "Now look here, son, we do not play our cricket like that in Derbyshire."

"The war was still so close," Tom Cartwright said. "People could see the consequences of doing wrong." Or, as Geoff Edrich put it, "You've got to take the rough with the smooth. You have your good days and your bad days. That's all there is to it. Cricket is a character-building game."

People may argue about the rights and wrongs of walking, but it has an idealism, a care for the purity of the sport, that has always struck a chord with me. It was not a softness, as some have suggested. Do not tell me that Geoff Edrich and Cliff Gladwin were soft. The men in those days were much harder than we are now.

The best of sport is when opponents respect one another and do not resort to sharp practice. England and New Zealand managed that in this summer's World Cup Final, as on the same afternoon did Novak Djokovic and Roger Federer at Wimbledon. The glow of both matches – one a team game, the other individual – should serve as inspiration to the next generation.

Cricket has so much power to do good in the world, to bring people of different cultures together, to inculcate good manners and respect. In our cynical age it is hard to write this without sounding soppy but, if played in the right spirit, cricket does teach lessons for life. All sports do, but cricket – with its strange mix of individual and team, of reflection and action – has a special quality that sets it apart. It is important that, in its search for a new popularity, cricket does not lose touch with that.

*

"You can be over-organised if you're not careful."

I love that sentence. Tom Cartwright was told it by Peter Cranmer, one of his first second-eleven captains at Warwickshire, and it stayed with him, not least in his last years when he was a lone figure, coaching all around Wales, refusing to fit into the new structure in which most of his time was meant to be spent sitting on a computer and filling in forms. He was Tom Cartwright so they let him be, but his successor was brought into line.

When I look at the way cricket has changed in my lifetime, it seems to me to be a more top-down game, with much greater control from the centre. We have raised standards but we have done so from the top, creating greater uniformity. There is much more regulation, covering everything from the training of club umpires to the overs that can be bowled by different age-groups. The quirky outgrounds have been removed from the county circuit, and pitches standardised, often by importing a common loam.

Much the same has happened in other parts of our society. Where once teachers were left to do things in their own way, now they work to detailed frameworks handed down from above, with performance monitored at every turn. Such a structure has raised the standard of the worst, but it has almost certainly knocked some of the creative life out of the best.

In television the network controllers stick more closely to pre-set, tried-and-tested formulae than they did fifty years ago, when creativity was given a freer rein. In 1969, when the Monty Python team first joined forces, they applied for a series to a BBC executive who was astonished by the lack of detail in their proposal. "You've got no title, nothing written down," he said with disbelief. "You've no idea what it's about, whether you need music or film, or who it's going to appeal to. I'm sorry, I can give you 13 shows, but that's all."

Life was hard for many people in the 1940s and 1950s. We were recovering from war, rebuilding the country. It was the same in cricket. A county club would be run by three or four administrators, and coaching for the top players was confined to pre-season and was often basic. That left people having to work things out for themselves, and from that came the greater mixture of batting and bowling styles. Add in a wider range of playing surfaces, and greater regional differences between the counties, and the result was a game with more variety. Cricketers came in different shapes and sizes, and the way they played was not so much moulded by coaching as by the expression of individual personality.

You can never compare eras satisfactorily. Modern cricketers would need to adapt to play on the pitches and with the equipment that existed in the 1950s, just as the cricketers of then would have to approach the modern game with a different mindset. The general assumption is that the overall standard has improved, certainly at the higher levels of the game, and that is probably true. But I cannot help feeling that there were aspects of the old game – its greater variety, its rootedness in community, the sense that the cricketers were having to find their own paths to success – that had a charm that we have largely lost.

We think we have greater freedom, but maybe much of it is an illusion. Maybe, beneath the different hairstyles and the choice of programmes on our iphones, we have become more beholden to corporately determined orthodoxies. And maybe, as a result, we have lost a little of the richness of our humanity.

*

The greatest administrative change in English cricket in my lifetime has been the transfer of power away from the old MCC, with its patrician loftiness. Initially, when the Test and County Cricket Board was set up in 1968, the personnel was much the same, with ex-cricketers of the right social class occupying all the leading roles. In 1997 the ECB was created, and the cricketers became subservient to businessmen, who were looking to inject greater financial acumen into the game. All four chairmen to date have come from the commercial sector, three of them from retail.

Back in the 1950s the President of MCC wrote to the Treasurer about the lengthening waiting list for membership. He mooted the possibility of 'a drastic rise in entrance fees or subscriptions' but acknowledged immediately the problem with this, summoning the horror of the club being over-run by self-made men of commerce, a view that may well have contained a tinge of anti-semitism: 'It is so important for us not to put membership beyond the means of the very people we want as members – the young, the "professional classes" and the Service members. If we apply too stringent an economic sanction, we will find the place full of Sir Julien Cahns.'

It is hard for us to read this in the 21st century and not to be appalled. Without question we are a better society for having rid ourselves of that prejudice and snobbery, for having created easier – if still not equal – paths to achievement for all those with talent.

Yet, in the world of cricket, the shift from a game run by a social elite to one run by men of money has had its disadvantages. For all its faults, and they were many, the MCC administrators cared about the character of the game, its special spirit, in a way that it is not clear that the money men of the ECB always do. Further, in their years in control, MCC had a vision for the game and were not as resistant to change as their popular image would suggest.

I was enchanted by Alan Rayment's story of his summer at Lord's in 1959, helping out with the coaching of the ground-staff lads. The Head Coach was old-school, teaching the boys, in Alan's words, "to play pretty shots, not score runs." Few, if any, of the boys had the talent to earn a living as cricketers, and Alan lost his cool one day, going into the net himself and whacking every ball as hard and as far as he could. "The game's not about impressing coaches and MCC toffs," he shouted. "It's about hitting the ball, scoring runs, winning matches."

His explosion caused a stir, and soon enough he was summoned to see Billy Griffith, MCC Assistant Secretary, and Harry Altham, Treasurer and guru of the MCC coaching scheme. "It was a bit like going to the headmaster's study. I was expecting to be sacked."

"Well, Alan," Harry Altham began. "We understand that you've been having some thoughts about the coaching we give to the boys. We'd like you to tell us what you think about your experience here."

Alan did not hold back, speaking his mind with clarity and with passion.

"We have been informed of all this," said Billy Griffith, "and we've discussed it in committee. It's been decided to offer you the post of Head Coach from next season."

It was not what Alan wanted, and it did not happen. But it reflected a side of MCC that is often forgotten, a side that is stronger now than ever: a care not only to look after the best of the game's traditions but to adapt to the challenges of the present and future.

Fred Rumsey hated the patronising attitude of the old MCC, yet he felt it necessary in his book to add a paragraph, stating his admiration for their 'age-long devotion to cricket'. Tom Cartwright, who never shed his socialist principles, ended his life wishing MCC were back in charge of the game.

Even Bomber Wells, another Labour man, hankered for the civilities of that old world: "Mary and I were watching a game at the King's School the other evening," he told me once. "The Sixth Form against the Masters. People were clapping one another. 'Splendid catch, Mr Robins,' the headmaster said. Then somebody dropped one: 'Gallant effort.' They were words you hadn't heard for forty years. Mary said to me, 'It's the most beautiful game in the world, played in this spirit.'"

Dear Bomber. Overweight, carefree. He may have been a great entertainer and taken nearly 1,000 wickets, but he would not get close to the first-class game today. And he knew it. Like Tom, he was no fan of the businessmen who had taken over, the men who were organising and standardising the game he loved. "It's the funniest, loveliest game under the sun," he said, "if you just let people get on with it."

*

"I don't know," Bomber said to me one day. "Maybe, when you get older and you watch the young people playing, you start to have the wrong thoughts."

For more than twenty years I have immersed myself in cricket's past, and I can see qualities of the old game that have been eroded. But so much has happened in cricket in recent years that has been a joy to witness: the growth of the women's game, the inspirational development of disability cricket, the pastoral care the game now shows towards its players, the rise of new Test-playing countries, not least the war-torn Afghanistan. The game's reach is greater than ever.

The Spirit of Cricket lives on. It is a wonderful time to be alive.

33

A cry from the heart

When my father was close to death, I took to reading to him at night. Years earlier, he had sent me up to his father's house to read from the large family Bible, a task that was always brought to an abrupt end when it was time for *The Archers*. Dad did not ask for the Bible so I read him a biography of the West Indian cricketer Learie Constantine. I am not sure he took it all in, but it was cricket and he liked it that I was sitting with him.

When I came home from my final university exams, he was having a spell in a nursing home. It was what we now call respite care, giving Mum a brief break from coping with his bulky frame and his near-incontinence, but in his three weeks in the home he had another stroke and died. On his last Sunday I sat with him in his room, watching cricket on a little television set. It was the first summer of the Sunday League, and a young Greg Chappell hit a magnificent 128, the first century in the competition. It is my last memory of my father.

Twelve years later, in 1981, Mum was diagnosed with an advanced cancer. I collected her first prescription for morphine, and the pharmacist was so shocked by the dosage that he rang the doctor to check it. For three weeks the three of us, her boys, stayed with her at Peter's house in Salisbury, and she gradually slipped away. The morphine gave her lovely visions – a ginger-haired girl standing at her feet, a gypsy child at the door, glorious sunsets – but we tried to keep her with us, playing games of Scrabble and watching cricket on television. She was awake and happy through most of Ian Botham's blazing innings at Headingley – she thought he had been too young for the captaincy and was glad Mike Brearley had been brought back – but she dozed in and out of Bob Willis's extraordinary bowling the next day. "Another wicket, Mum, wake up." A fortnight earlier it would have meant the world to her, but it was starting not to matter anymore.

The day after she died, the three of us went across to her flat to sort things out. When we finished, we turned on the television just in time to see Botham the bowler taking five quick wickets and winning another Test.

Cricket on television. When I look back, it was always there, so much of my life mixed up with it, a background flicker through all my summers.

I can see Andrew and me coming in from our cricket in the garden to discover in horror that England, so certain of victory at Old Trafford, had collapsed against Richie Benaud; I can see a group of us, after a day's community work in Bristol, huddled around a set to see Derek Underwood bowling out Australia at The Oval; I am sitting in a launderette in Edinburgh, watching Viv Richards hitting an imperious 291 to make Tony Greig grovel; I am going to buy a tent with Sue during a World Cup Final, coming home to find to my astonishment that the unbeatable West Indies are close to defeat against India; I am playing cricket at an Oxford college ground, seeing Devon Malcolm destroying the South Africans; and, in the summer of 2005, I am sitting on the sofa, Martha beside me, and we are rigid with tension till England at Edgbaston take that last Australian wicket and squeeze home by two runs.

And then nothing. Cricket on television, it was gone. Cricket as part of our national consciousness, as a central pillar of our sporting summer, it was no longer there for me nor for the bulk of the population.

On a recent edition of the quiz show *Pointless* five contestants failed to name a single England cricketer of recent years. The sixth and last, a young woman, also looked clueless: "I don't know why, I'm sure it's not right," she said, "but the name Alastair Cook has come into my head."

The viewing figures declined significantly when the sport moved from BBC to Channel 4, and they plummeted when, from 2006, live coverage was available only on the subscription Sky Sports channel. Then, for one glorious day in this summer of 2019, it was back, the World Cup Final on Channel 4, and once more everybody was talking cricket. Normally Martha and her husband do not turn on the television during the day, but they spent that afternoon watching cricket. A fortnight later I was reading *The Times*, with the paper open at a picture of Lord's, and their daughter, not yet two years old, pointed at it and said, 'Cricket'.

The people who made the decision back in 2005 meant well. They did what they thought was best for the sport, bringing in untold riches that have built the ECB into a highly staffed organisation that gives money aplenty to the game at all levels. A good proportion of it is spent promoting cricket, money much of which would not be needed if it were still on mainstream television.

When the ECB lobbied the government to remove all cricket from TV's 'crown jewels', the events that must be free to view – the Olympic Games, the All-England tennis championships, the FA Cup and World Cup football finals, the Grand National and the Derby, the Rugby Union World Cup and Rugby League Challenge Cup finals – they were relegating cricket to secondary status, no longer in the first division of the nation's sporting life.

I thought it a terrible decision at the time and, if I have changed my view at all since then, it is only that I would no longer use the word 'terrible'. I would say 'catastrophic'.

34

Through the remembered gate

I started the story of this book in the autumn of 1993, with the decision to improve my cricket with some coaching. I drove up to Stroud each Friday afternoon, and in the first three winters it never once occurred to me that the sessions would lead to anything more than, as Ken Biddulph put it, "a few more runs, a few more wickets, a few more years enjoying the game". Then, stimulated by the fizz of Hazel's evening class, I found myself writing a book about county cricket in the 1950s. Even then I had no idea that I would go on writing about cricket, certainly not that I would set myself up as a publisher. Life has its surprises.

The journey into cricket's past took me back to the world of my early years. As a child of the post-war baby-boom, coming of age in the 1960s, I had always seen my generation as a great force for progress, sweeping aside the stuffiness, the prejudice, the backward-looking conservatism of the prevailing culture. There was some truth in that perspective. Yet, as I journeyed back into the 1950s, walking through the gate the old cricketers opened for me, I started to see that world of my childhood with different eyes.

The continent of Europe had been ravaged by two wars in thirty years. The first, in which my father had spent four years as a stretcher-bearer in the trenches, saw more than one in nine British troops killed in action, with many more severely wounded or dying of disease. A generation was put through hell. The second war, following so close on its heels and lasting six years, brought even worse carnage: the aerial destruction of parts of many cities, the harshest of combat in the Far East and the mass extermination of peoples in concentration camps. Between those wars there had been the Great Depression, reducing many to unemployment and destitution, and the alarming rise of dictatorships, both fascist and communist.

Rebuilding Britain after the Second World War was a massive task. The people were worn down by the conflict, whole areas lay in rubble, and the settlement with the United States left the country stretched financially. "Never again" was a phrase I heard repeatedly in my childhood. There was a determination to create a better world, and that generated a spirit of optimism: both at international level, with the Universal Declaration of Human Rights and the formation of the European Economic Community, and domestically, with the National Health Service and the Festival of Britain. We look back with horror at the sprawling housing estates built in those years and the soulless city-centre developments, and we forget that they grew out of an idealism about shaping a new and better way of life.

English cricket was determined to be up and running for the start of 1946. There was little new talent, just men who were yearning to make up for the six summers they had lost to war, and at several grounds there was major repair work waiting to be carried out. Yet the crowds flocked back, a new generation of players started to emerge, and for seven years in the 1950s England's cricketers were on top of the world.

The salary for playing a summer of county cricket was meagre, the relationships almost feudal. Yet, compared with the long hours of working in a factory, a pit or a railway goods yard, it was a good life, out in the sunshine, playing sport in front of large, appreciative crowds. For a generation who had known war, there was an understanding of sport's place in the wider scheme of things.

Alec Bedser, born in 1918, was part of the Dunkirk evacuation, along with his twin brother Eric. "You've never seen such a shambles in your life," he told me, recalling the moment when in the middle of a cornfield they threw themselves to the ground, lucky to escape machine-gun fire from a low-flying German plane. "The war made men of us. It toughened us up. After that I was never nervous when I played cricket."

Geoff Edrich, also born in 1918, talked to me about his time in the Japanese prisoner-of-war camp: "You have to have a bit of luck to get through – and a bit of will power. Anybody can lay down and die. A lot of the boys died of a broken heart, actually. They couldn't see the end. If you thought, 'This is not going to finish,' that's it, isn't it?"

Bob Appleyard, born in 1924, was a seaman whose ship was in harbour in Malta at the end of the war. There he played cricket against the crewmen of two destroyers. Soon afterwards, the destroyers were blown up by mines, and he was fishing bodies out of the sea. "Both ships were going home, and floating in the bilge water were all these toys and dollies the crew were taking home to their families."

And Fred Rumsey, born in 1935 and living through the Blitz in London's East End: "I would go to school in the morning, and the boy in the next desk would be missing. The teacher would explain that he had been killed, and we would just carry on. I was aware that I had hardened myself to death; I made sure that it was not going to upset me emotionally. We all did, the boys and the girls. A war child is a different person from a child brought up in peace."

In the cricket of the 1950s there were no bowling machines or video analysis, and the equipment had little of the modern sophistication. Out on the field they had to think things out for themselves – how to bat and bowl on different surfaces, how to read the state of a game – and they had to develop the stamina to manage a six-day-a-week, summer-long schedule with many long, gruelling journeys by car, coach or train. It was a tough world, with a fine line between success and failure. As Fred Titmus, the Middlesex and England off-spinner, used to say, "They say the players now are fitter. They may be fitter, but they are not tougher."

That hardness extended to their standards of behaviour on the field. With the shadow of war still present, there was a collective understanding of the importance of fair play. At each county it fell to the senior professional, a veteran player, to uphold these standards, insisting that batsmen walked when they were out, that bowlers and fielders only appealed when they believed someone might be out and that umpires were treated at all times with respect.

It is hard for someone of my generation, a child of peace, not to feel that that world was too harsh at times, too regimented. I think of Frank Parr, banished from cricket for being too scruffy, for wearing a blue shirt to a House of Lords dinner and playing in a jazz band, and I shudder. I ran into that sort of discipline at public school, petty and vindictive, and I hated it. Yet that was the extreme. For the most part, from the testimony of the men whom I have met, there was a vibrant sense of community among the players – and a shared determination, almost idealistic in the early years after the war, to preserve and protect the best traditions of the game.

In time, as war receded from our consciousness and we started to enjoy a greater affluence, a professionalism of a different kind developed in cricket. The amateurs went, ridding the game of some of its outdated snobbery, and a new set of priorities emerged, with the winning at all costs gaining ground at the expense of those old standards that the senior professionals upheld. The introduction of one-day cricket, built around the excitement of the result, intensified that change, as did the surrounding youth culture, with its questioning of all authority.

I was part of that generation that questioned authority. I was inspired by Martin Luther King's 'I have a dream' speech, by the songs of Bob Dylan and by the young Czech student Jan Palach burning himself to death in protest at Soviet tanks on the streets of Prague. For a few heady years I believed, like so many, that we were a special generation; we were going to make the world a better place. It did not occur to me that most generations think like that. Certainly the one before mine did, the one that rebuilt the country after the war.

Cricket is such a tiny lens through which to view the wider picture but, by sitting with so many cricketers of that era, by recording carefully their testimony, I have come to see that wider world with a fresh perspective.

*

A few years ago at The Oval Micky Stewart was approached by a member of Surrey's marketing team. "Excuse me, Mr Stewart," he was asked. "Does the name Peter May mean anything to you?" Such is the way life moves on.

I interviewed the last two men to play county cricket in the 1920s, and they died some twelve years ago. I interviewed John Manners, the last man alive from the 1930s, and he is now 105. There are little more than a dozen county cricketers left from the 1940s and, of the twelve games from the 1950s featured in *Runs in the Memory*, only three are based on the testimony of men who are still with us.

Our points of contact with the past grow fewer with each passing year.

In the late 1970s Pat Murphy captured the memories of the veteran Warwickshire and England keeper 'Tiger' Smith, then in his nineties, but at that time such oral history projects with the elderly were not common. What a service it would have been to cricket's history if somebody had sat down with George Hirst or Charlie Parker, as Pat did with 'Tiger' Smith. How much richer might our understanding of our history be.

So many of the men with whom I have worked have gone now: Bomber Wells, Tom Cartwright, Ken Biddulph, Bob Appleyard, Keith Andrew, Geoffrey Howard. In my inner ear I can still hear all their voices, voices that it fell to me to record for future generations.

It was a privilege and a joy to be given that responsibility.

*

It has been a tiny project – recording the memories of old cricketers, publishing books by other authors – but it has given my life such a sense of fulfilment. I can only hope that people have had one-tenth of the pleasure in reading the books that I have had in working on them.

I would love to go back and do it all again but not from where I am now. Rather, I feel as Len Hutton did near the end of his life when he was asked if he would like to be playing in the modern game. "Yes, I would," he said. "I would like to be 21, 22 and start all over again. But I don't want to know what I know now because there's a lot of fun finding out."

*

On the last day before this book was set to go to the printers, Sue and I went to the annual lunch of the Cricket Writers' Club in London. The invitation came at the last moment and seemed important, so much so that I cancelled a trip to Leeds with Fred Rumsey. At the lunch, in front of many much more important people than me, I was presented with their Peter Smith Award for Services to Cricket, joining a list of recipients that included Alec Bedser, Richie Benaud, Dickie Bird, Christopher Martin-Jenkins and the Stewart family.

Had that pathetic duck at Warley, the nets with Ken Biddulph, the evening classes with Hazel, really led to this? It has been an extraordinary journey and, somewhat overwhelmed by the honour, I accepted it on behalf of all those who have made it possible: from Geoffrey Howard and Bob Appleyard to David Foot and John Barclay. Without them none of this could have happened.

There has been a great growth of media outlets in recent years, and in the room there were more than two hundred writers and broadcasters, some of them young and just starting out. I read them some words of Tom Cartwright: "John Arlott inspired me to play cricket. His voice was fascinating, and he painted pictures that made it inevitable that I wanted to play."

"May there be more John Arlotts among you," I said, "and may you inspire many more young people to play and follow this wonderful game."

*

There were years in my early adult life when I lost my way, when I lacked a sense of direction. Somewhere along the line my Christian faith got knocked out of me, and without it I struggled to find a way forward. I retained an ethical code based largely on Jesus's teachings, but I lost my belief in the central theological tenets: God creating the world, Jesus the son of God, the virgin birth, the resurrection, the after-life.

Bob Appleyard wrestled with the unbelievability of much of the Bible, but he was sure that there was something profound at the heart of it all. His Sunday morning visits to church played an important part in his life. "We try to get there about half an hour before the service," he told me. "I like to sit in the pew and think about all the people who have sat there over the centuries. What they were thinking. How they were dressed. What their attitudes were. I look at the great stones. I think how they must have humped them about, how they got them into place. There are so many memories in a church. All the years people have sat and worshipped. There's something solid about it, something that will last after we have gone."

I think that is what I miss most about my religious faith, that reminder of an eternity of time beyond our own brief lives. Modern culture is so much about the moment, everything consumed and thrown away, everything "got up to be exciting", and we struggle to retain a proper sense of perspective, an understanding that we are here for just a short while and that we have a duty to look after our world for future generations.

Fairfield Books

Full list of publications *(hardbacks, unless stated)*

Stephen Chalke

Runs in the Memory – County Cricket in the 1950s *(1997, softback 2002)*
Caught in the Memory – County Cricket in the 1960s *(1999)*
One More Run *(softback, 2000)*, with Bryan 'Bomber' Wells
At the Heart of English Cricket – The Life and Memories of Geoffrey Howard *(2001)*
Guess My Story – The Life and Opinions of Keith Andrew, Cricketer *(2003)*
No Coward Soul – The Remarkable Story of Bob Appleyard *(2003, softback 2008)*,
with Derek Hodgson

A Sporting Scrapbook – The Wimbledon Club 1854-2004 *(2004)*
Ken Taylor – Drawn to Sport *(2006)*
A Summer of Plenty – George Herbert Hirst in 1906 *(softback, 2006)*
Tom Cartwright – The Flame Still Burns *(2007)*
Five Five Five – Holmes and Sutcliffe in 1932 *(softback, 2007)*
The Way It Was – Glimpses of English Cricket's Past *(2008, softback 2011)*
A Long Half Hour *(softback, 2010)*
Now I'm 62 – The Diary of an Ageing Cricketer *(softback, 2010)*
Micky Stewart and the Changing Face of Cricket *(2012)*
Summer's Crown – The Story of Cricket's County Championship *(2015)*
In Sunshine and in Shadow – Geoff Cope and Yorkshire Cricket *(2017)*
Cricketing Allsorts *(2018)*
Through the Remembered Gate *(2019)*

David Foot

Fragments of Idolatry – From 'Crusoe' to Kid Berg *(2001)*
Harold Gimblett – Tormented Genius of Cricket (2003)
Sixty Summers – Somerset Cricket since the War *(2006)*, with Ivan Ponting
Footsteps from East Coker *(2010)*

John Barclay

The Appeal of the Championship – Sussex in the Summer of 1981 (2002)
Life Beyond the Airing Cupboard *(2008)*
Lost in the Long Grass *(2013)*

John Barclay & Stephen Chalke *(editors)*

Team Mates *(2016)*

Douglas Miller
Born to Bowl – The Life and Times of Don Shepherd *(2004)*
Charles Palmer – More than just a Gentleman *(2005)*

Peter Walker
It's Not Just Cricket *(2006)*

Simon Lister
Supercat – The Authorised Biography of Clive Lloyd *(2007)*

Mark Wagh
Pavilion to Crease ... and Back *(2009)*

Patrick Murphy
The Centurions – From Grace to Ramprakash *(2009)*
The Greatest Season – Warwickshire in the Summer of 1994 *(2019)*

Dudley Doust
Bradley Brook – An American Walks Down An English Stream *(softback, 2009)*

Anthony Gibson
Of Didcot and the Demon – The Cricketing Times of Alan Gibson *(2009)*
With Magic in my Eyes – West Country Literary Landscapes *(2011)*
The Coloured Counties – Literary Landscapes of the Heart of England *(2017)*

Anthony Gibson & Stephen Chalke *(editors)*
Gentlemen, Gypsies and Jesters – The Wonderful World of Wandering Cricket *(2013)*

Tony Ward
Typhoon Tyson to Twenty/20– A lifetime of watching Northamptonshire cricket
(softback, 2011)

Fred Rumsey
Sense of Humour, Sense of Justice *(2019)*

Brian Rose
Rosey – My Life in Somerset Cricket *(2019)*, with Anthony Gibson

INDEX

(for reasons of space, close family and incidental characters are omitted)

288